The American History Series

SERIES EDITORS
John Hope Franklin, *Duke University*
A. S. Eisenstadt, *Brooklyn College*

William L. O'Neill
RUTGERS UNIVERSITY

The New Left

A History

HARLAN DAVIDSON, INC.
WHEELING, ILLINOIS 60090-6000

Library of Congress Cataloging-in-Publication Data

O'Neill, William L.
    The New Left : a history / William O'Neill
        p.   cm. — (The American history series)
    Includes bibliographical references (p. 000) and index.
    ISBN 0-88295-960-3 (alk. paper)
    1. Ne Left—United States. 2. United States—History, 1961–1969.
    I. Title. II. Title: American history series (Wheeling, Ill.)

    HN90.R3 2001
    320.53'0973—dc21   00-050836

Cover photo: Antiwar activist Jerry Rubin, along with other defen-
dants in the Chicago Seven conspiracy trial, speaks to the press in
February 1970. Front row, from left: Rennie Davis, Rubin, Abbie
Hoffman. Back row, from left: Lee Weiner, Bob Lamb, and Thomas
Hayden. (Eds: Lamb was not one of the Chicago Seven.) *AP Photo,
courtesy Wide World.*

Manufactured in the United States of America
04 03 02 01 1 2 3 4 5 MG

FOREWORD

Every generation writes its own history for the reason that it sees the past in the foreshortened perspective of its own experience. This has surely been true of the writing of American history. The practical aim of our historiography is to give us a more informed sense of where we are going by helping us understand the road we took in getting where we are. As the nature and dimensions of American life are changing, so too are the themes of our historical writing. Today's scholars are hard at work reconsidering every major aspect of the nation's past: its politics, diplomacy, economy, society, recreation, mores and values, as well as status, ethnic, race, sexual, and family relations. The lists of series titles that appear on the inside covers of this book will show at once that our historians are ever broadening the range of their studies.

The aim of this series is to offer our readers a survey of what today's historians are saying about the central themes and aspects of the American past. To do this, we have invited to write for the series only scholars who have made notable contributions to the respective fields in which they are working. Drawing on primary and secondary materials, each volume presents a factual and narrative account of its particular subject, one that affords readers a basis for perceiving its larger dimensions and importance. Conscious that readers respond to the closeness and immediacy of a subject, each of our authors seeks to restore the past as an actual present, to revive it as a living reality. The individuals and groups who figure in the pages of our books appear as real people who once were looking for survival and fulfillment. Aware that historical subjects are often matters of controversy, our authors present their own findings and conclusions. Each volume closes with an extensive critical essay on the writings of the major authorities on its particular theme.

The books in this series are primarily designed for use in both basic and advanced courses in American history, on the undergraduate and graduate levels. Such a series has a particular value these days, when the format of American history courses is being altered to accommodate a greater diversity of reading materials. The series offers a number of distinct advantages. It extends the dimensions of regular course work. It makes clear that the study of our past is, more than the student might otherwise understand, at once complex, profound, and absorbing. It presents that past as a subject of continuing interest and fresh investigation.

For these reasons the series strongly invites an interest that far exceeds the walls of academe. The work of experts in their respective fields, it puts at the disposal of all readers the rich findings of historical inquiry, an invitation to join, in major fields of research, those who are pondering anew the central themes and aspects of our past.

And, going beyond the confines of the classroom, it reminds the general reader no less than the university student that in each successive generation of the ever-changing American adventure, from its very start until our own day, men and women and children were facing their daily problems and attempting, as we are now, to live their lives and to make their way.

John Hope Franklin
A. S. Eisenstadt

CONTENTS

PREFACE

Tom Hayden, a past president of Students for a Democratic Society (SDS) and a central figure in the book that follows, concluded his memoir *Reunion* (1988) with these words: "I miss the sixties and always will." In light of the terrible violence at home and abroad that began in the decade and continued beyond it—including the War in Vietnam, urban, campus, and police riots, the assassinations of John and Robert Kennedy, Martin Luther King, Jr., and Malcolm X, the rise in crime and drug use, and other problems too numerous to mention—this is an absurd statement.

Yet anyone who lived through this era and was even marginally connected with its great movements, especially those for civil rights and against the war, can understand and perhaps even echo Hayden's sentiment to a degree. With all its evils, of which SDS became one, the sixties was a time when politics and ideas mattered; and college classes mattered also—not as tickets to be punched *en route* to business careers but as forums for discussion and debate. In the sixties, off-campus social ferment generated on-campus issues, students often taking the lead in arguments and almost always in organized protests. Campus radicals formed their own crusade, a political, social, and cultural movement usually called the New Left today, but then very often simply called "the Movement" by activists. The New Left was responsible for much of the violence on college campuses, but it also generated a level

of political, and to some extent intellectual, excitement seldom
seen before and never since in academia.

Although the majority of New Leftists were students, SDS,
with its increasingly radical political agenda, was far from the
only organization or group with a tendency to call for radical
change. Young Marxists wanted to make America as much like
Communist China as possible. Hippies, mainly through example,
wanted to transform society by promoting such ideas as peace,
love, community, and freedom from serious employment. Yippies
wanted both the political revolution of SDS and the Hippie way of
life. Together with like-minded men and women, these groups became known collectively as the New Left.

A feature not often remarked upon by analysts of the New
Left is that many in the Movement were historicists, that is, they
believed if they understood the past correctly they could shape the
future. The idea of historicism was old-hat even then, and more
than a little dubious. The point, however, is that the fervor it inspired made teaching history, American history in particular, a far
more spirited and demanding task than those of us who did this
work had ever anticipated. Once residents of the Ivory Tower, we
found ourselves embattled, literally, when the police and National
Guard were called out, figuratively, during classes. Although incidents of classroom violence were rare, we instructors had to prepare ourselves every day to meet challenges and charges by
students that we were peddling official propaganda, defending imperialism, or worse. This could be unpleasant, yet also stimulat-
ing, because, though we teachers were often at odds with our students, many of us felt that in our classrooms we were debating
urgent issues in a way that might affect history as well as illumi-
nate it. But with the end of the Vietnam War and the collapse of
the civil rights and student movements, this sense of engagement
passed away too. That is what I miss about the sixties.

In 1971 I published a book on the recently concluded decade
called *Coming Apart,* which included a chapter on the New Left.
When I was asked to write this volume for The American History
Series, it meant returning to a subject that I had not studied or
even thought much about for almost thirty years. Given the large

number of books about the New Left that have appeared in the interim, I was curious about what I would learn that I had not known at the time. I did find numerous details and bits of information that were not public knowledge in the 1960s, but I have been surprised by the extent to which discussions and analyses of the Movement still follow the same course as they did when it was alive. Although a few historians have taken a long view of the Movement so that it can be seen in historical context, or have examined it in unique ways, the battle lines are essentially unchanged. Defenders of the New Left still maintain that it was a powerful force for good, praising it for fighting racism, helping to end the Vietnam War, reforming universities, politicizing students, and, often, much more. Critics of the Movement fall into one of two camps. Conservatives see nothing of value in it, holding that even the New Left's worthy goals were hopelessly corrupted by violence and authoritarianism. Liberals tend to admire the early New Left, which did, in fact, contribute to the struggle against racism and addressed public affairs in a high-minded and even original way. But they agree with conservatives that the violence, factionalism, and revolutionary posturing of the Movement's later years not only destroyed the New Left, but compromised the causes that it professed to serve. The New Left is not a subject that anyone approaches neutrally. All the literature is partisan, my own included, because in writing about the Movement and the sixties one is also writing about people and issues that did not end with the decade or even with the twentieth century. The New Left itself may be dead, but most of its former members were still alive at century's end, many in the prime of life and exerting considerable influence—particularly in higher education.

What has changed, therefore, and what makes the New Left still worth writing about—apart from its inherent interest—is the long shadow it cast. From the ashes of the Movement a new political impulse was born that would play an important role in the culture wars that still rage today. One could successfully criticize the New Left in its time, and describe it with considerable precision. What could not be known then was its outcome, which only the passing of time has revealed.

William L. O'Neill
Highland Park, New Jersey

CHAPTER ONE

The Rise of SDS

The 1960s were the most turbulent years since the "Red Decade" of the 1930s. Like the thirties, the 1960s were marked by antiwar demonstrations, left-wing agitation, and considerable violence, particularly over labor issues. Labor organization was the key issue to radicals then, and affected them in much the same way as the fight against racism would influence radicals in the sixties. Both were seen not just as important movements but as moral crusades, sanctified by the blood of martyrs. At the same time, and often involving the same people, the sixties was a time of tremendous social and cultural change. Before it the 1920s had been the benchmark for innovation in these areas. It had been the Jazz Age, noted for flappers, short skirts, bathtub gin, and the sexual revolution. The sixties would go further in every respect, from the miniskirt to marijuana, and would feature a genuine sexual revolution, unlike that of the 1920s, which was more apparent than real. And, unlike the twenties again, women in the 1960s would not only assert their right to have more fun, but would demand equality in practice virtually across the board.

Among the negatives of the sixties was the rate of crime, which had been declining in the 1950s but now began to rise again, skyrocketing thereafter. Family life was another casualty of the decade. The divorce rate, which had fallen during most of the 1950s, began to climb in the sixties and, like the crime rate, rose until the 1990s, by which time half of all marriages ended in divorce—twice the rate of the fifties. The increase in sexual promiscuity had much to do with the rising divorce rate, and also with the flood of illegitimate births the nation experienced. Rare in the fifties, illegitimacy began to increase during the sixties until by the 1990s, 70 percent of all black children were born out of wedlock, as were more than 20 percent of white children. Illegal drug use, previously uncommon, became popular in the 1960s, and not just among the underclass. Soon conservatives were routinely blaming everything that seemed to them dysfunctional or immoral in America on the legacy of the 1960s. This was, perhaps, to overstate the case, but there is little doubt that more so than any other decade, the sixties shaped the society we live in today.

The New Left was not wholly responsible for these cultural changes. The Vietnam War, the civil rights movement, the sexual revolution, the counterculture, and the emergence of television as the principal news medium and molder of popular taste (no longer merely a novel form of entertainment) were catalysts for change as well. So too was the astounding economic prosperity that began during World War II and continued into the early 1970s. The New Leftists hated the rising consumer culture based upon the very large real income growth enjoyed by a majority of Americans during the fifties and sixties. Ironically, it was that same wealth that made it possible both for college enrollments to rise and for college students to worry less about their personal futures, as somehow money could always be found when needed.

During the Red Scare (1946–55), radicalism had been discouraged and thousands of people lost their jobs because of real or imagined ties to the Communist Party. Senator Joseph McCarthy of Wisconsin was the leading witchhunter, and the word *McCarthyism* was coined to describe his reckless slanders and destructive investigations. But by 1960 the Red Scare was (to students) a distant event, and radical dissent seemed, if not risk free, to pose few problems to one's economic health.

Thus a host of elements came together in a few short years that would change the nation forever. The Vietnam War and the civil rights movement stimulated much of the era's passion, wealth, technology, new ideas about art, culture, personal conduct, and the rise of the pleasure principle—which held that self-gratification was the purpose of life—eroding old standards and creating new ones. But if the New Left was only part of this rich mixture, it was one of the most spectacular ingredients and would have far more lasting effects than its critics at the time believed. As it happened, these results were not usually the ones New Leftists had wanted, but the law of unintended consequences took hold and generated many ironies.

Birth of the New Left

The New Left originated in the Eisenhower Era of the 1950s, still often seen as an age of conformity by historians, and also as an age of mindless consumerism and trivial pursuits—much like the 1980s and 1990s except lacking the social pathology of these later decades. But, unlike the eighties and nineties, which were driven by business and technological changes but produced little in the way of political and social gain, the fifties were wracked by fierce political struggles that had important consequences. The Red Scare is usually blamed for stifling dissent in the society at large and contributing to the blandness of Eisenhowerism. It did that to a degree, but the Red Scare had other effects. For one, by essentially destroying the Communist Party USA, it nearly wiped the left side of the political slate clean, making possible the creation of a new radical movement untainted by espionage or rationalizations of Stalin's repressive regime and mass murders in the former Soviet Union. Although the Red Scare weakened civil liberties at first, its long-range effect was to strengthen them. By the end of the fifties the Supreme Court was reversing its earlier rulings and extending the protection of the First Amendment to unpopular ideas and associations. On college campuses, too, there was much more concern for free speech and a strong desire not to allow a repeat of McCarthyism. The New Left would benefit greatly from these developments, particularly during its early years.

The fifties was also the time during which the black civil rights movement took to the streets. Previously the fight against racial segregation had been primarily a legal one—culminating in the Supreme Court decision in *Brown* v. *Board of Education* (1953), which struck down the doctrine of separate but equal schools for blacks and whites. Two years later the black population of Montgomery, Alabama, was in full revolt against segregated buses, marching, demonstrating, and boycotting the bus company by walking to work.

The Montgomery boycott made its leader, Martin Luther King Jr., a world figure. It combined virtually all known methods of protest together in a more imaginative way and on a greater scale than movements for equality had ever achieved before. Also new in this context was King's philosophy of nonviolence, a doctrine holding that the use of force even in self-defense was wrong, and that one should seek to convert the oppressor as well as fight oppression. It is hard to say if nonviolence converted many segregationists, but it made the use of force by racists a weapon that could be used against them in the court of public opinion. The civil rights movement pioneered direct action techniques that could be used by others as well, giving radicals a wider range of political options in the future.

The fifties was also the age of the Beat Generation. Leading Beats, such as the writers Jack Kerouac and Allen Ginsberg, did not have a political agenda. But they despised authority, convention, and orthodox morality, and lived bohemian lives. Their opinions and antisocial behavior became widely known as they shocked traditional Americans and generated enormous publicity. Art was their religion, but it was often a defiant art, based on contempt for both middle-class values and artistic convention. The Beats seemed freakish at the time, a passing sensation, grist for the mills of the media, who were then, as now, always in search of novelty and perversion. Unbeknownst at the time, the Beats were spreading ideas that would profoundly affect the next generation.

Less dramatically, the revival of political liberalism probably gave impetus to the Movement too. Liberal Democrats secured big gains in the 1958 elections. The election of John F. Kennedy two years later put a president in the White House who, while not especially liberal himself, inspired many liberals. His advocacy of the Peace Corps, a program that sent young Americans to work in the Third World, and its immediate success, excited young people and showed that youth had an untapped potential for disinterested service.

During his campaign Kennedy had raised the idea of establishing a Peace Corps to channel the energies and high-mindednes of college graduates. They would live among Third World peoples serving as nurses, teachers, and in other capacities desperately needed by the poor. Soon after taking office Kennedy established the Peace Corps by executive order, naming his brother-in-law, Sargent Shriver, to head it. Popular with students, the Peace Corps won over Congress as well—even the conservative Barry Goldwater liked it. By 1964, 10,000 Peace Corps volunteers were helping people to help themselves in forty-six countries.

Another wild card thrown into this mix was the rising birth rate. The arrival of that huge generation known as the "baby boomers" had caught everyone by surprise. Previously it had been a rule of American life that each generation gave birth at a lower rate than the prior one, population increase being merely a function of immigration. But starting in World War II, young Americans began having more, rather than fewer, children. The resulting baby boom strained the nation's lower schools in the fifties. In the sixties it would have a similar effect on institutions of higher education—the number of college students more than doubling during the decade. Indeed, the ratio of college-age youth actually enrolled in institutions of higher education rose from 38 percent in 1961 to over 50 percent a decade later. Thus, the pool from which sprang campus advocates of new ideas would be larger than ever before.

Finally, by the sixties, college students were physically more mature than their predecessors, a fact to which universities had not adapted. When the modern university was formed at the beginning of the twentieth century, the average age of puberty was about six-teen years. By the 1960s puberty began around age fourteen. As a result, men and women entering college were well beyond adolescence in terms of physical maturity, and yet universities still treated them as children, enforcing dress codes, limiting their political expression, and even making female students retire to their single-sex dormitories at set hours every evening. The anger students were soon to express was probably, at least in part, owing to the survival of universities' doctrine of *in loco parentis*—that they took the place of the students' parents—which no longer made sense in terms of human biology.

As the sixties dawned, few Americans believed that students would soon influence history. In the 1950s the level of political apathy on campus was considered to be so great that critics labeled college-aged youth the "Silent Generation." This tag was misleading in several respects. For one, it ignored the student activism of the period, which, while not usually attracting national attention, was meaningful. The University of Texas at Austin, for example, was the scene of a number of civil rights and civil liberties test cases that aroused strong feelings locally. UT, Austin was home to a lively form of Christian liberalism that concerned itself with such topical issues as alienation, widely used in the fifties and sixties to describe, for example, the rejection of the political system by blacks and poor people generally. Emerging leftists organized protests as well, notably against the UT president's refusal in 1957 to allow a black student to star in the opera *Dido and Aeneas*. A leader among religious student radicals at UT was Sandra "Casey" Cason, who went on to become a civil rights activist and, after marrying Tom Hayden in 1961, an important voice in Students for a Democratic Society. Hayden, a future president of SDS, was not religious, so their marriage united the Christian and secular wings of the New Left. Apart from being tall, blond, and beautiful, Cason's rise to eminence in the New Left was explained by Hayden as a function of "her ability to think morally, express herself poetically, and have practical effects." Others like Cason played similar roles as catalysts at a number of universities. At the University of California, Berkeley, student activists formed their own political party named SLATE in 1957. Harvard had a similar body called Tocsin. At more than a few other campuses, rivulets of agitation were beginning to trickle.

The "Silent Generation" label misled in another way, since it implied that American college students traditionally had been in the forefront of social action. In some other countries that was certainly true, but not in the United States, where there was little precedent for student militancy and more for student misbehavior, such as panty raids and football riots. Even in the "Red Decade" of the 1930s, college radicals, who were not all that numerous, had belonged to student chapters of adult organizations that determined their agendas.

SDS Takes the Stage

That practice still seemed to be the case in 1960, when the surviving handful of campus political groups affiliated with adult bodies, the Student League for Industrial Democracy (SLID) among them, were suffering from what looked like terminal indifference. In 1960 SLID was reduced to having three barely functioning chapters when, out of desperation as much as anything else, its membership decided to change the organization's name to Students for a Democratic Society (SDS). At this point the newly named organization had no thought of breaking with its parent body, the League for Industrial Democracy (LID), a nonprofit organization of democratic socialists identified with the labor movement, which provided SLID with small amounts of money and considerable amounts of unwanted advice. But SDS, as the nation would soon know the group, unfurled its sails just as the winds of change were about to strengthen. Its new name was officially adopted in January 1960.

Only weeks later, on February 1, four black students sat down at a whites-only lunch counter in Greensboro, North Carolina, a form of nonviolent resistance and a daring challenge to the Jim Crow laws in effect. Their protest would transform the nation. Thus, the sit-in was born. The sit-in took nonviolence to another level. Instead of protesting against segregation from the outside, black students began entering segregated facilities and refusing to leave. They endured the resulting insults, beatings, and arrests with stoic dignity, reaping a harvest of publicity, embarrassing southerners, and inspiring sympathizers elsewhere in the nation.

That first modest and nearly spontaneous nonviolent sit-in was followed by many others, acts that galvanized not only black students in the South but northern whites as well. Within months perhaps 100 student groups had been formed to support the recurring sit-ins. At the University of Michigan in Ann Arbor, the newly renamed SDS chapter joined the effort, this at the urging of one of U.M.'s few student radicals, Al Haber, age twenty-four. The early growth of SDS, and the central place in it occupied by Ann Arbor, was, to a large extent, Haber's doing. In the fifties Al Haber, whose father was a faculty member at the university and a supporter of LID, occupied a lonely position as Michigan's "resident radical." But his wilderness years were over. Even as the sit-ins were taking place, Al Haber was organizing a conference on "Human Rights in the North." Few expected much to come out of this obscure conference, but when it opened in May, stars of both the old and new civil rights movements were on hand—people such as Bayard Rustin, master organizer of the black left, James Farmer, a veteran of the civil rights movement who was about to make the Congress of Racial Equality (CORE) famous, Michael Harrington of LID and the Young People's Socialist League, who was soon to become famous with his book on poverty *The Other America,* and, most significant, representatives of the newly formed Student Nonviolent Coordinating Committee (SNCC, pronounced "Snick"), which was leading the new sit-in movement.

That conference made SDS. By summer it had eight chapters and 250 members. President Al Haber established its first, full-time national headquarters in New York. His position in Ann Arbor—and soon in SDS as a whole—was taken by Tom Hayden, editor of the influential student paper the *Michigan Daily.* Hayden, who was born in 1939, had been recruited by Haber and quickly established his value as a leader and spokesperson. After graduation, and marriage to Casey Cason, now the Young Women's Christian Association's (YWCA) liaison to SNCC, in which the religious influence was strong at first, Hayden became the first field secretary of SDS. The job had no real description so it would be what he made of it. It paid $62 a week, poverty wages at the time, but all SDS could spare. Hayden opened an office in Atlanta, Georgia, SNCC's home base, and was soon in the thick of the fight for integration as SDS's link to SNCC's voter-registration drive, which was entering its most bloody phase. Over the next four years dozens of registration workers would be killed by racists, culminating in 1964's Freedom Summer, a voter-registration campaign in Mississippi and Alabama during which fifteen SNCC members would be slain.

On October 11, 1961, a segregationist in McComb, Mississippi, gave Hayden a beating that made the young activist famous. On his second day in McComb, while stopped at a traffic light, Hayden was approached by a burly young man who knew an outside agitator when he saw one. The man dragged Hayden from his car and worked him over. By sheer chance a news photographer saw the beating and managed to take pictures of it without being seen. One of those photographs went out on the Associated Press wire and was printed by many newspapers. It showed a neatly dressed Hayden on the ground in the approved nonviolent crouch, while a young man in blue jeans threw a punch at Hayden's unprotected head. The McComb police, always on the mob's side when it came to race, arrested Hayden and his male associate, and then ordered them out of town.

When they arrived at the Atlanta airport FBI agents met them and arranged for the two to fly to Washington for an interview with Burke Marshall, the assistant attorney general for civil rights. Burke sympathized with SNCC's voter-registration campaign, but urged Hayden to persuade SNCC members to stay out of dangerous places like McComb, as the government could not protect them. Although deflating to Hayden, who expected more from the federal government, his well-publicized beating, together with his writings from the South, which SDS had been distributing, made him—at the age of twenty-one—a hero.

By the fall of 1961, SDS had twenty chapters, and Haber was sending out 10,000 free copies of its newsletter containing

Hayden's reports from the South. Although SDS was still very small compared to adult political organizations like Americans for Democratic Action (ADA) or the National Association for the Advancement of Colored People (NAACP), its members had already begun to think of themselves as actors on the stage of history. Some of them were "red diaper babies," whose parents were, or had been, members of the Communist Party. But all understood that history required them to issue a manifesto.

SDS assigned Hayden, its best writer, to compose the SDS manifesto—which became known as the *Port Huron Statement.* He did this in Ann Arbor during the spring of 1962. The most often cited document produced by SDS, it is interesting now chiefly as a thermometer registering the temperature of young radicals at the start of their fateful journey through the sixties. On the whole, it was a moderate and thoughtful paper, rooted in the liberalism to which most "SDSers" were still residually attached. It was also infused with a kind of wounded patriotism, a sense that American ideals had been lost and Americans needed a new sense of commitment. Hayden began by saying, "We are people of this generation, bred in at least modest comfort, housed now in universities, looking uncomfortably to the world we inherit." What made SDSers uneasy were the same things that bothered liberals—nuclear weapons, racism, world poverty and hunger, and overpopulation.

Hayden maintained that American leaders offered no solutions to these problems, nor did the universities, which brushed aside human values in favor of "empirical" research. The principles of SDS, on the other hand, began with such values—human potential, fraternity, honesty, a desire to end human loneliness and isolation, and a belief that power should be based not on possessions or privilege but on "love, reflectiveness, reason and creativity," words that would soon take on a spectral quality given the hate and violence to come. "Participatory democracy" was the method Hayden put forward to cure the world's ills, although it was more a slogan than a plan, and Hayden never clearly spelled it out.

Hayden's criticisms of America's political and social ills were more specific. The American political system appeared to offer a choice, he posited, but in reality did not because the differences within the the two major parties were greater than those separating one from the other. As such, the party system squelched debate on fundamental issues. Americans were dehumanized by a "remote control economy" run by the wealthy and a handful of large corporations for their own benefit. The "military-industrial complex," a new term then, having been coined only the year before by President Eisenhower in his farewell address, loomed over everything, nurturing the Cold War for its own power and profit. Even organized labor, because it was part of the establishment, offered little hope to individuals caught up in the tentacles of this overarmed state. Technological advancement was perverted for militaristic ends. Around the world rebels were rising up against Western domination, a process the United States sought to prevent in the name of anti-Communism.

According to Hayden, the solutions to these problems included disarmament and an end to the nuclear and other arms races. It should be America's national policy, he argued, to eliminate hunger, poverty, disease, ignorance, violence, and exploitation, replacing them with "abundance, reason, love, and international cooperation." Fifty years should suffice to achieve this, Hayden wrote innocently, probably thinking that his timetable was, if anything, too conservative. But he did recognize that American democracy as then constituted would be inadequate to the challenge, hence the need for a different America, one based on the principles outlined here.

It would be easy to make fun of this document, filled with the hopefulness of youth and a mind-numbing lack of experience with the real world and with history. Yet the *Port Huron Statement* compels respect even so. Although Hayden succumbed to the radical vice of utopianism, having no clear idea how to implement change, the paper was specific in many areas, well-reasoned given its assumptions, and refreshingly inclusive by today's standards. Hayden believed that his proposals would benefit nearly everyone, not simply members of one or another victimized minority. He was concerned not just with material needs but with individual isolation and alienation, topics of great interest at the time which have since fallen from sight for no good reason. While Hayden was its principal author, the *Statement* was adopted by SDS as a whole and must be viewed as a collective expression of its members' hopes and dreams. In their youthful ardor SDSers possessed, Hayden would later write, what the novelist Doris Lessing called "the power to create through naivete."

Today the Port Huron meeting of SDS is chiefly remembered for the *Statement*. At the time, however, its composition shared center stage with a generational struggle that broke out between young SDSers and older radicals. A total of fifty-nine people, including perhaps a dozen observers, averaging about thirty-five attendees at each session—met in Port Huron, Michigan, on June 12, 1962, at a summer camp loaned to SDS by the United Auto Workers. As membership dues were only a dollar a year and often not paid, SDS relied for its support on small donations in cash or kind provided by a few unions, erratic support from the LID, and an occasional grant. The UAW was its major supporter because Mildred Jeffrey, the mother of founding SDS member Sharon Jeffrey, was a high official in the union.

As soon as the meeting convened, an angry debate broke out between Michael Harrington of LID, at thirty-four already an experienced socialist, and the youngsters led by Hayden. Harrington laced into them for failing to attack Communism strongly enough and for not including labor and liberal groups as a part of their program for reforming America. Later Harrington regretted his behavior at the meeting, believing he had overreacted to the young people's dismissive attitude toward veteran radicals. But after Harrington left in a huff the SDSers did take his criticism seriously and revised the *Statement* enough to win Harrington's subsequent approval. The face-off with Harrington notwithstanding, the Port Huron meeting was considered by SDSers to have been not only successful but a historic event, which it was. Hayden was elected president of the chapter, to Haber's considerable relief— he was not much of an organization man. And the *Port Huron Statement* enjoyed wide circulation, despite the fact that no one knew exactly what "participatory democracy" meant.

Over the next several years SDS struggled to find a place for itself in the political spectrum. Member growth continued, although slowly, and the issues continued to be argued. These dialogues led to the publication of another statement, *America and the New Era,* after the 1963 general meeting held near Pine Hill, New York. Written by Hayden and Richard Flacks, a graduate student who would separate from SDS the next year after marriage and the beginning of his academic career, *America and the New Era* was both shorter (fifteen pages) and more narrowly focused on domestic issues than the *Port Huron Statement,* which remained the signature document of SDS. For Flacks, as well as many other SDSers, the summer of 1963 was the best time they would ever know. The civil rights movement was blossoming. The nuclear test-ban treaty between the United States and the Soviet Union awaited signature. And on June 10, at the American University in Washington, D.C., President Kennedy gave a speech in support of the treaty that was free of his customary Cold War bombast.

SDSers had not been fans of the young president. Indeed, his 1960 campaign was notable for its hawkish rhetoric. Soon after taking office Kennedy launched a huge increase in defense spending (which the Soviets would match); then an abortive U.S.-backed invasion of Cuba came to grief at the Bay of Pigs. In 1962 he and Chairman Nikita Khrushchev of the Soviet Union had hovered on the brink of nuclear war during the Cuban Missile Crisis. Kennedy greatly expanded the military, sent the first American combat troops to Vietnam, faced down Soviet leader Nikita Khrushev during the missile crisis, and otherwise lived up to his reputation as a cold warrior. But the test-ban treaty and the American University speech seemed to herald a possible change. On June 10, 1963, he said of the Soviets, "If we cannot end now all our differences, at least we can help make the world safe for diversity. For, in the final analysis, our most basic common link is that we all inhabit this small planet. We all breathe the same air. We all cherish our children's future. And we are all mortal." Accordingly, Kennedy's assassination in November 1963 strongly affected some in SDS. Hayden, who would always have a foot, or at least a toe, in the doorway of the real political world, believed that the "tragic consciousness of the sixties generation began here."

But the practical consequences of JFK's death were few for SDS, since it was already moving beyond liberalism, as the debate with Harrington indicated. The slide was further evidenced in October 1963, when leaders of the democratic, anti-Communist, Old Left met privately in a Manhattan apartment with leaders of the New Left, hoping to bridge the gap between them. The Old Leftists were editors of the mildly socialist journal of opinion *Dissent,* among whom the literary critic Irving Howe was best known. The New Leftists included Tom Hayden, Todd Gitlin, and Paul Potter, past, present, and future presidents of SDS. The discussion went downhill quickly, Hayden and Howe in particular clashing. To Howe, the SDSers were uncritical of Cuba's Fidel Castro, failing to recognize the dead hand of totalitarianism when they saw it, and showed too little respect for democratic values. Hayden was "fanatical," in Howe's opinion (Gitlin thought "dynamo" more descriptive). Hayden also—and contradictorily in Howe's view—made a strong pitch for nonviolence in foreign affairs, which the *Dissent* crowd, their memories of Hitler and fascism still fresh, considered ridiculous. To SDS leaders, intellectuals like Howe were part of the failed past, inactivists, while they themselves were the wave of the future.

Afterward Howe wished he had been more temperate, for fierce debate was a way of life among New York intellectuals but repugnant to SDSers, who at the time thought discussion should lead to consensus rather than turning into a forum in which one idea prevailed over another. In any event, a widening gap existed between the two sides that could not have been bridged by conciliatory words. Realists and democratic to the core, the editors of *Dissent* were far removed both in age and experience from the youthful romantics of the New Left.

By this time college students, as well as recent graduates, were routinely becoming politically active in a variety of ways not dreamed of a few years earlier. President Kennedy's creation of the Peace Corps had officially sanctioned the idea that young people could make a difference in the world. The Freedom Summer Project of 1964 would test that thesis in a much more dangerous way. Conceived by SNCC, Freedom Summer was sponsored by the Council of Federated Groups, which included other civil rights organizations and the National Council of Churches. Its aim was to send 1,000, mostly young, white volunteers to join SNCC's field force in registering black voters. The project organized 40,000 blacks into the Mississippi Freedom Democratic Party and started some thirty Freedom Schools in nineteen counties. But the cost was very heavy. Among the fifteen civil rights workers killed that summer were James Chaney, Andrew Goodman, and Michael Schwerner, who had been missing since June and whose bodies were found near Philadelphia, Mississippi, in August. Freedom Summer was the last straw for black militants, who were preparing to drive whites out of the civil rights movement and abandon nonviolence before the summer began, and believed that its casualties proved their point. This was an emotional decision on the part of the black militants, born of rage, and made little sense, as white support had been crucial to the movement and nonviolence highly effective, despite the casualties inflicted by racists.

SDS began its own project that summer, known as the Economic Research and Action Project (ERAP). It was directed by Sharon Jeffrey, who had been one of SDS's first recruits in Ann Arbor and was a gifted organizer. The funds were contributed by the UAW, still a supporter of SDS and a union with a large minority membership. Under Jeffrey's direction, 125 SDSers moved into northern black ghettos as community organizers bent on creating political and self-help structures among the very poor. Al Haber was ERAP's nominal director, but had doubts from the start, fearing that ERAP meant action for its own sake and that it was guided by emotion rather than intellect. He was soon replaced by Rennie Davis, a true believer.

Tom Hayden went to Newark, NJ, as an organizer, remaining a resident for several more years after the ERAP folded. Although Sharon Jeffrey supposedly led the effort in Cleveland, leadership was going out of style. SDS had been organized in the usual way, with formal meetings and elected officers, but by its nature participatory democracy made leadership suspect. ERAP projects involved spending a great deal of time in marathon talks aimed at achieving unanimity. This was hard to reach, and organizing ghetto-dwellers, whose dysfunctionality was much greater than expected, proved to be harder still. SDSers had not been prepared for the high rates of alcoholism and drug addiction they encountered, as well as domestic violence, illiteracy, and other problems that characterized the ghetto. They failed to understand that people without any political opinions could not be radicalized. At a national meeting of ERAP organizers in January 1965, eight days were wasted trying to reach agreement on methods and goals. By the spring ERAP was virtually dead, a victim of organizational incoherence, and a growing belief in radical decentralization. Then, too, the Vietnam War was beginning to crowd out other issues popular among leftist students.

Although it failed, ERAP had attracted favorable publicity. ERAP made participatory democracy seem more real, and the apparently successful communal living arrangements of organizers seemed to point the way to a higher form of social service, one based on selfless brotherhood rather than careerism and bureaucracy. ERAP inspired untold numbers of communes, clinics, and free schools for years, despite its failure to significantly influence ghetto life anywhere.

For SDS, ERAP was a stop on the highway to fragmentation, and by the end of 1964 factionalism was rampant. SDS meetings had degenerated into free-form exercises leading nowhere. Tom Hayden, whose marriage to Casey had broken up in 1963, contributed to the disorder with ambiguous remarks and unanswerable questions, such as "What would happen to professors if poor people could give lectures on poverty?" For SDS, the days of reasoned debate and coherent agendas were just about over.

Meanwhile, the War in Vietnam was getting harder to ignore. On February 8, 1965, American aircraft bombed targets in North Vietnam in response to a raid on an airbase in South Vietnam by the Viet Cong. Three days later President Johnson announced the doctrine of "sustained reprisal" against the Viet Cong, which would soon lead to an enormous increase in American air operations over the North. At this point SDS decided to organize a protest in Washington, a historic move for SDS, and the country. On March 25 the first improvised "teach-in" against the escalating war was held in Ann Arbor. The teach-in was not a takeover of public buildings like the sit-in. It was a scheduled event during which faculty and students gave talks on aspects of the war, denounced the Johnson administration, and proposed policy changes.

Some teach-ins had a scholarly tone, while others resembled political rallies. Within days teach-ins—some lasting all night—were being organized at colleges and universities across the country. Well over 100 such events took place, culminating in Washington with a twelve-hour National Teach-in.

It was against this background that SDS staged a march on Washington on April 17, 1965. The event was small compared to future protests against the war, but expecting at most 10,000 participants, SDS was thrilled when the actual turnout came to between 15,000 and 25,000 persons—the largest demonstration for peace in history some believed. The usual lineup of personalities addressed the crowd—I. F. Stone, an independent journalist and proprietor of the influential newsletter *I. F. Stone's Weekly,* Senator Ernest Greuning of Alaska, one of the first antiwar politicians on the national stage, and the legendary Bob Parris (Moses) of SNCC. Joan Baez and Phil Ochs, popular folksingers and antiwar activists, performed, as did Judy Collins, who sang Bob Dylan's powerful "The Times They Are A-Changin'." Finally, everyone sang "We Shall Overcome," the anthem of the civil rights movement. The sixties and the antiwar movement were now fully joined. Ominously, however, the specter of left dogmatism also raised its head, as some participants mocked liberalism, angering I. F. Stone. He was a liberal himself, Stone told the crowd (and a former Stalinist too, he might well have added), and had "seen snot-nosed Marxist-Leninists come and go."

SDS now decided to break with LID completely and relocate its headquarters to Chicago, moves that made less difference than the leaders had hoped. For one thing, SDS still could not decide what its true mission was and failed to take advantage of the momentum that had started in Washington. Decision making, never easy for SDS leaders, was made more difficult by the increasingly anarchistic and bohemian character of the membership. The rapid pace of change is summed up by a photograph—the earliest group picture of SDS that survives—of the National Council meeting in Bloomington, Indiana, in September 1963. It shows a group of clean-cut young people, fists raised self-consciously in an awkward salute. The 1965 general meeting held in northern Michigan from June 9 to 13, 1965, in contrast, featured men and women wearing long hair and a great deal of leather and denim. Another sign of the rapidly changing times was that people smoked marijuana at this major SDS meeting, yet another first. Increasingly, New Leftists were coming to look and behave like hippies.

Observers at the 1965 general meeting came from other groups on the left—the National Student Christian Federation, the (Marxist) Progressive Labor Party, and, poignantly it would later seem, representatives of SNCC, who were making their final appearance at an integrated function. Black Power advocates would soon expel their white membership, setting in motion a process that undercut and finally destroyed the civil rights movement. At the conference talk was more rambling than ever, the hostility to elitism, hierarchy, and even structure itself more manifest. Plenary sessions were chaired by members picked at random. Workshops debated whether to have chairmen at all. Attempts to frame another SDS manifesto were denounced as repressive examples of "statementism." Position papers were disregarded. In a token nod to the past, a new president was elected—or acclaimed, it was hard to tell—as a replacement for Paul Booth, a voice of reason who vainly urged participants to avoid identifying themselves with the Viet Cong. His successor, Carl Oglesby, was a member of just four-months' standing. Otherwise, the only decision to come from the meeting was to admit Communists as members, to SDS a blow on behalf of a more radical democracy. This claim was made by people whose commitment to actual democracy had all but disappeared.

Without a program, local SDS chapters were on their own, all the more so since in Chicago the national office was floundering. The lack of direction in SDS was bad enough, but worse still was the new "office democracy," which essentially meant that the mundane work of filing, mailing, and answering letters was to be done voluntarily, according to the dictates of an individual's conscience. Since most consciences rejected dictation, the necessary paperwork never got done. At the National Council meeting in September, office democracy was defended by members who admitted that it did not work. At the end of the year SDS had perhaps 10,000 members and no plan for its future. Paul Booth, named national secretary in September, reduced the administrative chaos a little, only to be voted out of that office at the next national meeting in Clear Lake, Iowa, the following June—along with the rest of the "Old Guard." He was then all of twenty-three years old. The 1966 convention did launch a program of sorts, known as "student power," which was meant to radicalize undergraduates. In practice this did not make a whole lot of difference, SDS being blown hither and yon by increasingly fickle winds.

While the rising tide of anarchy paralyzed SDS, Tom Hayden had come to see in the Vietnam War a cause to which he could give himself completely. In December 1965 Hayden visited Hanoi, the capitol of North Vietnam, along with Herbert Aptheker of the Communist Party USA, and Staughton Lynd, a historian, Quaker, and a veteran of the civil rights and peace movements. The invitation had been sent to Aptheker by Communist leaders in Hanoi, who specifically requested that he bring two non-Communists along with him. Lynd and Hayden fit the bill and gave Hanoi its money's worth by propagandizing on its behalf afterward, notably with their book, *The Other Side* (1966), which gave the Communist version of the war.

Lynd, like Hayden, was a romantic, and the two found it easy to represent the Communists in Vietnam not simply as victims but as just about perfect. According to the authors, North Vietnam's social and economic system could hardly be improved, nor could the emotional life of the people. A leading poet had cried while composing a poem to Norman Morrison, an American who had immolated himself to protest the war and was being lionized in North Vietnam. (Morrison had been inspired by the example of Buddhist monks in South Vietnam who torched themselves while demonstrating against a Saigon regime.) Lynd and Hayden had seen a factory manager in Hanoi break down while thinking about Morrison and Abraham Lincoln—workers, too, became teary-eyed whilst contemplating these great men. North Vietnam, one-party rule to the contrary, had even developed its own form of democratic government, the authors wrote, "rice-roots" democracy, as also a "socialism of the heart" that entailed hearty handclasps, poetry, song, and a good deal of weeping.

Enraptured by their own propaganda, Hayden and Lynd failed to observe that North Vietnam fell somewhat short when it came to civil liberties. Ruthlessness overlaid with bathos proved to be a winning combination for other visitors as well, such as the actress Jane Fonda—Hayden's future wife—who would soon herself gladly bathe in the healing waters of Vietnamese Communism. In 1967 Hayden flew to Bratislava, then still part of Communist Czechoslovakia, where he met a delegation of Vietnamese and gave a fiery speech proclaiming that "We are all Viet Cong." He also, in his self-appointed role as secretary of state for the New Left, negotiated the freedom of three American prisoners held by the Viet Cong—the first POWs released by Vietnamese Communists.

Meanwhile, in SDS itself chaos still ruled. SDS had refused to concentrate on the war for fear of becoming a single-issue organization. It was also against developing its student base because that would have meant ignoring others—workers, professionals, artists, mothers—who in theory would make SDS a grand national coalition but who, in practice, wanted nothing to do with the Movement. Nevertheless, by the summer of 1965, SDS was getting enormous publicity for its antiwar stand, although it had yet to develop an antiwar program and was playing the Vietnam issue by ear. Its membership grew anyway, for increasing numbers of young people were sick of society, or the war, or both. However, in the absence of a viable program, how this momentum might be used was anyone's guess.

Some SDSers busied themselves by forming "free universities," which offered courses in everything from the theory and practice of revolution to "Zen Basketball" and "Paper Airplanes and People." Hundreds of such schools sprang up, most of them short lived, some ending up being absorbed by real universities or liberal groups such as the National Student Association, which in 1968 received a large grant from the Ford Foundation to explore the usefulness of free universities as agents of reform. Publishing "underground" newspapers was another outlet favored by many

SDSers. And, from time to time, antiwar demonstrations did break out, notably in the fall of 1966, at which time there were some 200 campus chapters of SDS.

By the spring of 1967 many, perhaps half, of all SDS chapters had become involved in draft resistance. Instead of trying to reach the general public, this strategy entailed persuading men eligible for military service to burn their draft cards as an act of defiance. SDS urged resistors to accept prison terms rather than serve if inducted, or go underground, or leave the country. The National Office did what it could, putting out buttons—one read simply "Resist"—and publishing a special issue of its newsletter, *New Left Notes,* devoted entirely to draft resistance, which sold 10,000 copies. Others were doing similar work, but SDS enjoyed particular success at its April 15 Spring Moratorium in New York City that featured a mass draft-card burning during which 100 or so unidentifiable pieces of paper went up in flames. It is not clear if this is what *Time* magazine had in mind when it named the new generation as its "Man of the Year" in January because of its devotion to "decency, tolerance, brotherhood."

At this point so many demonstrations, sit-ins, and direct actions were being staged that it was impossible to keep track of them. An ironic protest, in light of future events, took place at Cornell University when the local district attorney attempted to confiscate copies of the student literary magazine. Some 2,000 students blocked his act, and when five were arrested, the crowd liberated them from police custody by force. Thirty years later, students, usually racial minorities, would "confiscate" student publications as a matter of course—politically correct sympathizers endorsing these acts, or turning a blind eye. But in the sixties—for a while—free speech still was still important.

The riots and demonstrations of spring gave way to "Vietnam Summer," named after the fabled Freedom Summer of 1964 during which at least fifteen voter-registration volunteers had been killed. Fortunately no one died during the demonstrations of Vietnam Summer, in which SDS participated, but by no means organized. It now had a total membership of perhaps 30,000, with chapters on some 250 campuses. But SDS was running on momentum and adrenaline, as much carried along by the rush of events as exercising any control over them. Every convention saw a turnover in leadership, and that of 1967 held in Ann Arbor from June 25 to July 2 was no exception.

SDS now came under assault by the tightly organized squads of Progressive Labor, an attack that was hard to resist, as SDS had no membership requirement and was forced to accept anyone, regardless of age or status. The Progressive Labor Party (PL) was a small band of Maoists who had broken away from the Communist Party USA in 1962. Infatuated with Mao's dream of Third World revolutionary movements, doctrinaire and sectarian PLers brought to the formless SDS meetings an obsession with revolutionary theory that proved contagious. They also meant to take over SDS, launching prolonged theoretical discussions aimed at not only developing a correct "party line" in the Leninist tradition, but at seizing power. The resulting agonizing debates ranged all over the Left's intellectual landscape in pursuit of partisan objectives. It also led to considerable posing and pretense as each speaker or faction sought to validate its revolutionary credentials. Gone was the old effort to arrive at consensus. Gone too was the idea of participatory democracy, since Leninism (and/or Maoism) were antithetical to democracy of any kind.

On the other hand, SDSers' tradition of openness made their meetings easy to disrupt. And that is exactly what had happened in June 1967 during a Back-to-the-Drawing-Boards meeting at a wooded camp in central Michigan organized by the Old Guard to figure out where the New Left ought to be going. That meeting, however, never got off the ground because Hayden's keynote speech was interrupted by a invasion of Diggers (so named after seventeenth-century English communists), a group of anarchistic, existential, and profane bohemians with vaguely political notions. Three of the Diggers, who had just arrived from San Francisco, seized the stage, high on drugs or their own self-importance. At this point, their spokesperson, a man named Peter Berg who for unknown reasons called himself Emmet Grogan, engaged in a long incoherent rant, obscenely condemning SDS, the Kremlin, and "fags," among others, after which he knocked one woman down and slapped around (or pretended to slap around—eyewitnesses disagreeing) a few others. The Diggers left the next day, but the Drawing Boards meeting never recovered, adjourning without having arrived at anything meaningful. This fiasco, SDSer Todd Gitlin would later write, explained why the New Left's efforts to outgrow its student base always failed. Having rejected old beliefs while failing to arrive at new ones of comparable weight, the New Left had no vital center.

In October 1967 the Dow Chemical Company of Midland, Michigan, returned to Madison, the University of Wisconsin's main campus. The previous winter Dow's job-recruiters had touched off a major sit-in because Dow manufactured napalm. A jellied gasoline that could not be extinguished with water, napalm symbolized to students the inhumanity of the Vietnamese War, for it was both a horrible burning agent and an indiscriminate weapon that turned landscapes into seas of flame. Unlucky civilians in Vietnam were often scarred or burned alive by napalm attacks misdirected to their villages. The first Dow sit-in had led to arrests but no real violence. The second sit-in began peacefully on October 18 at the Commerce Building, where job interviews were being held. The sit-in was broken up by club-wielding riot police, who cleared the building but inflamed the large crowd outside, which became ever more agitated, especially after the police attacked with tear gas—the first time students on a major campus had been exposed to this chemical agent. The crowd recoiled but later counterattacked with boots, bricks, rocks, and fists, the police responding with Mace and other weapons. After a long day of turbulence, sixty-five students and seven policemen were treated at local hospitals, three for broken bones. More rallies followed, and a boycott of classes lasted several days. Although nothing had been decided when students returned to class, the transition from nonviolence to rioting had been made—and not just by those at Wisconsin.

On Monday, October 20, with SDS participation, 10,000 people marched on the draftee induction center in Oakland, California, as part of "Stop the Draft Week." Some sat-in to block the building and were hustled off to jail. Sporadic violence on Tuesday was met by an overwhelming police response. A peaceful demonstration on Wednesday accomplished nothing. On Friday the demonstrators returned to the center equipped with helmets and makeshift shields and signs mounted on stout wooden poles, which they wielded in battle against the police. Cars, potted trees, benches, newspaper racks, and other moveable items were pushed into street intersections. Afterward, demonstrators boasted of having "held" the streets of Oakland for four hours and scrawled revolutionary graffiti—"Che (Guevara) Lives," and "Free Oakland"—on walls and sidewalks. (Ernesto "Che" Guevara was a leader of the Cuban revolution who was later killed by security forces in Bolivia.) This made for bad public relations but was thrilling to participants. Thereafter attacking police and public and private property would be standard practice for "revolutionaries."

The philosophy of nonviolence that had destroyed racial segregation and enfranchised southern blacks thus perished, without fanfare or debate. Not all future demonstrations would be violent, but nonviolence was now merely a tactic, not a faith. In the New Left's view nonviolence had been useful in its time, but that time had passed. More likely, since nonviolence had been highly effective as an instrument of social change, the discipline nonviolent protest required was simply no longer there. Civil rights, as always, paved the way for other segments of the Movement, SNCC having abandoned nonviolence for the heady illusion of Black Power. Then, too, at a time when armed revolutionaries like Che Guevara and Chairman Mao were becoming folk heroes of the left, when countercultural gurus were urging everyone to "do their own thing" irrespective of the consequences, such a turn was probably inevitable. It was, after all, far more satisfying to break a window or a policeman's head than to put one's own body at risk by passively sitting-in. Movement people rationalized this change as a simple matter of moving from "protest" to "resistance," a so-called higher form of political action. Tom Hayden went along with this at the time, only later coming to see the resort to violence as a pathological response born of hatred and frustration. In any event, violent resistance carried the seeds of terrorism within it and ultimately would be the death of the Movement.

The event in 1967 that engendered most publicity for the antiwar cause was the "March on the Pentagon" which began on October 21 and overshadowed the campus violence in Berkeley and Madison. It was organized by an umbrella group called the National Mobilization Committee, or "Mobe." The Mobe's project director for the March was Jerry Rubin, a Berkeley activist. He was aided by Abbie Hoffman, an independent organizer of theatrical protests. Rubin had met Hoffman only the previous August during a demonstration in New York City at which a group of protestors dressed as "hippies," the blanket term for devotees of the counterculture, had thrown $300 in singles on the floor of the New York Stock Exchange. Their reasons for doing so were murky, but the event attracted much media attention and made Hoffman, who had organized the stunt, famous—or infamous, or notorious, depending on how you looked at it. Rubin recruited Hoffman for the Mobe, and it seems to have been Hoffman's idea to climax the March on Washington by attempting to levitate the Pentagon.

The March was the biggest antiwar demonstration yet, with perhaps 100,000 people showing up. It was remarkable also for the variety of its participants, which included SDSers of course, Yippies—as followers of Rubin and Hoffman would soon be known—and a broad range of Americans including many distinguished figures. Norman Mailer, the country's most celebrated novelist, was there—and would immortalize the occasion with his autobiographical account, *Armies of the Night* (1968). Also present were Robert Lowell, the country's foremost poet, Dwight Macdonald, a radical in the 1930s who was now a prominent media critic, and Paul Goodman, another thirties radical who was something of an icon thanks to his *Growing Up Absurd* (1960), a treatise on alienated youth that had anticipated the Movement and helped define it. Dr. Benjamin Spock, whose book on child care was the rock upon which parents of the baby boomers stood, attended as well—advising parents to save their children's lives by stopping the war.

Protestors sang songs and gave speeches as usual, but many young radicals had lost their taste for planned events and conventional forms of expression. After arriving at the Pentagon, which was defended by armed troops, nonviolent protestors made gestures by inserting flowers in rifle muzzles. According to Jerry

Rubin, "beautiful naked chicks went up to GI's and suggested they take off their uniforms and come home with them." Aggressive young men rushed the lines of soldiers and U.S. marshals, thousands forcing their way onto the Pentagon's lawns. In his stream-of-consciousness memoir *Revolution for the Hell of It* (1968) Abbie Hoffman described the action as follows: "Homecoming Day at the Pentagon and the cheerleaders chant 'Beat Army! Beat Army!' It's SDS at the 30-yard line and third down. Rubin cuts the rope with a hunting knife and the Charge of the Flower Brigade is on."

The flag of the National Liberation Front was raised to show solidarity with the communists in South Vietnam, and seers, mystics, witches, and sorcerers staged their exorcism and attempted levitation of the massive five-sided building. At night campfires burned, songs filled the air, and love was made freely, until, at midnight, soldiers attacked with clubbed rifles, tear gas, and other instruments of persuasion, arresting perhaps 700 people—Mailer among them—and bloodying hundreds more. At dawn, most of the multitude folded their tents, Hoffman and some others remaining on the Pentagon's steps until the following night. "The Battle of the Pentagon," as Mailer called it, was over. Although it achieved little, the March was an epic moment of the sixties, the event at which the New Left and the counterculture came together most spectacularly.

Although marchers were deadly serious about ending the War in Vietnam, and not all were happy with the methods of Rubin and Hoffman, the bizarre happenings and events staged by them in Washington were well thought out. Both had considerable experience at manipulating the media and knew that the more bizarrely they behaved, the greater the coverage. They had taken to heart a popular slogan, "the medium is the message," which meant to them that what mattered was getting on television, not how they got there. Rubin and Hoffman never worried about bad publicity, believing that only failing to get publicity for their causes was bad. The media came to realize that they were being manipulated, but when the two made news the media had to cover it.

SDS was delighted by its successful participation in the biggest and broadest protest yet, but the problem of how to capitalize on the publicity such events garnered still eluded it. Theories and strategies came and went. The essential dilemma of how to convert what was still a rather narrow student, or ex-student, movement into some kind of nationwide revolutionary force remained. While the SDS National Office was still committed to resistance, PL favored what it called "base-building," the development of a worker-student coalition. The union of these disparate bodies was based on the popular, although self-evidently absurd, belief that students were a victimized rather than a privileged group in society, a conviction summed up in a popular underground essay entitled "The Student as Nigger." Both approaches, but especially that of PL, were threatened in the spring of 1968 by Senator Eugene McCarthy's strong showing in in the New Hampshire Democratic presidential primary, which led Robert Kennedy to throw his hat in the ring as well. Many Democratic leaders agreed with McCarthy that the War in Vietnam had to be ended, but none were willing to challenge President Johnson who seemed unbeatable. Only the junior senator from Minnesota had the courage to do so. However, as McCarthy lacked money and political support, few gave him much of a chance. Accompanied by actor Paul Newman, poet Robert Lowell, and 10,000 student volunteers, McCarthy ran a leisurely campaign and nearly beat Johnson in New Hampshire even so.

Senator Robert Kennedy of New York, the slain president's brother, had wanted to run, but was afraid of Johnson. After McCarthy's moral victory in New Hampshire, Kennedy, who was much better known than the senator from Minnesota, realized that he could win the nomination. Because McCarthy depended so heavily on students (some called his run the "children's crusade"), he aroused hopes on campus that conventional politics still offered a way of ending the War in Vietnam and that students could be part of the solution. Kennedy appealed to students as well and was strongly backed by minorities. Both candidates were potentially subversive of organizations such as SDS that had turned their backs on democracy.

CHAPTER TWO

SDS: Decline and Fall

SDS's National Council met on March 28, 1968, less than two weeks after Robert Kennedy's announcement of his presidential candidacy, and was completely befuddled. Its membership had never been larger—280 chapters and growing—or the road ahead less certain. Its plan for the spring, ten days of protests and student strikes, had been taken over by the Student Mobilization Committee—the youth wing of the Mobe. Barren of ideas, the Council decided to organize blacks in some undisclosed manner, even though it was a white organization and Black Power groups like SNCC monopolized the recruit pool. According to historian Staughton Lynd, the only explanation for this pointless and futile gesture was white guilt, which SDS members were always denying they felt but whose actions revealed otherwise. Draft resistance went out the window just when Vietnam had become the dominant political issue. Polls, for example, showed that one-third of all Americans now opposed military conscription.

SDS's pathetic excuse for a plan was mainly an emotional response to the great urban riots of the sixties. Urban riots, beginning with the one in the Watts section of Los Angeles in August 1964 (with thirty-four deaths), and running through Newark, New Jersey, in July 1967 (with twenty-five deaths), and Detroit the same month (with forty-three deaths), had become a regular feature of summertime in America. Then, the murder of Dr. Martin Luther King, Jr., on April 4, 1968, ignited the worst violence of all. During the next twenty-five days riots broke out in some 100 cities—notably Wilmington, Delaware, Baltimore, Chicago, and Washington D.C,, leaving more than sixty dead and thousands injured. These seasons of violence remain poorly understood. In the past, race riots occurred when white lynch mobs invaded black neighborhoods. Although terrible in their effects, traditional race riots are easily explained. Racial tensions would mount, and then a precipitating event would create a mob mentality, and the violence would begin. The urban riots of the sixties were different. Usually reacting to some action by the police, blacks rioted inside ghettoes, looting and burning commercial districts, and fighting pitched battles with police and National Guard units. The great majority of those killed and wounded were black, as rioters were poorly armed compared to law enforcement agents. The commercial districts that served blacks would lay in ruins for decades, imposing hardships on the entire population. But the riots thrilled SDS because they conformed to its ideology. What to others seemed random, self-destructive outbursts of violence, to SDS was clearly state-sponsored genocide on the one hand, and revolutionary uprisings on the other. As the authorities sought vainly to understand the riots and find solutions to them, SDS thought it knew exactly what was needed: more protests and demonstrations.

While the National Office focused on race, the scheduled Ten Days of student protests against the war went forward also, often with the active participation of SDS chapters. It climaxed on April 28 when participating students at some fifty campuses went on strike by skipping classes for the day. But these actions were eclipsed by unrelated events at Columbia University that would become the stuff of legends. The Columbia chapter of SDS was divided between a moderate group, the "praxis axis," and a more militant "action faction," a division characteristic of most SDS chapters by this time. In March the action faction won out, electing Mark Rudd as chair, and on April 23, SDS occupied Columbia's administration building, nominally in protest against a university plan to build a new gymnasium on property inhabited by poor blacks. Such was the spirit of the times, however, that events soon took on a life of their own. Initially a black-white coalition, the protestors soon were occupying different buildings, self-segregated by race. Within days other buildings were seized, several by protestors who had no connection with SDS, including hippie or Yippie groups such as the Motherfuckers—a name chosen for its shock value. (Their full name was "Up Against the Wall, Motherfucker," taken from a poem by the radical playwright known in those days as LeRoi Jones). Hayden and other Movement celebrities turned up also. After eight days the police moved in, breaking heads and arresting over 700 people. A student strike followed that lasted a month and forced the university to cancel final exams.

The Columbia SDS chapter that had started everything profited little from the strike, for, true to pattern, members could not decide how to exploit their fleeting advantage. In the end, liberal students successfully pressed for "reforms," more student participation in university affairs, the offering of more relevant classes—the usual menu of changes designed to make college easier and more pleasant for students. Oddly, despite the wrenching nature of this experience, Columbia suffered less academic damage than did other universities faced with similar demands, managing to hang on to the core curriculum that would make it increasingly distinctive in later years.

But if all publicity truly is good publicity, SDS as a whole had gained greatly. Since the Columbia takeover happened to be held in America's news capital, every aspect of the affair received close attention. SDS, which no longer reminded anyone of the Age of Chivalry, became an accredited revolutionary menace. Numerous state legislatures entertained bills to ban radical student organizations and deny them funding, and to deny funding to college administrations lacking the requisite counterrevolutionary spirit. And Congress passed legislation denying funding to universities that banned military recruiters and authorizing the president to dispatch U.S. soldiers to unruly campuses. The FBI stepped up its already considerable surveillance of the New Left. While in the Pentagon, a "domestic war room" was created to supervise armed responses to radical threats.

Educational leaders worked both sides of the street, while also taking a harder stand against violent protests. At the same time no fewer than 72 percent of colleges and universities expanded opportunities for student participation in campus governance. Most universities, if they had not already taken such steps, also responded to other student complaints. For example, restrictions on student conduct, such as dormitory hours and dress codes, went by the board. The concept of *in loco parentis,* whose unpopularity among students was equaled only by the unwillingness of adults on campus to enforce it, died a sudden death. Graduation was made easier by abolishing foreign-language and other unpopular requirements. Although not a matter of official policy, course standards were lowered as well, a process that came to be know as "grade inflation." Most of these changes remained in place at the century's end, having long outlived the New Left and the sixties.

No university could end the war in Vietnam or bring about racial justice. But what they could do to mollify students was done, producing the much more user-friendly campuses students enjoy today. While they may have been effective over time, in the short run these changes accomplished little. The protest at Columbia was followed by the greatest wave of student strikes, demonstrations, and protests yet, which took place up and down the academic ladder and all across the country. According to the Educational Testing Service there were 3,463 protests during the 1967–68 academic year, mostly in 1968. Perhaps one-third included sit-ins, strikes, hostage-taking, and building seizures. Few involved violence or serious property damage, and those that did were often incidents to which the police responded. As a rule, universities made further concessions—where there was anything left to concede.

All this, but especially the Columbia takeover which it had led, further radicalized SDS. Although united on the need for extremism, SDSers agreed on little else. At their annual meeting in June 1968, an epiphany of sorts was reached when a relative newcomer named Bernardine Dohrn—a beautiful, fiery lawyer whose eloquence and sexuality deprived Movement men of their remaining shreds of good sense—was nominated for one of the three top jobs, interorganizational secretary of SDS. When asked from the floor if she considered herself a socialist, Dohrn replied, "I consider myself a revolutionary communist." She was elected unanimously. PL launched its most determined effort yet to take over SDS, reducing the convention to a struggle for power between itself and the National Office faction. For the last time, as it still had the votes, the National Office prevailed. But with internal disorder at its highest level yet, and with the delegates refusing to pass any resolutions whatsoever, this victory was meaningless.

Events, however, did not wait on SDS. Planning was already far along for demonstrations to coincide with the Democratic National Convention in Chicago—a train wreck waiting to happen. Under the auspices of the Mobe, Hayden and Rennie Davis were organizing a series of events based on the proposition that institutions must be forced to change. Mayor Richard J. Daley, the last of the big-city bosses, had a different idea: that the way to save civilization was by breaking heads. His 12,000 police officers were to work twelve-hour shifts—with 6,000 regular troops and 5,000 National Guardsmen on call as needed. That they would indeed be needed was the hope of Abbie Hoffman and the Yippies, who intended to cause all the mischief they could, and the fear of veteran pacifist David Dellinger and the Mobe, which was still committed to nonviolence.

The New Left's rendezvous with destiny began on Sunday, August 25, 1968, with a Yippie demonstration in Chicago's Grant Park that ended in what everyone later called a "police riot." All the frustration engendered by years of being called out to quell protests and defiant acts, and having been called "pigs" by hippies and New Leftists countless times—the Yippies brought an actual pig with them, "Pigasus," their candidate for president—gave way to an orgy of violence, the police swinging clubs at everyone within reach. As the preparations for the commencement of the

CHAPTER TWO   3 3

Democratic national convention continued, so did the beatings and arrests in the park. On Monday, the day the convention opened, Hayden was arrested twice. He was far gone by this time, lost in fantasies of a revolution being made on the street. Darting from riot to riot in a variety of disguises that baffled even supporters, he tried simultaneously to encourage his troops while avoiding arrest.

On Wednesday, the one day for which the Mobe actually had a permit to hold a rally, the heart of the action moved from Grant Park across Michigan Avenue to the Hilton Hotel. Now more arrests and beatings took place in full view of television cameras, the bright lights of the media illuminating the scene as the protestors chanted "The Whole World is Watching," which, indeed, it was. As it turned out, how onlookers and television viewers perceived the events surrounding the convention differed markedly. Some, including prominent members of the media, saw just another, if a particularly violent, police riot. Others, including most of middle-class America, saw a bunch of long-haired hippies cursing the police and waving Communist flags. Although the numbers could not be known for certain, it was believed that more than 100 demonstrators ended up in hospitals and perhaps 700 were arrested. One young man was shot dead by the police. According to President Johnson's National Commission on the Causes and Prevention of Violence, which issued a special report (*The Walker Report*) on the convention episode, of some 300 newspersons who covered these events, sixty-three were injured and/or arrested. Despite the drama outside its walls, the convention proceeded as expected, and Hubert Humphrey, the favored candidate of Lyndon Johnson and the rest of the Democratic leadership, received his nomination on schedule. He would narrowly lose to Richard Nixon come November.

After the convention SDS kicked itself for not having been more on top of things during this historic encounter. About 500 SDSers were present and did what they could to cause trouble, but it was the Mobe and especially the Yippies who got most of the credit—if that is the right word—for the unrest. Even so, SDS continued to profit from the worsening mood on campus. Applications for new chapters poured into the National Office, which, given its disarray, could not cope with the flood. By year's end there were perhaps 400 chapters with some 80,000 members, although the actual figures were anybody's guess. Whatever the tally, it did not take account of the much larger number of sympathizers who would turn out given the right incentives.

For Hayden, however, it was nearly the end of the line. Alone, and mentally and physically spent, he moved to Berkeley, where he joined a collective and tried to rebuild his life. But his dreams of revolution soon collided with reality when in March 1969 he, Rennie Davis, David Dellinger, Abbie Hoffman, Jerry Rubin, Bobby Seale of the Black Panthers,* and two others were indicted for conspiracy to incite a riot in Chicago during the Democratic National Convention. The alleged conspiracy existed only in the imaginations of law enforcement officials, since the accused disagreed on a host of issues and had never worked together as a group. For Hayden (and for Hoffman) the trial was an ordeal. Long separated from SDS, Hayden had never been more famous or more isolated. No longer admired by liberals because he had advocated violence, he also was mistrusted by radicals for having flirted with the powerful at various times—including Robert Kennedy, whom he knew and believed would be a catalyst for change. RFK's assassination was a personal blow to Hayden, another reason for his state of depression. The columnist Murray Kemptom, himself a veteran of 1930s radicalism, called Hayden a candidate without a party—which had the ring of truth and foreshadowed Hayden's later career. In February 1970 when Hayden was convicted—along with four others of the Chicago Eight, (which initially included Bobby Seale)—of incitement to riot, there were protests at campuses across the nation. (The trial is covered in more detail in Chapter Three.) Still, for Hayden the years of free-wheeling radicalism were nearly over.

SDS owed much to publicity, some of it even favorable, particularly at first. Now, with the country wracked by violence, it offered the media comfort to think that one easily recognizable organization was responsible for the spread of anarchy. *Life, Look,*

*a radical paramilitary group that had evolved out of a street gang

Newsweek and other publications all agreed that SDS was at the bottom of things. *Fortune* magazine took a poll in October that revealed that the campus leaders were further to the left than had been supposed—half of them believing that America was a sick society, two-thirds that the United States' participation in the Vietnam War was wrong. Che Guevera, the ubiquitous symbol of revolution, was more admired by them than were Nixon, Johnson, or Humphrey. A million young people, in college and out, regarded themselves as part of the left—although no one at this time was entirely sure what it meant to be radical.

But appearances were misleading. SDS had no control over events and was in no condition to capitalize on student feelings of anger and alienation—which for most would prove to be transitory. SDS meetings had become forums dominated by agonizing and sterile debates over such irrelevant matters as which faction was the true beacon of Marxist-Leninist hope for the oppressed masses. Progressive Labor was relentless and highly disciplined, big advantages in what were for the most part relatively small chapter and national meetings. And while the National Office still opposed PL, it too now saw itself as Marxist and allied with freedom fighters in the Third World and black revolutionaries at home. These internal obsessions, increasingly divorced from reality, had little attraction for the much larger student audience that wanted to act but was not caught up in dreams of street-fighting glory.

Then, too, the government had big teeth and was well-equipped to defend itself, especially against these pseudo-revolutionaries. SDSers were always reviling the state and its monstrous powers, while at the same time acting as if it were a feeble thing that they could easily brush aside. As events in Chicago ought to have demonstrated, this was a dangerous way of thinking. The New Left was under heavy surveillance. In Chicago police informants had been everywhere. Army Intelligence, as well as the FBI, tracked student radicals. Over 300 FBI special agents were on the job, infiltrating SDS, among their other activities, and seeking to worsen the organization's factional disputes—as if they could get any worse. Campus police forces were beefed up and often armed as well. University administrations were quicker to call in the local police, who themselves tapped phones, employed snoops, and otherwise expanded their arsenals. Arrests and/or expulsions were ever more frequent and effective. With confrontations becoming so violent, and bombings and other forms of property destruction taking place on many campuses, it was inevitable that protestors' force would be met with greater force. In an arms race between student radicals and the criminal justice system—the latter backed up by the U.S. military—there could be no question as to who would prevail. Meanwhile, as noted, universities were cutting into the radicals' base of support with timely concessions, a carrot-and-stick approach that would ultimately work.

Even so, 1969 began with another in a series of student strikes at San Francisco State College that lasted for four and a half months and resulted in at least 700 arrests. At Cornell in April armed black students took over the student union and threatened violence if their demands were not met. A terrified administration quickly conceded virtually every point. The militants' triumphant departure from the union, weapons and ammunition proudly displayed, received wide publicity and encouraged radicals who were promoting the use of force, although not an appalled general public. Along with the posturing and angry rhetoric, and in part because of it, people were dying. A bomb killed a custodian at UC, Santa Barbara. Police shot a white protestor to death in Berkeley and a black student at North Carolina A&M. Assailants, reportedly factional rivals, killed two Black Panthers at UCLA. But although many campuses were marked by protests and acts of violence, student radicals seldom got their way, the incident at Cornell being the major exception.

San Francisco State College was a particularly troubling case in point. In 1968, after a violent strike over racial issues, semanticist S. I. Hayakawa, the college's new president, was brought in to restore order. He attempted to do so by stationing city police on campus, which prompted another violent student strike that lasted for months. During the turmoil, class attendance fell to below 20 percent, many programs were curtailed or eliminated, and some of the best faculty members resigned. As many as 600 SFPD officers patrolled the campus. In December police arrested 150 students; in January 1969 at one rally they took into custody 450 students and faculty members, after which the strike fizzled out. All told, police charged about 700 activists, some serving as much as six months in jail, while Hayakawa fired two dozen faculty members and expelled every student who had been arrested. Both sides gained something from the struggle. Hayakawa's truculence appealed so much to Californians that they subsequently elected him to the U.S. Senate. The Black Studies Department, which had been the center of agitation, was enlarged, and more minorities gained admission. Only the college lost.

As a result of these violent protests, SDS lost its constituency. College students, most of whom rejected the turn to violence, increasingly spoke out against it. Various efforts by SDS leaders to recruit members among high school students, working-class youth, and soldiers failed. The women's liberation movement—some of its leaders, like Casey Hayden, former SDSers—was growing outside of the organization. For feminists this was a necessary break, since male SDSers, and women like Bernardine Dohrn who were wedded to the Marxist-Leninist line, displayed intense hostility to the idea that women were a victimized gender. They believed singling out women, white women in particular, diverted attention from the more urgent needs of workers and people of color. The problem with this argument was that workers never demonstrated any interest in SDS or the revolution, and Black Power organizations were hostile to whites, ruling out transracial alliances. For the first time SDS was shrinking, not growing, beset by forces from without and within.

Further, the Progressive Labor threat to SDS was getting worse. After having first supported the idea of Black Power, PL was now against it and in favor of integration. Following Red China's lead, it also opposed Castro's Cuba, the North Vietnamese and Viet Cong, use of recreational drugs, the wearing of long hair, the youth culture, and virtually everything that radical students liked and that SDS believed in or was trying to assimilate. A student strike at Harvard in April, prompted when PLers seized a building and were evicted by force, ended up being taken over by moderates and liberals after PL refused to compromise with the administration. PL gained control of Harvard SDS, but lost otherwise and remained at the margins of student life. No matter, in PL's view, political integrity had triumphed. For others in SDS as well, being right had become an end in itself, while accomplishing anything took second place.

Meanwhile, the federal government was increasing its efforts to suppress radicalism. President Nixon's attorney general, John Mitchell, a future Watergate defendant, had made the student left a particular target. Perhaps 2,000 FBI agents were assigned to "Red Squad" duties, in addition to thousands of informants with whom student organizations were salted. Even divisions marginal to the effort, such as the Internal Revenue Service (students had no income to speak of) and the Civil Service Commission (few if any radicals expected to become Civil Servants), were on the lookout for leftist tax delinquents and aspirants to public service. In addition, numerous state and local authorities cooperated with, or duplicated the work of, federal agencies. And even as the demonstrations and the attendant violence raged on, the battle for public opinion had already been lost, decisively so. One poll showed that 82 percent of respondents thought that student protestors should be expelled from their colleges, while another found that half the U.S. population opposed student demonstrations, even when peaceful and legal. It is little wonder, then, that twenty state legislatures enacted laws to punish colleges and students for political misconduct. As usual during crises, free speech was falling victim to exaggerated fears.

After the spring demonstrations the majority of New Left campus organizations, SDS chapters in particular, suffered from arrests, expulsions, and withdrawals of campus support. California banned SDS from its public schools, and in some colleges sympathetic faculty members lost their jobs. Across the nation SDS leaders were being arrested as a matter of course by local police, for assault, vagrancy, or whatever charge could be made to stick. This was inevitable: as with advocates of Black Power, who were being treated even more harshly, white leftists' resort to violence had provided all the sanction needed for officialdom to respond in kind and with overwhelming force. By sneering at nonviolence young radicals had sowed the wind and were now reaping the whirlwind. They did not see it this way, of course. To dedicated leftists, state-sanctioned repression only proved that the state was just as evil as they had always claimed, and clearly ripe for overturning.

It was against this backdrop of swelling student discontent, internal factionalism, and official attempts to crush the whole Movement, that SDS self-destructed. The climactic events took place during June 1969 in the Chicago Coliseum, where SDS met for its final convention. Thousands of people were on hand, delegates, observers, informants, police, reporters, and miscellaneous hangers-on. Delegates were greeted with a special edition of *New Left Notes* that featured the longest piece it had ever run by a group calling itself "Weatherman." The title of the article was "You don't need a weatherman to know which way the wind blows," taken from a Bob Dylan song, "Subterranean Homesick Blues." Its eleven signers included Mark Rudd and Bernardine Dohrn—one of only two women signatories. In this document the future Weathermen asserted that the job of white Americans was to promote black and Third World liberation struggles against American imperialism. The mechanism for this was to be "armed struggle." SDS should transform itself into a revolutionary party with cadres, collectives, maximum secrecy, and central direction—something like the Bolsheviks of old, that is to say. In reality this meant abandoning efforts on behalf of the working class, a move that socialist historian James Weinstein later called the "politics of despair and adventurism."

As a weapon in the class struggle, and also in the factional struggle between PL and the National Office of SDS, this policy failed to work. Tensions were high and became higher still on the second day of the convention when a member of the Illinois Black Panther Party, ostensibly an ally of the National Office, digressed onto the subject of "pussy power." When the audience reacted with catcalls and cries of disbelief, he announced that Superman was a "punk" because of his failure to take carnal advantage of Lois Lane. Amid chants of "Fight Male Chauvinism" the convention broke up, never to meet again. Now the Weathermen and its allies, amounting to slightly more than half of the delegates, held their own meeting. Weather leaders maintained that as blacks were the only true revolutionary force, it no longer made sense to try to recruit whites into racial organizations, and attempting to do so was, in fact, "objectively racist."

Although SDS would have collapsed anyway, the odd alliance between the Black Panthers and the National Office faction sped things along. The relationship was based on white guilt, naturally, a powerful force in the New Left that seemed to grow in tandem with Black Power, which had deprived white leftists of their natural black allies, notably in SNCC and the Congress of Racial Equality. This left only the Panthers, a relationship that black SDS allies took at face value, ignoring the evidence that the Black Panther Party (BPP)—founded mainly by ex-convicts—was more of a criminal gang than a political organization. Out of necessity as much as blindness, many in SDS insisted that the BPP was actually a vanguard party, persecuted by the police for political reasons rather than for its cache of guns and violent tactics, or its involvement in the drug trade—although these were certainly cause enough for the often bloody raids on Panther offices and residences.

After its last convention, SDS divided openly into two factions, each claiming to be the true SDS, plus various groups, or grouplets, which aligned themselves with one side or the other. Weather leaders took over the National Office, which they now called the Weatherbureau, and attempted to put their ideas into practice by forming revolutionary collectives in working-class neighborhoods. But, like ERAP before them, Weather didn't get far using this tactic, as youthful workers were sadly uninformed about the fundamentals of Marxism and declined to be radicalized. Raids on public schools designed to mobilize youth were equally futile. These failures led the Weatherbureau to lose interest in white youngsters and further glorify the black liberation struggle and the role ostensibly played in it by the Panthers, a strategy that ran aground because the Black Panthers had their own agenda.

Only weeks after the last SDS convention, the Black Panthers held a meeting in Oakland, California, the Conference for a United

Front Against Fascism. Rather than calling for urban warfare, Panther leaders demanded that the white left devote all of its efforts to protecting Black Panthers from attacks by the state and the police. When Weatherman held this to be counterrevolutionary, the Panthers responded in their usual style. David Hilliard, Panther chief of staff, declared: "We'll beat those little sissies, those little schoolboys' ass if they don't straighten up their politics. So we want to make it known to SDS that the first motherfucker that gets out of order had better stand in line for some kind of disciplinary actions from the Black Panther Party." That put an end to the United Front against Fascism.

Although completely without allies, the Weathermen in October gathered in Chicago for what had been billed as "Four Days of Rage," during which they were to "liberate" the streets and achieve other revolutionary goals. Only about 300 protestors turned up, bolstered by an equal number of sympathizers. On the first night, October 8, Tom Hayden assured the group of his support, then simply walked away. Undiscouraged, Weather guerillas stormed into an affluent Northside district known as the Gold Coast, breaking windows and attacking vehicles with revolutionary gusto until they ran into a wall of policemen. The next day, police officers broke up an attack by "women militia," and also a final kamikaze attack by the massed legions (200 strong) of this new Red Army. About all the so-called Days of Rage produced were 284 arrests and bail charges in excess of $1.5 million. In addition to the injuries suffered by members of Weather, some fifty-seven police officers were hospitalized.

This was the end of SDS for all intents and purposes. The campus chapters faded away. Protests and demonstrations still took place, sometimes organized by various other groups, sometimes spontaneously in response to particular events, such as stepped-up bombing attacks on North Vietnam by the U.S. military. Only the Weather faction of SDS lived on, growing ever more secretive and deranged—at one meeting Bernardine Dohrn hailed the grisly Tate-LaBianca murders in Los Angeles by the notorious Charles Manson gang of cultists and drug addicts as revolutionary acts. Owing to continued government surveillance of them, and their own plans for terrorist operations, Weathermen now separated into cells. Although few in number—two or three hundred people at most—their spirits were high since, as they often reminded themselves, Fidel Castro and General Giap of North Vietnam had begun their revolutions with even fewer people. Apparently, the smaller the number of revolutionaries, the better the chances of success. By this tortuous reasoning, when only one Weatherman remained it would be time for the mighty to tremble.

The sixties came to an end amidst a welter of violence. It began slowly in 1968, but the 1969–70 school year witnessed at least 174 on-campus bombings or attempted bombings, and perhaps seventy more off campus. These were directed mostly at ROTC buildings, Selective Service offices, and like targets. In addition, students vandalized property, sometimes government buildings, other times the shops of merchants whose mistake had been to cater to students. The American Council of Education estimated that these acts took place in the context of 9,400 protests, 731 of which led to police responses.

In America life as a whole took a turn for the worse. Crime of every sort rose, as did actions against the police. There were a record number of assaults on police officers in 1969—33,604 (as compared with 16,793 in 1963) of which eighty-six resulted in death. Most of these acts were the work of criminals, but a few were conducted by organized terrorist groups, such as Weather and the New Year's Gang in Madison, Wisconsin.

But when it came to violence, the Weathermen seemed to be their own worst enemies. In March 1970, shortly after they had gone underground, three members died when a "bomb factory," a Greenwich Village townhouse, exploded, killing Diana Oughton, Ted Gold, and Terry Robbins, all founders of Weather. They had been in the process of making nail bombs, weapons designed to mutilate and kill, which were highly effective against their unintended victims (themselves)—although Kathy Boudin and Cathy Wilkerson, whose parents owned the townhouse, escaped the burning building. Robbins' body was so shredded that it took weeks to identify him on the basis of thumb fragments. Oughton was not identified for ten days. If martyrs were all that a movement required for success, then the Weather Underground was on its way.

Although Weathermen went on to commit perhaps twenty bombings in later years, some radicals believed that the townhouse explosion marked a turning point for the New Left as a whole. It was a loss of innocence for some. Other radicals came back to reality at last, remembering that words had practical consequences that could be just as lethal as any unjust war. There were different turning points for different people, but there is no question that this highly publicized Weather fiasco had a sobering effect: it involved persons well known on the left, who were making bombs to mutilate and kill people.

The greatest wave of white political violence followed the invasion of (or incursion into, the official euphemism) Cambodia by American troops in search of an enemy headquarters, which President Nixon announced on April 30, 1970. In protest to this escalation of the Vietnam War into neighboring Cambodia, student strikes erupted on many campuses, including Kent State University in Ohio. On May 4, 1970, National Guardsmen fired into a crowd of unarmed students there, killing four and wounding nine others. Ultimately antiwar demonstrations or protests took place at about half of the nation's colleges and universities, of which 536 were shut down for some period of time—at least fifty-one for the balance of the school year. Some 100,000 demonstrators poured into Washington D.C.; there they blocked traffic, broke windows, assaulted police and property, and otherwise expressed their indignation. In August an independent terrorist group, the "New Year's Gang," attempted to destroy the Army Mathematics Research Center on the Madison campus of the University of Wisconsin with a huge car bomb. Instead it blew up the physics department, killing a young postdoctoral fellow who had a wife and three young children. Like the townhouse explosion, this bombing had a chilling effect on radicals who had been proclaiming the merits of violence. Not among those who now harbored regret, unfortunately, was Professor Harvey Goldberg of the UW history department, who had been advocating violence in his classes and would later testify for the defense at the trial of Karl Armstrong, one of the bombers.

Nonetheless, polls showed that all this violence had led most Americans to see campus unrest as the nation's leading problem, overshadowing the Vietnam War, racism, poverty, urban riots and even crime. The New Left no longer existed as any kind of recognizable political movement. All that remained of it, but not for much longer, was rage and violence on both sides of the barricades. Ironically, conservatives were the only people who benefitted greatly from the left's turn toward violence.

Protests continued into the early seventies. On April 24, 1971, for instance, 200,000 people gathered for more demonstrations in Washington D.C. But during the 1970–71 academic year there were fewer protests than in the previous year, and in 1971–72 fewer still. President Nixon did a great deal to end the New Left by *Vietnamizing* the war. Ostensibly, *Vietnamization* was a program for arming and equipping the South Vietnamese to defend themselves, making possible a withdrawal of the American military. Actually, it was a scheme to declare victory and get a defeated U.S. force back home before South Vietnam fell to the enemy. Either way, it extinguished the fires on campus. By the end of 1972 only 24,000 American troops remained in Vietnam, too few to stimulate peace demonstrations at home. In January 1973 Nixon ended the draft, delivering the *coup de gras* to antiwar activism, since it had been the draft that had made the war an on-campus issue. Without it, college students were no longer personally at risk and therefore could return to the comfortable politics of indifference. In short order, protests dropped off the front pages of newspapers, and, while the tradition of campus marches and protests never died out entirely, the student revolution was over.

CHAPTER THREE

Hippies and Yippies

The Counterculture

SDSers were never sure what to make of the counterculture. The speed with which young people had transformed themselves physically took everyone by surprise. One minute men had short hair and women favored full skirts, the next minute men were sporting beards and long hair, and women were donning miniskirts. Khaki pants gave way to blue jeans, the neat buttoned-down look of the fifties replaced by a mixture of grunge and exotica. Women bathed in bikinis or nothing at all—nudity for men and women alike quickly becoming popular in public places ranging from swimming holes to rock concerts. It also became commercial: "topless" and "bottomless" bars sprang up everywhere and pornography entered the mainstream as "adult entertainment." Urged on by gurus such as Timothy Leary—a Harvard scientist turned prophet of dope—youngsters "tuned in, turned on, and dropped out" in alarming numbers. The word *hippie* was coined to describe these new bohemians. Rock and roll, already a great industry, became the sacred music of the young and marijuana their holy communion. Everyone was urged to wear flowers in their hair and to "make love, not war."

LSD, the hallucinogen espoused by Leary, enjoyed a vogue among young people but had unpredictable effects, with many users experiencing a "bad trip." This kept LSD, also known as "acid," from attaining the ubiquity of marijuana. Some young people took to the road, many crash landing in San Francisco's Haight-Ashbury district, the new Mecca of hippiedom. The first hippie phrase, "flower power," was soon on every lip, but the notion proved ephemeral. The much-heralded "Summer of Love," a pilgrimage of young people to California (1967), turned sour, ending in a welter of bad trips, criminal assaults, and police interventions. But, while the hippie "movement" was short lived, the hippie ethic, fueled by a seemingly endless supply of runaway youth, communes, incessant references to peace and love—plus dope and sexual freedom— proved more durable and dragged on for years.

While hippies were never as numerous as they appeared to be, since huge numbers of young people adopted their dress and some of their habits without going all the way, the appeal of sex, drugs, and rock and roll was so great that the New Left could not ignore it. Many leftists were themselves attracted by rock and roll, free love, and marijuana. Others understood that what lured such a large part of their own generation was impossible to ignore. This was not an either/or situation, for one could at once enjoy the pleasures of narcotics and the flesh and see them as instruments of revolutionary change, as SDS and the Weathermen did at various times.

The Yippies

But it was the Yippies who most famously embodied both strains of the sixties—the self-indulgent world of the hippie with its preference for shock effects and the desire to make a revolution of some unspecified kind. No one embraced these traits more conspicuously than did Abbie (Abbott) Hoffman, who, for a while, brought the two worlds together, and whose life serves as a lens through which to view this facet of the New Left—a neglected one in some respects, since historians are more comfortable with political parties than political theater.

Hoffman was born in 1936 and educated in Worcester, Massachusetts, and at Brandeis University, where he studied under Herbert Marcuse—an emigre whose neo-Marxist philosophy was soon to make a considerable impression on Movement intellectuals. Another of Hoffman's professors, Abraham Maslow, was a rebellious psychologist who preached sexual freedom, communal living, and self-actualization. Maslow had a profound effect on Hoffman, known to that point chiefly as a petty hustler and small-town Romeo. After graduating from Brandeis in 1959 Hoffman entered UC Berkeley's graduate program in psychology. Already an activist of sorts, Hoffman joined the effort to save Caryl Chessman, the so-called "Red Light Bandit." Chessman had been convicted of multiple rapes and sentenced to death on the ground that moving his victims from their cars to his own amounted to kidnapping. In prison Chessman—who admitted to little beyond a misspent youth—became a writer and apparently was rehabilitated, inspiring many citizens to work for a commutation of his sentence. He was executed in 1960 anyway, but the struggle on his behalf was a sign of changing times in California. So was the demonstration against House Un-American Activities Committee (HUAC) hearings on Communist schoolteachers in San Francisco on May 13, 1960, that resulted in many arrests, mostly of students, in which Hoffman participated as well.

Hoffman married his pregnant girlfriend in 1960 and worked at the Worcester, Massachusetts, State Hospital for two years. Other jobs followed, as did volunteer work for the Committee for a Sane Nuclear Policy (SANE), the National Association for the Advancement of Colored People (NAACP) and the Congress of Racial Equality (CORE). With his marriage failing and his interest in activism on the rise, Hoffman joined the Student Nonviolent Coordinating Committee (SNCC). He worked briefly in Mississippi in 1964 during Freedom Summer, returning in 1965 to register voters again. In 1966 he obtained a divorce and moved to New York City, where he opened a store to sell handicrafts made by the

Poor People's Corporation of Mississippi. But Hoffman's career as a champion of black civil rights was just about over. In December 1966 SNCC voted by a narrow margin to expel whites from the organization. In response Hoffmann, who would soon turn his store over to black management, fired off an angry blast at SNCC and its leader, Stokeley Carmichael.

Published in the *Village Voice* as "SNCC: The Desecration of a Delayed Dream," the article was signed "Abbie" rather than "Abbott" Hoffman, the first time he used this name professionally. The article heralded the birth of a new writing style by which the nation would soon come to know Abbie Hoffman, a style that was personal and somewhat fictionalized. But his coming stream-of-consciousness form still lay ahead, as did his expletives and playfulness. In the *Village Voice* article, Hoffman was clearly angry and hurt. He not only condemned Black Power as such, he also exposed the sexual and financial exploitation of white women, as he saw it, by blacks in the civil rights movement—a revelation widely regarded by leftists as an act of betrayal. Then, in an early display of the demons that would plague him throughout his life, Hoffman went into hiding. Apparently this was a manifestation of his first attack of manic-depression, the illness that would lead to his suicide. He was also smoking marijuana and taking LSD at the time, a self-prescribed treatment that would always work badly for Hoffman.

Nevertheless, his search for a fresh beginning was powerfully influenced by his immersion in the New York City counterculture, which was then entering into full bloom. Hoffman enjoyed the music of the Fugs, a hippie group whose name was a euphemism for sexual intercourse. He also liked "happenings"—street theatrical events—and the multimedia presentations of pop artist Andy Warhol. Hoffman seems to have actually studied Zen Buddhism, which many hippies claimed to admire but few knew anything about. He also studied the writings of the Beat Generation, poets and novelists such as Allen Ginsberg, Lawrence Ferlinghetti, and Jack Kerouac, and visited the avant-garde theater, seeing such plays as *The Persecution and Assassination of Jean-Paul Marat as Performed by the Inmates of the Asylum at Charenton under the*

Direction of the Marquis de Sade—known familiarly as *Marat/ Sade*. On Easter Sunday in March 1967 he took drugs, wore flowers in his hair, and attended the New York Be-In, a celebration of peace, love, and hanging out together inspired by a San Francisco Be-In where the Beat Generation had mingled with hippiedom. Soon Hoffman married again. His second wife, Anita Kushner, was a fellow spirit in some ways, although unlike Hoffman, she believed in monogamy.

By the spring of 1967 Hoffman had combined his experiences with the counterculture, his reading, and a close if unscientific study of the mass media to produce the concept that would soon become famous as "Yippie." It was foreshadowed on April 29, 1967, when Hoffman organized a "Flower Brigade" to join a "Support Our Boys in Vietnam" march sponsored by the Veterans of Foreign Wars. The flowered few were promptly beaten up, which Hoffman had counted on when he had alerted the media. The result was a flurry of stories about peaceful hippies being victimized by warmongers. In the Movement weekly *WIN,* Hoffman playfully wrote that his group might have fared better, except that, "We were poorly equipped with flowers from uptown florists. Already there is talk of growing our own. . . . The cry of Flower Power' echoes through the land. We shall not wilt."

The Hoffman brand of political expression was outrageous, to be sure, very hard on peace marchers (*peaceniks* was the invidious term), but eye-catching and highly effective in its own way. In any event, a new form of political theater never dreamt of in SDS's philosophy had been loosed on an unsuspecting nation. In August came Abbie's (aforementioned) raid on the New York Stock Exchange, when Hoffman and his coconspirators threw handfuls of dollar bills on the trading floor to the detriment of Exchange business. Although the meaning of this gesture was somewhat opaque, it drew much publicity, reason enough, in Hoffman's view, to make the effort rewarding. It also made him famous, a reputation he would consolidate as an organizer of the March on the Pentagon in October.

Already skilled at staging events that would draw media attention, Hoffman learned that it was easier to attract radio and TV reporters than to manipulate the establishment press. Before the March on Washington he appeared on a panel put together by the National Mobilization to End the War in Vietnam (MOBE). His spiel on the planned exorcism of the Pentagon was featured on television news shows, but, while the *New York Times* ran a picture of the panel, he claimed to have been cut out of it. What he learned from this apparently was that television was the better medium for him. In any case, his performance style was more suited to television than to the print media.

Hoffman had a keen sense of what would play well on the "tube." In general, speeches got little attention, a sound bite or two perhaps, but television reporters in New York had been very impressed by an acting troupe called the Bread and Puppet Theater, which since October 1965 had regularly appeared at antiwar demonstrations, often dressed in black robes and death masks—on occasion bearing a black coffin symbolizing the dead in Vietnam. To Hoffman, the best kind of antiwar street theater was the kind that inspired assaults on the participants. He loved it when during his Flower Brigade march young women were punched and kicked and American flags torn to shreds by outraged bystanders. To someone who believed in symbols as much as Hoffman did, the televised results were sublime.

Sometimes there could be too much of a good thing, however. One such case appears to have been the Yip-In at Grand Central Station in New York on March 22, 1968, which was organized by Hoffman. Thousands of supporters showed up, and many were clubbed senseless by police angered by a Yippie attack on the stations's great clock. Hoffman himself was beaten unconscious and suffered vertebral damage. He dubbed the event "The Grand Central Massacre" and later said it was worse than the rioting during the Democratic National Convention in Chicago.

Although events did not go exactly as planned at Grand Central, Hoffman was by 1968 an accomplished media exploiter. While his strategy was hard to pin down, since he contradicted himself as a matter of principle—"confusion is mightier than the sword" being one of his numerous slogans—and borrowed freely from many sources, a few ideas stand out. He admired the hippies' style, but not their lack of purpose. He liked the fact that SDS had a purpose, but criticized SDS's lack of style, frequently slandering it as bureaucratic and denouncing its academic roots, which he believed—rightly, to be sure—SDS never quite outgrew. He was closest to the Diggers, whom he had seen at work in San Francisco—at the aforementioned SDS Drawing Boards conference in June 1967. Because a handful of them reduced the affair to a shambles, the Diggers had earned his respect. In his manifesto, *Revolution for the Hell of It* (1968), Hoffman had a section called "SKULLDIGGERY" in which he identified himself with the Diggers, citing their Zen-like personas, existential devotion to the moment, and also their flamboyance.

But if Hoffman was one with the Diggers in certain respects, his differences with them were major. The Diggers, although superficially resembling them, looked down on hippies as mere "consumers" and disliked the counterculture as a whole. Hoffman, on the other hand, saw the hippies as potential revolutionaries and borrowed heavily from the counterculture. He also fell out with Digger leaders like Emmet Grogan, who believed that the colorful Hoffman was stealing their thunder. The Diggers, however, were far from being the only ones in this position, since Hoffman was an industrious scavenger of other people's ideas, and one who did so on principle, often calling himself "Free" (the pseudonym he used when writing *Revolution for the Hell of It*). This work was followed in 1971 by *Steal This Book,* which neatly captured his position.

Hoffman also differed from the Diggers in favoring the planned event and the calculated use of the media. His "spontaneity" was well-thought out and designed, in the short run at least, to achieve specific ends. Planning was not entirely foreign to the Diggers—Grogan's disruption of the Drawing Boards conference was widely believed to have been rehearsed during the road trip from California to Michigan—but Hoffman's plans were far more elaborate. The events in Chicago constitute a case in point. He began organizing for the Democratic National Convention as early as January 1968, opening an office in Manhattan for that very purpose. When asked if offices were consistent with Yippie anarchism, Hoffman explained that they left the door to their offices unlocked so anyone who might drop by could answer the phone and thereby become a Yippie spokesperson.

Although "Yippie" was basically an idea, or "myth," as Hoffman always put it, Yippie founders acquired the trappings of a real political party—buttons, leaflets, posters, and press conferences. Later the founders came up with the name Youth International Party so that Yippie would be an acronym rather than just a word. Although appealing to the young, nearly all of the founders, including Hoffman, Jerry Rubin, Ed Sanders of the Fugs, and Paul Krassner of the *Realist* magazine, were veteran radicals and over thirty, the age beyond which no one was worthy of trust as an ad-age of the era held.

In theory they were organizing a "Festival of Life" to take place in Chicago at the same time as the Democratic Party's "Convention of Death." Yippie ads invoked the gods of the counterculture to attract masses of rebellious youth. Hoffman knew that, given a little encouragement, the establishment could be counted on to use force, perfect grist for the mills of the media and certain to produce great images. Although Yippie propaganda was couched in playful terms, its leaders were deadly serious and spent long hours planning how to reap maximum political benefits from the expected mayhem.

Events nearly derailed the Festival of Life. President Johnson stunned everyone on March 31, 1968, by announcing that he would not be a candidate for reelection. Even Hoffman was impressed by Johnson's move, writing admiringly of him that by dropping out "Lyndon is out-flanking us on our hippie side." America was still reeling from the Tet Offensive of January, technically a military defeat for the Viet Cong (who had suffered more casualties) but a political win for Vietnamese Communists, as the attack had taken the American forces by surprise and proven that the war's end was not in sight, contrary to the line maintained by U.S. generals. Americans were further stunned by the murder of Martin Luther King, Jr., on April 4, 1968, the subsequent riots in urban ghettoes, the entry of Senator Robert Kennedy into the presidential race and his June assassination, soon after winning the

Democratic presidential primary in California. For a while there were fears on the left that Kennedy, who had real charisma, would channel rebellious youth back into the swamp of electoral politics. His tragic death erased any such worries, however, and with Senator Eugene McCarthy's campaign in disarray, it looked like the 1968 DNC would prove to be another boss-run affair—in other words, a perfect target for the Yippies to display their style of protest.

It was with high hopes, therefore, that Hoffman and his company descended on Chicago in August. To ensure a maximum police response Hoffman floated numerous rumors: that Yippies were going to contaminate Chicago reservoirs with LSD, sending everyone in the city on a bad trip; that they would paint cars to resemble taxis and spirit convention delegates to the wilds of Wisconsin; that Yippie girls disguised as hookers would dose the delegates' drinks with hallucinogens; that the Chicago Amphitheater would be subjected to mortar fire; that 100,000 men would burn their draft cards; that 10,000 nude Yippies would frolic in Lake Michigan; and that sex and drugs would be everywhere to the detriment of public morals. Spread by the mainstream newspapers, these and other rumors kept Chicago police in hot pursuit of nonexistent conspiracies and events, raising their temperatures as well as that of Mayor Richard J. Daley in particular

The radical turnout was actually quite small, probably amounting to a few thousand people at most, many of them Chicago youths out for a good time. Nevertheless, the crowd was sufficient for Hoffman's purpose. He started off by reading a list of eighteen demands he had composed, including an end to the war, freedom for imprisoned Huey Newton of the Black Panthers "and all other black people," the legalization of recreational drugs, and universal sexual congress. His demands were widely ignored, but he and Pigasus, the Yippie candidate for president, and a real pig, got a great deal of attention, and Jerry Rubin and a few other Yippies were promptly arrested. All of this happened before the Festival of Life began on August 25 with a rally in Lincoln Park that was violently broken up by the police, who attacked reporters and photographers as well. And so it went for days on end.

Hoffman—in the grip of the manic phase of his disease—appeared here, there, and everywhere, giving speeches that made little sense yet were perfectly in keeping with the moment. He was arrested as usual, for obscenity, having written the F-word on his forehead with lipstick, and thereby missed some of the fun.

Afterward Hoffman was ecstatic, crediting the Yippies with ruining Hubert Humphrey's presidential campaign at the start and making Richard Nixon president. Hoffman had jubilantly predicted this outcome in September. He and others on the left believed that only a conservative such as Nixon could end the war in Vietnam because any Democrat would be red-baited mercilessly for attempting to do so and must of necessity fail. In this they were correct, although it would take much longer for Nixon to get America out of Vietnam than radicals expected. Whether the spectacle in Chicago actually caused Humphrey's defeat is problematic. Although Nixon won by a very narrow margin, with an edge of less than 1 percent of the total vote, he would have prevailed handily if George Wallace, the racist governor of Alabama, had not run on a third-party ticket. Wallace garnered 13.5 percent of the total vote, most of which otherwise would have gone to Nixon. Thus, questions about the presidential horserace aside, what the election of 1968 showed was that the country was turning to the right, just the opposite of what organizers of the Festival of Life—who saw it as a great radicalizing effort—meant to achieve.

HUAC and the Yippies

This national turn to the right was far from apparent at the time, and the Yippies were soon staging another theatrical event, this time before the House Un-American Activities Committee. Committee members should have known better than to go up against the Yippies, especially after Jerry Rubin—a free-style Berkeley radical before he became a Yippie—had made fools of them in 1966. Unlike most New Leftists, Rubin, who was born in 1938, actually came from a working-class family. He earned a diploma from the University of Cincinnati, visited Israel and Cuba, and began graduate studies at Berkeley, dropping out after participating in the 1964 Free Speech Movement to become a full-time revolutionary. During his three years in Berkeley he became known as the P. T. Barnum of the revolution. Among his accomplishments was to have helped organize Vietnam Day demonstrations, teach-ins, and the International Days of Protest. He was especially proud of having nearly become mayor of Berkeley in a four-way race.

Rubin had been subpoenaed to appear before HUAC in 1966 as a member of the Vietnam Day Committee, welcoming the chance to send up HUAC and propagandize against the war. Advised by Communist Party members not to testify, a self-defeating tactic that had hurt them in the 1950s, Rubin recalled—in his Hoffman-like memoir *Do It!* (1970)—telling the Communists and their lawyers "Fuck You! I'm not going to miss this chance to tell the world where it's at." Planning to embarrass the committee with political theatrics, he consulted a leading authority, Ronnie Davis of the San Francisco Mime Troupe, who advised Rubin not simply to wear the hat of a Revolutionary War soldier as planned, but the entire uniform. Rubin was warned by others not to make a display of himself, since HUAC was hoping to pass a bill that would make the kind of dramatic protests Rubin had been staging in Berkeley felonious, advice which he naturally disregarded.

Stoned and sweating in his wool uniform—which looked highly authentic from the stock at his throat to its elaborate fac-ings—Rubin sat through four days of testimony only to have his opportunity to testify aborted when HUAC's chair called off the circus. Rubin, who did not take this at all well, was carried out bodily by federal marshals and charged with disorderly conduct. It was not what he had hoped for, but satisfyingly well-publicized just the same. "Joe McCarthy turned over in his grave," Rubin noted cheerfully. The hearings so embarrassed Congress that the anti-Berkeley bill died in committee. Rubin returned home to a hero's welcome.

Given this exciting background, Rubin was overjoyed at be-ing subpoenaed by HUAC again. Hoffman, David Dellinger, Tom Hayden, and dozens of others held to be responsible for the events at the DNC in Chicago were subpoenaed as well and, as always, shared Rubin's enthusiasm for such an opportunity. On October 1, 1968, opening day of the HUAC hearings, Rubin appeared wearing a Black Panther beret, Viet Cong pajama bottoms, a Mexican bandolier with live ammunition, bells, bracelets, and earrings. His feet, face, and naked chest were painted with psychedelic designs and peace symbols. He carried a toy M-16 rifle. Guards took away his ammo but allowed Rubin to keep his pretend weapon. Hoffman chose a vaguely Indian motif for the occasion, sporting feathers in his hair, a hunting knife and a bullwhip. A band of women calling themselves the Women's International Terrorist Conspiracy from Hell (WITCH) carried brooms and formed a circle around Rubin, burning incense while dancing and chanting.

At various times Hoffman accused HUAC of being soft on Communism, and further infuriated committee members by wearing an American flag shirt, which officers tore to shreds before making him spend a night in jail for desecrating the flag—the irony being, no doubt, unintentional. Hoffman became the first person to be prosecuted under a new federal statute that made defacing or defiling Old Glory a criminal offense. A Yippie could hardly ask for a better response. Although he refused to testify before HUAC, Hoffman did testify at his trial for flag-desecration, telling the court "I regret that I have but one shirt to give for my country." The judge gave him thirty days in jail for his crimes, a sentence reversed on appeal. Rubin was green with envy, for on the very day of Hoffman's arrest, Rubin had been wearing the Viet Cong flag as a cape, which nobody seemed to notice.

Rubin wanted to testify before HUAC, at which time he planned to name as fellow Yippies everyone in the Chicago and Washington phone books. He also had some choice names he intended to call committee members, but was thwarted once more when the hearings were suspended for two months. When they resumed, Rubin was faced yet again with his perennial problem: what to wear to Congress. As it was Christmas time, he choose a Santa Claus suit, for which offense guards denied him entry to the hearing room. "HUAC Bars Santa Claus," were the headlines in newspapers the following day, just as Rubin had intended. HUAC later proposed a bill that would have criminalized insulting Congress through "cultural means," which he proudly called the Rubin Bill. "Make yourself illegal" he urged in *Doing It!*

The End of the Yippies

The Great Chicago Conspiracy Trial was even more newsworthy than the baiting of HUAC, although not nearly as much fun. The indictment against Hoffman, Rubin, and of the rest of the Chicago Eight was issued in March 1969, the delay having been caused by doubts on the part of Attorney General Ramsey Clark, who was losing his taste for trying antiwar activists—in time he would become an active leftist himself. John Mitchell, President Nixon's first attorney general, had no such qualms, and, being new to office, failed to appreciate the risks involved in putting heroes of the Movement and the counterculture on trial. The defendants had been at the March on the Pentagon, the Columbia takeover, and in Chicago; some were articulate and all were hard to intimidate. An odd choice to include in the nonexistent conspiracy was Panther leader Bobby Seale, whom none of the other defendants except Rubin knew personally. The Chicago Eight would be defended by, among others, William Kuntsler, soon to become America's most famous radical attorney. The trial would be presided over by Judge Julius Hoffman (no relation to Abbie), soon to become infamous. It was later learned that throughout the trial Judge Hoffman had been in close touch with the FBI, part of a real, if official, conspiracy against the defendants.

The defense was handicapped by sharp differences among the Chicago Eight, who, not actually having been co-conspirators, entertained very different ideas about strategy. Seale wanted the trial to concentrate on racial issues and to defend the Black Panthers. Dellinger, Rennie Davis, Hayden, and John Froines wanted the Vietnam War to be put on trial. The Yippies favored more theater of the absurd, dramatizing the divisions in America and putting the judicial system on trial.

In the second edition of *Revolution for the Hell of It* (1970) Hoffman tried to put a brave face on his courtroom experience, but the trial was a low point in Hoffman's life, after which he would never be the same. The trial was hard fought on both sides, the government bringing in hordes of police and official witnesses, and Judge Hoffmann acting ruthlessly against the disruptions of Bobby Seale, first having him chained and gagged, then removed from the courtroom, and finally, in November, separating Seale's case from that of the others and sentencing him to four years in prison for contempt of court.

Abbie testified in December, giving a good performance as usual, but the prosecution was more interested in *Revolution for the Hell of It* than in Hoffman himself, making it one of the few books in American history to be used as evidence in a criminal case. While Judge Hoffman forbade the jurors to read it, prosecutors quoted long sections from the book to prove that the defendant was a dangerous man. For its part, the defense brought in witnesses from the counterculture, persons such as the Beat poet Allen Ginsberg, to establish the context out of which Yippiedom had emerged. The trial ended in bedlam. David Dellinger, then fifty-five, was sent to jail for the remainder of the trial in February. Abbie slandered Judge Hoffman, having earlier called him a "disgrace to the Jews," in Yiddish. Hoffman and Rubin came to court in judicial robes worn over Chicago police department shirts to signify that Judge Hoffman was a policeman in disguise—their last act of political theater in a courtroom. Judge Hoffman sentenced all of what was now the Chicago Seven plus Kunstler to prison for contempt of court, the length of each sentence differing according to how much each defendant had irritated him. Kunstler was apparently the most annoying, getting the longest sentence (four years and thirteen days), while Weiner received the shortest (two months and eighteen days). Abbie Hoffman was sentenced to just eight months, his frequent outbursts in court notwithstanding.

On February 18 a verdict was reached. Froines and Weiner were found not guilty, Hoffman, Rubin, Hayden, Dellinger, and Davis were found not guilty of conspiracy, but guilty of crossing state lines to foment violence. Judge Hoffman gave the convicted the maximum penalty, five years in prison and $5,000 fines. Afterward the expected protests took place around the country, most of them organized by the defendants and the Chicago Conspiracy staff, who had kept their office in Chicago open so as to raise money and generate propaganda. The defendants appealed, and in November 1972 a U.S. Court of Appeals reversed most of the convictions and rebuked Judge Hoffman and the prosecutors for failing to give the Chicago Eight a fair trial. All of the original charges against Bobby Seale were dropped, as were his convictions for contempt of court in 1973. The government had the option of retrying the Chicago Eight but wisely decided to spare itself any further embarrassment. So after four years and millions of dollars spent, the Chicago Eight were free at last.

All the same, time was running out for the Yippies. Hoffman, Rubin, and others went to Miami in 1972 for the Democratic National Convention, but local authorities had learned a lesson from Chicago and rolled out the red carpet instead of police vehicles. Yippie leaders spoke to the city council and to patrolmen. They were permitted to camp in Flamingo Park, parade on Collins Avenue, and commit acts of political theater pretty much as they pleased. Reminiscent of the early days of Flower Power, minus the violence, the Miami convention was also the swan song of the Yippies. The convention itself, which nominated George McGovern on the basis of his primary victories, was packed with female and minority delegates and voted for the most radical platform in memory, giving the Yippies little to protest. They were also upstaged by the Zippies, a younger generation of leftists who hoped to displace their elders, a meaningless competition in the new political era dominated by conservatives such as Richard Nixon. For the Yippies, Zippies, and the other proponents of theatrical leftism, it was all downhill from there.

CHAPTER FOUR

Fadeout

By February 1970 the Weathermen had gone underground, all members who opposed this decision having been expelled, and the last SDS office in Chicago was abandoned. SDS sold its records to the State Historical Society of Wisconsin for $300, a best buy for that worthy institution. The several hundred surviving members of Weather spread across the country in small "cells" of from three to five people. The townhouse explosion that killed three bombmaking members in New York the next month failed to produce a change in strategy but did alter Weather tactics. Weathermen resolved to minimize harm to bystanders by giving up nail bombs and phoning in pre-explosion warnings—thus some vestige of humanity reared its head.

After the killings at Kent State and elsewhere in May, the group issued its first manifesto, written by Bernardine Dohrn and signed "Weatherman Underground." She called it "a declaration of a state of war." For the first time Weather identified itself with the counterculture, foreshadowing yet another policy change. Subsequently the Weather Underground took credit for various bombings around the country, even as federal indictments naming numerous Weathermen and their aboveground accomplices were being handed down.

After the townhouse explosion, Weathermen had actually lost some of their taste for blowing things up and were searching for more benign revolutionary tactics. Their most conspicuous effort was to help spring Timothy Leary from confinement. In February 1970 Leary had been given a ten-year prison sentence for possession of marijuana. He was being held at the California Men's Colony at San Luis Obispo, from which he intended to escape. The unlikely joining of Leary and Weather was arranged by one of Leary's LSD suppliers, a member of a shadowy network of manufacturers and dealers known whimsically as the Brotherhood of Eternal Love. On September 13, 1970, Leary got over the prison fence and was smuggled all the way to a Black Panther compound in Algeria by elements of the Weather Underground and their supporters. It would be the beginning, Weathermen hoped, of an alliance between themselves, Leary's white following, black revolutionaries, and Hispanic militants. In addition, having been sharply criticized by Women Liberationists, Weather was trying to lose its macho image and recast itself as gender-friendly. The cells were renamed "families," as an instance. For lack of alternatives, however, random bombings and manifestos remained Weather's essential tools. Thus, in 1974 Weather applauded the kidnapping of Patty Hearst by a tiny fringe group impressively named the Symbionese Liberation Army. The SLA specialized in armed robbery, the very touchstone of radicalism in the New Left's degenerate phase.

By this time the Weather Underground had been reduced to perhaps fifty members and had backed away from the counterculture, having discovered at long last that sex, drugs, and rock and roll were so much a part of consumer capitalism that they had become counterrevolutionary. The defeat of George McGovern in the presidential campaign of 1972 (sealing the ascendancy of the conservative Richard Nixon) the winding down of the Vietnam War, and the passing of the sixties, in short, led to further reflection, a smattering of additional bombings, reorganization, and name changes that signified little and accomplished less. In 1977, depressed by the obvious futility of their lives, Weathermen began surfacing and turning themselves in to the government. Among them was Mark Rudd, still under indictment for his actions at the Columbia takeover and the Days of Rage. He and others with similar records generally received fines and probation, since no evidence directly linked them to the various bombings for which Weather had taken credit. In 1980 Bernardine Dohrn and Bill Ayers, now married and with two children, surfaced as well. That same year, after giving herself up, Cathy Wilkerson was sentenced to three years in prison because of her role in the townhouse explosion.

A few refused to quit and suffered the consequences. On October 20, 1981, Kathy Boudin, Dave Gilbert, Judy Clark, and Black Liberation Army member Sam Brown were arrested while attempting to rob a Brinks armored truck to finance the BLA. They killed two policemen in this bungled effort, and those arrested, including some apprehended later, received long prison terms. In 1983 former Weatherman Linda Evans and several others formed a new group and committed a string of bombings. Evans and two other women were arrested a few years later, Evans being sentenced to forty years in prison. In 1994 one of the last of those charged in the Days of Rage, Jeff Powell, surfaced after twenty-five years underground. He was fined $500 and placed on probation, having suffered longer for so little purpose than anyone on the deflated New Left.

In later years some former Weathermen, such as Mark Rudd, had a change of heart. Others, including Dohrn and Ayers, remained unrepentant about their time in Weather. Nevertheless, in the early 1990s an interviewer found that the recalcitrant couple had rebuilt their lives in remarkably conventional ways considering their background and notoriety. Ayers had earned a Ph.D. from Columbia University and was teaching in the Education School of the University of Illinois, Chicago; Dohrn, a law school graduate, was working at the Children and Family Justice Center of Northwestern University: both safely back in the ivory towers that they had excoriated in the sixties. Neither expressed any regrets about their former lives, and Dohrn went so far as to reinvent her past by try-ing to erase the violence. She had never believed in force, Dohrn now explained, but only sought "ways to act that were nonviolent but more militant," a quest that seems to have gone wrong consid-ering Weather's bombings and the Days of Rage. According to Dohrn, the bombings were purely symbolic. "We called it propa-ganda of the deed," she said artlessly, seemingly unaware that the term had been coined by anarchists in the nineteenth century. Comparing the New Left in this country with its counterparts abroad, she observed that "we see how restrained, temperate, and appropriate the American movement stayed." That people died at the hands of Weather apparently did not come up in the interview, but if it had those deaths probably would have been appropriate too, according to Dohrn's logic, and trivial in number compared to Vietnam and other imperialist outrages.

In the absence of reliable data it is hard to say how many New Leftists made this kind of transition. For the great majority who did not go underground or become bombers, life after the sixties was much less difficult. Todd Gitlin became a distinguished pro-fessor at New York University and a historian of the Movement. Richard Flacks, who had begun his academic career early, re-mained active in protest politics while also writing extensively about the New Left. He had been viciously attacked in his Univer-sity of Chicago office in 1969 by a never-identified man with a crowbar who nearly severed Flacks' left hand, but Flacks contin-ued his career at the University of California, Santa Barbara. Jane Addams, who had been a student at Antioch College in 1964 when she went south for Freedom Summer, later became executive sec-retary of SDS. After the breakup of SDS she returned to school, earning a Ph.D. in anthropology and gaining tenure at Southern Il-linois University. Many other members of SDS, most less well known, also ended up teaching in the once-despised university, upon which they would have a profound effect.

Tom Hayden, the most famous leader of SDS, continued to be its most visible veteran as a result of his decision, rare among Movement people but not surprising in light of his past contacts with Robert Kennedy and other mainstream figures, to take up electoral politics. In 1976 he ran in the California Democratic primary against U.S. Senator John Tunney. Although defeated, Hayden remained active as a political organizer and in 1982, with the aid of his wife, the actor Jane Fonda whom he had married in 1973, won election to the California State Assembly. Although he and Fonda later divorced, Hayden's political career prospered, and by the end of the nineties he was a member of the California State Senate, leaving it because of term limits in 2000. Despite Hayden's success, his radical past was always a liability, and a man of his gifts, not otherwise hobbled, might well have become a United States senator.

In the 1970s Rennie Davis joined the following of the adolescent "perfect master" Maharaj-Ji. Casey Hayden (Sandra Cason) dropped out of the feminist movement, became a Buddhist, and after years marked by personal difficulties returned to Atlanta to work for the administration of Mayor Andrew Young. Paul Booth became a labor organizer. Al Haber moved to the San Francisco Bay Area and, while supporting himself as a cabinetmaker, remained active in left-wing causes. Sharon Jeffrey became a feminist. Peter Berg, who had helped found the Diggers in 1966, became an environmentalist; in the 1990s he was still active in the Planet Drum Foundation, which he had created in 1974. Timothy Leary, after years on the run, returned to the United States, completed his prison sentence, and became president of Futique Inc., a company that designed interactive software for personal computers. His enthusiasm for cyberspace was as great as it previously had been for LSD. When he contracted what proved to be a fatal form of cancer, he established an Internet Web site with a live camera, enabling all the world to share in his death, which came peacefully in May 1996.

Abbie Hoffman's later life can only be regarded as pathetic or, to use his brother's word, a "shipwreck." He became deeply involved in drug trafficking as part of a cocaine distribution ring, for which he was arrested in August 1973. This was so inconsistent with all that he purported to stand for that Hoffman lied about it for the rest of his life. But, although his then-wife Anita (they were divorced in 1980) defended him bravely, he had been caught red-handed with three pounds of cocaine that he intended to sell for $36,000. To avoid certain conviction, Hoffman went underground in the winter of 1974, surfacing now and again at fashionable restaurants and events. Under the name Barry Freed he became an environmental activist in upstate New York, working to save the St. Lawrence River, for which he received the thanks of Senator Daniel Patrick Moynihan and Governor Hugh Carey. Middle-aged, stout, and bearded, few recognized Freed as the lithe Yippie leader of old—despite his transparent name change. (*Revolution for the Hell of It!* had been marketed under Hoffman's pen name, "Free.") Hoffman also continued to write articles and yet another memoir, *Soon to Be a Major Motion Picture* (1980).

Hoffman turned himself in to authorities on September 4, 1980, receiving a three-year sentence on his drug-trafficking charge, much of which he served in a work-release program in which he was a drug counselor by day and an inmate by night. He remained a celebrity of sorts throughout this period, and he continued to lecture and write after his release. Nevertheless, his manic-depression, which he continued to treat with alcohol and narcotics, continued to dog him. After a failed attempt earlier, he successfully committed suicide in April 1989 in Bucks County, Pennsylvania, where he resided. He died a rebel—if also something of a fraud, which he had been for most of his life—a victim of the sixties, as well as of his illness. His ex-wife Anita, who had been as loyal to his memory as she had been to him in life, died of cancer in January 1999.

The life of Jerry Rubin, with whom Hoffman's name will always be linked, took an opposite course. After the sixties Rubin gave up politics for his interest in fitness, nutrition, and entrepreneurship, turning his hand with some success to various business ventures. He often granted the media interviews, engaged in debates with Hoffman, among others, and remained preternaturally youthful, the fit, clean-cut, youngish man of his later years bearing little resemblance to the bearded, pudgy Rubin of the 1960s. When asked if he had any regrets in one interview, Rubin answered quite seriously that he wished he had invested in real estate during the sixties. In one of those senseless acts of fate, Rubin was accidentally killed while jaywalking in Los Angeles in 1994. Unlike Hoffman, who has been the subject of at least four biographies (plus several novels and a film) there is not much literature on Rubin except what he wrote himself. He embarrassed radicals to the end, business being the enemy they had all made war against.

Michael Harrington outlasted the New Left by many years, dying of cancer in 1989 at the age of sixty-one. Although he never wrote another book as successful or important as *The Other America* (1962), until his death he remained the most influential socialist in the United States. Harrington was the real thing, not a pseudo-revolutionary but a man who through his many books and innumerable speeches clung stubbornly to his beliefs and never stopped trying to win others over to them. He was the mirror image of a New Leftist and a standing reproach to all who had once called themselves radicals.

In the end, everything turned out quite differently from what the New Left had expected. There was no revolution. Instead American politics became more conservative, the left moving to the center and the right flourishing. Most of the luminaries of the New Left burned out quickly. In 1966 Jack Newfield, a journalist and early member of SDS, had predicted "that in fifteen years Bob Dylan's poems will be taught in college classrooms, that Paul Booth, Julien Bond, and Stokeley Carmichael will be the leaders of adult protest movements, that the Beatles movies will be revived in art houses, and that Tom Hayden, Norman Fruchter, Robb Burlage, Mario Savio, Dick Flacks, Bob Parris, and Carl Oglesby will be major social critics." He was right, more or less, about Dylan and the Beatles, wrong about everyone else. Indeed, most of the names he listed are unknown to the general public today and some were obscure at the time. The very title of Newfield's book on the New Left, *A Prophetic Minority,* soon rang hollow.

Why the New Left Failed

Various reasons have been put forward to explain the demise of the New Left. The disappearance of the theatrical left is easily explained. The Yippies, Diggers, and similar bodies had little in the way of form or structure, no real roots, and, tied as they were to the counterculture, could hardly have been expected to outlive it. The Yippies in particular owed their strength, such as it was, to the enemies they made, and when people stopped taking offense at their pranks, there was not much point in remaining a Yippie.

SDS, which was much more ambitious and enjoyed a longer life than did the theatrical left, has attracted considerable scholarly attention. Among the most valid explanations offered by historians for its collapse was its failure to develop a real constituency, even though the need for one had been obvious to SDS from the beginning. Indeed, the history of its efforts to find a target group is almost a history of SDS. Students, as a group, who had seemed a lost cause because of their political apathy in the early sixties, proved to be more responsive to SDS than expected. But efforts to expand beyond the campus invariably met with failure. ERAP demonstrated that the poor had little interest in what young radicals were preaching. Such success as ERAP did enjoy came from mobilizing poor women on specific issues, not from infusing the needy with class consciousness. The rise of Black Power deprived SDS of the race issue, which had so powerfully influenced the Old Guard and remained a bleeding wound in SDS's side—its repeated attempts to say "farewell to white guilt" notwithstanding. White working-class youngsters were no more supportive of SDS than were poor minorities, and appending SDS to Third World revolutionary movements did not work either, since this amounted to a tacit admission that nobody in America was organizable except college students. Finally, college students were never a reliable membership base because of their volatility and unfortunate tendency to graduate.

Another very real problem with garnering the support of college students was that while events in the mid-sixties radicalized them to some extent, the proliferation of radical activities in the late sixties had the opposite effect, increasing the proportion of those who identified themselves to pollsters as conservatives, and diminishing those who sided with the left. Additionally, studies made at the time showed that those twenty-nine years old and under, of whom college students were a minority, showed more support for the Vietnam War than did older people—refuting yet again the New Left slogan about not trusting anyone over the age of thirty.

The high rate of membership turnover was another burden on SDS. None of the early SDS leaders still held leadership positions by the end of the sixties. Although Hayden, Rennie Davis, and other high-profile members remained activists for most or all of the decade, by 1965 even they were mostly working outside SDS, which reincarnated itself every year or two. Turnover had always been characteristic of American leftists. In its prime during the 1930s, the Communist Party USA, for example, was believed to have lost half its members annually. Nevertheless, the half that remained was fairly stable and the party's leadership was especially so, providing a continuity utterly lacking in SDS.

Still another explanation for the collapse of SDS was its rapid devolution from a political movement to more of a religious cult. The Weathermen held apocalyptic views and believed that by going underground they would hasten the day of America's destruction, which was, in any case inevitable. And, even if they failed to hasten that day, they themselves were to be the saving remnant upon which a new and more glorious communist order would be built. That radicals were more pious than political was argued by Paul Goodman at the time. A guru of sorts to New Leftists in the early sixties, by 1969 Goodman had become their critic, seeing them as experiencing a religious crisis that was bound to end badly. "Alienation," he wrote, "is a powerful motivation, of unrest, fantasy, and feckless action. It can lead . . . to religious innovation, new sacraments to give life meaning. But it is a poor basis for politics, including revolutionary politics."

What this description fails to explain is why an organization pledged to democracy and fresh ideas became a hotbed of sloganeering, empty Marxist cliches, and finally terrorism. Here the "external" thesis, as it might be called—that SDS devolved into a cult because external pressures—police repression, the continuing war in Vietnam, Richard Nixon's election, and other outside forces and events—is of little help. These forces all put pressure on SDS and created an environment ill-suited to reasoned debate, but they did not predetermine what SDS would become.

Historian Richard J. Ellis offers an internal explanation for the descent of SDS by defining it as an organization characterized above all by its devotion to radical egalitarianism. There is plenty of evidence for this thesis, beginning with the *Port Huron Statement* itself. Among the forces at work in SDS from the start was a tension between the radicals' need to work within the system so as to change it, and their longing to disengage from society in order to protect the qualities of brotherhood, honesty, and equality that they admired. In Ellis's view, ERAP was attractive because by organizing poor people who were outside the system, SDSers could work for radical change in society without compromising their integrity.

By the same token, those in SDS who believed in change by means of electoral politics, notably through the Political Education Project (PEP), were an embattled minority, which by 1964 had been silenced or alienated from the main group. Steve Max, who was active in PEP, blamed its destruction on the newer, younger SDS members who came out of the counterculture and believed that Congress and other government organs were irrelevant. This was a common belief among Movement veterans, but the attack on Max's faction was led by Hayden and the ERAP communes, leaders of the Old Guard. In short order the need to be relevant had given way to demands for "counter-institutions," "parallel structures," a "counter-society," in order to escape corruption at the hands of seductive America. Hayden, who had praised SNCC at first for its courage and commitment, was now admiring its "position as an effective force largely unintegrated into American society." According to this reasoning, the main enemies of radicalism were not conservatives—an easily identifiable and unifying threat—but liberals, insidious corrupters of all that was pure and good. Liberals were bad when they fell short, as when the 1964 Democratic National Convention refused to seat delegates from the Mississippi Freedom Democratic Party. But Liberals were bad when they succeeded, too; at the 1964 SDS convention Johnson's Great Society was denounced as a pernicious example of "corporate liberalism," the scorned many-tentacled monster that co-opted radicals by *appearing* to work toward similar goals. And, to the degree that Johnson's generous antipoverty measures actually worked, they distracted the poor from the radical cause, clouding their vision.

As Ellis sees it, the influx of new members into SDS inspired by opposition to the Vietnam War was as much a danger as an asset since it threatened to dilute the radical authenticity of SDS. Similarly, the moderate antiwar movement was hazardous because it put SDS in league with false friends who would sooner or later betray it. The solution of SDSers was to retreat into communes, demonizing society as a whole while practicing a radical egalitarianism that, while the opposite of capitalist America, proved very hard to maintain. This pattern was well established years before Weather took control of SDS.

The turn to violence by factions in SDS that followed was attributed by Hayden and others to external forces, the police, the war, critics, and opponents. But SDSers made few efforts to pursue their goals through established channels, and once let down by the poor, they easily embraced the argument that violence was good when practiced by themselves for lofty purposes, but bad if employed by government. The SDS principle that means and ends are intimately related, expressed in the *Port Huron Statement* fell by the wayside. First the idea of revolutionary violence, and then its employment, followed, prefigured by SDS's idealization of figures like Che Guevera and Chairman Mao. Again, this turn took place in the middle sixties and was made by the Old Guard. As early as 1964 the influential Swarthmore College chapter of SDS drafted a statement for the National Convention that proposed revolutionizing the country "by force of example or by guerilla warfare. . . ." Swarthmore's founders, Quakers and pacifists whose mark was still on the college, must have turned over in their graves. Yet here SDS was only following the example of SNCC. The Swarthmore chapter had both a large number of red diaper babies and extensive civil rights experience, notably in struggles that had taken place in Cambridge, Maryland, from 1961 to 1963. Leading members of the Swarthmore Political Action Committee who had participated in that effort became leaders of SDS, moving their field of action from Cambridge to Chester, Pennsylvania, under the auspices of ERAP.

Ellis puts the blame for SDS's failings squarely on radical egalitarianism, which was inherent in SDS from the beginning and determined its outcome. Egalitarianism is to him the poisoned fruit that drives radicals to violence however good their intentions. Although Ellis made many astute observations, as an abstract proposition his thesis is debatable. For example, monasticism rests in part on the same foundation as egalitarianism, and while there have been warrior monks in the past, religious communities are generally nonviolent. Further, unlike monastic orders whose members sign on for life, secular communes seldom last long and rarely condone violence. More than a century before SDS was founded, America had been peppered with utopian communities of many types. The ones that lasted more than a few years, notably those of the Shakers, were invariably religious. Secular communities, inspired for the most part by the teachings of Robert Owens and Charles Fourier, were typically fleeting and nonviolent—despite their radical egalitarianism.

Rather than positing an intrinsic egalitarian dynamic that drove SDS relentlessly to embrace force, it seems more fruitful to look elsewhere for the causes of their resort to violence, for example at what one might call the "black mystique." SDS was always imitating the Student Nonviolent Coordinating Committee (SNCC), whose force of example can hardly be exaggerated. What gave SDS vitality at the start was not changing its name from the Student League for Industrial Democracy to Students for a Democratic Society, but the southern sit-ins that erupted soon afterward. SDS's program ERAP was deliberately based on the success of SNCC in organizing southern blacks, figures of romance to SDS, who attributed their humanity and virtue to their isolation from white society and closeness to the earth. It was understood that northern blacks did not till the land, but otherwise SDS believed that what had been done in the rural South could be replicated in the urban ghettos of the North—"one oppression, one movement" being a common slogan.

Casey Hayden was an early critic of this theory. The first white organizer invited to join SNCC, she had been forced out of SNCC by Black Power in 1965 and soon thereafter joined the Chicago ERAP. Once there, it took her only a few months to discover the marked differences between North and South. In the South, issues were clear and the enemy highly visible, making it comparatively easy to organize against segregation and the Ku Klux Klan and for voter registration. In the North, poor people had no clear enemies but numerous problems with respect to housing, welfare, and supporting their families, the causes of which were neither dramatic nor obvious. Solidarity among blacks was all but impossible to achieve, and blame for their problems tended to be scattered or directed inward. Also, whereas in the South radical organizers had a clear field in which to operate, the North was already filled with agencies working to help poor people, making ERAP one of many alternatives for people in need—and among the more demanding. Finally, the urban poor were different from poor people in the rural South, unused to working together, lacking both institutions of their own and resources of every kind. "People in this area," Casey Hayden wrote of Chicago, "don't belong to anything and nothing belongs to them." She spent fewer than six months in ERAP before turning her allegiance to feminism and then disappearing from the Movement altogether.

Having failed to organize the underclass, SDS conveniently argued that since the very poor were too downtrodden to help themselves, it was necessary for radicals to act on their behalf. This led to what is called "vanguardism," the idea that revolutionaries must take the initiative, dragging the masses behind them. In the 1960s Leninism was still their obvious model, leading SDSers to idealize what were seen as Leninist states: notably Cuba and North Vietnam. These countries had the further appeal to SDSers of being nonwhite, wholly in the case of Vietnam, partially in that of Cuba. As the Communist Party USA had done with the Soviet Union, SDS held these countries up as shining examples of model societies—although this entailed glorifying police states, whose faults were held to be nonexistent, temporary, or, in any case, minor, compared to those of the United States.

Yet, at the same time SDSers were looking to the Third World and finding inspiration in brutal left-wing dictatorships, SDS's organization itself was moving closer and closer to anarchy, condemning every proposal for action as an effort at manipulation and every individual initiative as elitism. In one sense, formlessness was an expansion of direct democracy, but it was also democracy's antithesis. An essential feature of democracy is majority rule, but if every determined minority wields a veto, then the majority is powerless and there can be no rule at all. Similarly, that leadership in SDS could not be exercised openly did not mean there were no leaders, only that no one knew for certain who they were. This put a premium on charisma, as manifested by Tom Hayden early and Bernardine Dohrn late. It also eliminated accountability—another principle upon which real democracy depends. In 1965 when Paul Booth argued that SDS was too big to make consensus a requirement for arriving at decisions, the answer to problems arising from participatory democracy was more of the same—endless discussion.

As the SDS National Council, which was supposed to make policy between conventions, could agree on nothing, the National Office became more important by default. A 1967 "reform," according to which the offices of president and vice president were eliminated in favor of three coequal secretaries, strengthened the National Office even more since it gave the national secretary freedom from oversight. As the gap between leaders and followers widened, the National Office came to see itself as the vanguard and the rank-and-file as its troops. Factionalism within SDS became more intense, partly as a result of this change, leading to SDS's ultimate disintegration. Only then did the merits of representative democracy come to be seen in a more respectful light, too late to make any difference.

But SDS's embrace of radical egalitarianism does not fully explain this sequence of events. The internal dynamic (egalitarianism) explains much about SDS, but not its turn toward Leninism, a blueprint for taking power by force and the antithesis of participatory democracy. The question remains, how did Students for a *Democratic* Society end up despising the real people of America—as opposed to the mythical people of America for whom they claimed to speak—and embracing failed political doctrines such as Leninism that were the very opposite of what they had originally believed in?

There have been many answers to this question. A partial explanation was offered at the time by the sociologist Nathan Glazer, a member of the old radical, anti-Stalinist intelligentsia who became a neoconservative in reaction to the New Left. To him, the corrupting element of the New Left was its anti-institutionalism, which flew in the face of modern realities, had little popular support, and encouraged destructive tendencies without producing a viable alternative. In theory all institutions were seen as corrupt by the New Left, but in practice it was the universities that most felt the effects of radical attacks on authority. It was to save the university that Glazer moved to the right, as did many other academics who had themselves—like Glazer—been critical of higher education in many respects.

Another contemporary explanation of the New Left's souring was given by the philosopher and social scientist Lewis S. Feuer. In *The Conflict of Generations: The Character and Significance of Student Movements* (1969), Feuer put his finger on a crucial point, which might seem obvious but is often overlooked. The New Left differed from previous American radical impulses above all in being a student movement, which distinguished it from utopian socialism, the Socialist Party of Eugene V. Debs, and the Communist Party USA, all of which included young people but were led by, and often consisted mainly of, adults. The New Left, in contrast, was always peopled by students or young people who had not yet put their student years behind them.

This meant that, unlike movements of workers that are united, or have the potential of being united, by class consciousness, the New Left's animating feature was generational consciousness, a more or less self-aware revolt of middle-class children against their parents. Indeed, the term "generation gap" came into common use during the sixties because for the first time, political dissent was associated with an age group rather than a region or class. In addition, because they were students, New Leftists were deeply concerned with ideas. Feelings won out in the end, but ideas always remained important to the group, even to the Weather Underground, as shown by its search for a consistent theory.

The New Left was, in fact, the only true student movement in American history. For comparative purposes it is best understood not by looking at earlier forms of radicalism in America, but by looking at its counterparts overseas, and at earlier student movements such as the *Narodniks,* or Populists, of nineteenth-century Russia. Feuer drew innumerable comparisons between the New Left and its historical and contemporary equivalents, although he noted what was genuinely new in the Movement as well—participatory democracy on the one hand, the use of illegal drugs on the other. Sexual freedom, however, which some in the New Left seemed to think they had invented, was anything but novel. One New Leftist wrote of a shared belief that the "movement that screws together glues together. Or to be specific, that Socialists who sleep together creep together." Only the language was fresh; the idea behind it was deeply rooted in radical theory and practice.

If viewed solely as a student movement, the New Left had a predetermined fate. According to Feuer, radical student politics are conducted at such a high emotional pitch that activists eventually crash and burn. Also, political actions arising from generational revolt tend to be self-limiting. They end when the generation's independence drama has played itself out. "Meanwhile," Feuer says, "the leading political student leaders are often disabled by extreme commitments from assuming the role of leadership they might otherwise normally have filled." Such was the fate of Tom Hayden, Bernardine Dohrn, and others who, if gripped by less primal passions, might have gone far—or, in Hayden's case farther— thanks to their intellect and eloquence.

Whatever the reasons for its collapse, the New Left's place in American history remains considerable, if also somewhat elusive. It seems safe to say, however, that its place in history is not what Movement activists had envisioned. They failed to create the good society, still less a socialist state. They did not end the war in Vietnam. Richard Nixon accomplished that for geopolitical reasons of his own. Whether the New Left helped build opposition to the war is a moot point. Certainly it did so at first, but by the late 1960s everything touched by leftists had become so wildly unpopular that their endorsement was the kiss of death. Probably the New Left can lay some small claim to the gains made by African Americans during the decade, but, again, its useful role in the black civil rights efforts was limited to the early sixties. Later, New Left efforts to link racial equality with the Black Panther Party and Third World revolutionaries did more harm to than good African Americans. The rebirth of feminism owed a good deal to the New Left's inherent male chauvinism, which inspired radical feminists to break with it and form a movement of their own. Although male leftists came to see the error of their ways and tried to catch up to the women, their legacy in this area is, at the very least, ironic. And while the New Left did have a short-term effect on the Democratic Party, pushing it away from the center and contributing to the nomination of George McGovern for president in 1972, this had such a dire effect on their chances for electoral success that the Democrats have been backpedaling ever since.

The long-term influence of the New Left lies in three areas, of which the modern university would be first. This is such a complex subject that Chapter Five will be devoted to it. Next, as indicated above, the New Left contributed mightily to the growth of conservatism. This probably would have happened in any case, for the civil rights revolution and the Great Society were shocks to the body politic that were certain to create a backlash. But the New Left aided and abetted this trend to the right by providing conservatives with figures to demonize before the American people, which they did with such success that Republican intellectuals and politicians were still campaigning against the left and the sixties thirty years afterward—despite the point of diminishing returns having long since been reached.

But Republicans could not have exploited the New Left so successfully and for so long were it not for the deep distrust Movement people aroused among their own generation. A survey made by the magazine *Rolling Stone* in 1988 demonstrated that distrust, as well as how long the negative influence of the New Left lasted. The survey covered persons who were then between the ages of eighteen and forty-four, that is, those who had come of age in the 1960s, 1970s, and 1980s. By a large margin this groups was more opposed to welfare abuse than in favor of programs aimed at benefitting the homeless. Only 8 percent of the respondents believed it was important "to promote general social concern/less materialism in young people." Thus, after twenty years, the rejection of a core New Leftist doctrine could hardly have been more complete.

The third most profound influence of the New Left on American life regards personal conduct. The rise of sexual freedom, and with it the soaring divorce and illegitimacy rates, and the rapid spread of sexually transmitted diseases such as AIDS, were not directly the work of the New Left. American culture underwent a remarkable change in the 1960s, away from respect for authority, traditional values, and the family, and toward individualism, freedom from responsibility, and the pleasure principle. But the New Left, together with the counterculture, the hippies, the birth-control pill, the collapse of censorship, possibly even the appearance of the unprecedented report of sex researcher Alfred Kinsey and Hugh Hefner's *Playboy* magazine, were among the forces working to break down the old America that largely disappeared in the 1960s and 1970s. "Doing your own thing" became not just a Movement slogan but a national mantra. Although, thankfully, the phrase is seldom heard today, the selfish impulse behind it remains alive and well. It was not by accident that young people in the 1970s were dubbed the "me generation," for to some extent their ethos was similar to that of the New Left, stripped of its social and political consciousness. Later cohorts although given different names—Generation X, for example—were all "me" generations too.

These consequences were hardly what the New Left wished, and are not mentioned in books written by former New Leftists and historians sympathetic to the Movement. The truth about the New Left, which tends to get buried when accomplishments are highlighted, is that it had one original idea, participatory democracy, and one great passion, civil rights. Otherwise the Movement tended to be opportunistic, piggybacking on other causes with larger constituencies. The rhetorical convention, when writing about New Left accomplishments, is to list every popular cause, from ending the war to saving the environment, that anyone on the left ever expressed interest in, and assign certain people a share of the credit for whatever was eventually accomplished. But it hardly serves posterity to pick and choose in these matters. If the New Left helped in any way to end the War in Vietnam, it also encouraged, even reveled in, sexual abandon and self-indulgence, as well as in contempt for authority and the family. The legacy of the sixties, the good and the bad together, is the legacy of the New Left as well—not exclusively, to be sure, but as part of the mixture. That there have been gains in personal freedom and race relations cannot be denied. But that these have entailed very substantial costs to society cannot be denied either. The New Left was part of a great historical engine that transformed American life. Too small to have been the causative agent, the New Left was still large enough to materially shape the outcome. By 1980 at the latest, America was a country that New Leftists had helped create, even though it bore little resemblance to the land of their dreams.

CHAPTER FIVE

The Academic Left

On May 4, 1991, President George Bush chose "political correctness" as the subject of his commencement address at the University of Michigan in Ann Arbor. This term would appear frequently in the media during the next few years to describe a great variety of controversial practices, some not unique to the campus but all deeply entrenched there. Bush was most concerned with the proliferation of "hate speech" codes, designed to make the university a more comfortable place for women and especially minorities. The codes had become newsworthy because in recent years a number of students around the country had been disciplined, or even expelled, for making indelicate statements. This was the work of the Academic Left, the New Left's direct descendent and its most important legacy.

"The notion of 'political correctness' has ignited controversy across the land," Bush said. "And although the movement arises from the laudable desire to sweep away the debris of racism, sexism and hatred, it replaces old prejudices with new ones. It declares certain topics off-limits, certain expressions off-limits, even certain gestures off-limits. What began as a cause for civility has soured into a cause of conflict and even censorship."

Bush had chosen Ann Arbor quite purposefully as the site for his defense of the First Amendment. He was running for reelection and his numerous academic critics had been rendered vulnerable by the new norms on campus. Michigan's speech code, while by no means unusual, since hundreds of colleges and universities had similar rules, was among the most extreme, so much so that in 1989 it had been declared unconstitutional by a U.S. District Court. In its original form the university's policy on "Discrimination and Discriminatory Harassment" proscribed "any behavior, verbal or physical, that stigmatizes or victimizes an individual on the basis of race, ethnicity, religion, sex, sexual orientation, creed, national origin, ancestry, age, marital status, handicap, or Vietnam-era veteran status." The list of those who might be victimized was so inclusive that only extraterrestrials were omitted, accidentally no doubt. In response to the court's decision, U.M. had made cosmetic changes to its code, but the university administration was still vigorously prosecuting students for abhorrent expression.

Bush's speech, however self-serving, drew attention to a debate that had been going on for several years without attracting much notice. This was soon to change. A search of the NEXIS database of American publications found that *political correctness* appeared only sixty-six times in 1990, 1,553 times in 1991, and 4,643 times in 1993, after which mentions dropped off fairly sharply. What critics called political correctness, PC for short, went far beyond free speech codes. It included attacks on Western Civilization (the course), and the promotion of "multiculturalism," which in practice meant elevating Third World studies and eliminating or curtailing more "Eurocentric" curriculums. This took place on all educational levels, but had started in universities. The policy of affirmative action in accepting new students was a central feature of PC, and as a result many of the nation's best colleges and universities routinely enrolled minority students who did not meet the institution's usual scholastic standards. The same principle was applied to faculty hiring, although with less success, as the pool of black and Hispanic Ph.D.s was small, and affirmative action in faculty hiring was often a euphemism for raiding other schools' personnel. Increasing the proportion of women faculty had been much easier owing to the large and growing number of female Ph.D.'s. Except for outstanding senior women, still in short supply in the nineties, raiding other faculties to acquire female professors was uncommon. All of the above practices were justified in the name of diversity, a principle which held that the greater the proportion of selected minorities—and sometimes women—the better. Rules against sexual harassment were politically correct as well. Most cases brought under this rubric involved the victimization of women, once in a while heterosexual men, and sometimes homosexuals.

Perhaps the most difficult aspect of PC for outsiders to fathom was the growing influence in academic disciplines of *postmodernism*, a blanket term for a variety of theoretical approaches, which, however, had much in common. Postmodernism rested on the principle that the written word never actually meant what it said. The scholar's job, therefore, was to "deconstruct," that is, tease out the hidden meaning of books and other documents, called "texts." When postmodernists "deconstructed" the canon of classic texts written by white male writers, the works invariably were shown to be sexist, racist, homophobic, imperialistic, or otherwise reprehensible. Writing was seen as the exercise of power. Accordingly, there was no longer such a thing as literal truth, only partisanship, the critical scholar's biases apparently being preferable to those of the writer undergoing deconstruction.

This remarkable transformation of the university from an institution that cherished higher learning to a political agency obsessed with issues of race, gender, and power was made by survivors of the New Left—together with their heirs and allies. In the 1970s, had anyone thought about it, the likelihood of such a takeover would have seemed remote, for the New Left had been crushed, and the university seemed to have survived its onslaught relatively unscathed—save for minor changes such as grade inflation and the removal of unpopular graduation requirements. Further, there appeared to be no reason for radicals to embrace higher education. The New Left had devoted untold amounts of time and paper to denouncing the "multiversity" for its links to the military-industrial complex, and thus to the War in Vietnam, as also for its sexism, racism, and general failure to meet the expectations of revolutionary youth.

Yet time made it clear that nothing was more natural than the return of the repressed to academia. The collapse of the New Left as a movement did not mean that the impulse behind it was gone; nor were its former members and sympathizers dead. The problem for radicals in the seventies, seen as a personal one after the New Left's extinction, was how to be true to leftist principles and ideas and yet live productively in a nation dominated by conservatives and consumers. The solution for many was obvious—to attend graduate school. Bright young people in the sixties were not misled by their own rhetoric to the point where they could not tell the difference between academia and capitalism. To a radical, the advantages of the one over the other were self-evident. New Leftists had never believed in the ideal of disinterested scholarship, indeed, they doubted that such a thing existed. But the New Left at its most intellectually ambitious had been intoxicated by ideas, and many of its survivors still were. With political action in the nation at large having failed, the university became an increasingly attractive venue for leftover radicals.

Although much was made at the time of the distinction between early New Leftists, such as the thoughtful founders of SDS, and later New Leftists, who were believed to be wilder, younger, less educated—and more addicted to television and movies rather than to books—these differences meant little in subsequent years, as their generational similarities were stronger and more lasting. The crucial point was that the student body of the sixties contained a great many men and women who would enter academic life in the 1970s and 1980s. Many of these people were still New Leftists at heart. They became academics not necessarily because they had decided to replace politics with scholarship, but because the university—owing to its tradition of tolerance and relative distance from the money culture—was one of the few places in American life, and easily the most important, where it was possible to be both politically radical and professionally successful. In addition, there was always the hope of doing well by doing good, that is, of advancing in one's scholarly field and at the same time molding the thoughts of future generations of students, through whom it might still be possible to effect the changes the New Left itself had failed to make. It was a delusion, to be sure, since undergraduates never became politicized again in the twentieth century, but a congenial one all the same.

This is not to suggest that a conspiracy was formed in the post–New Left years to subvert higher education. There was never a convention at which someone like Bernardine Dohrn ordered leftists to infiltrate the university with conquest in mind. It was more a matter of tens of thousands of individuals coming to similar conclusions. The effect, however, was much the same as if a concerted effort had been made to retreat to the university and make it a place fit for Movement veterans, allowing for the fact that as they grew older their conception of what fitness entailed was bound to be different from what it had been in their rebellious youth. Even so, because the university of the 1990s was a hotbed of tenured professors and administrators who had once been New Leftists, or who shared many of their beliefs, by looking at the contemporary university much can be learned about the New Left itself. To study what is called political correctness is, therefore, to study the New Left in middle age.

Almost inevitably the former New Leftists who came to have such a powerful influence on academia mostly were products of the Movement's second phase, that of pseudo-revolution. The Academic Left did not believe in participatory democracy. Indeed, some mistrusted democracy itself and retained fond feelings for Castro's Cuba. America was never more than an object of criticism, while they glorified the Third World and ignored its faults. Racial minorities were as psychologically important to the Academic Left as they had been to the New Left, and spanned a greater range as racial preferences were extended to include Hispanics and American Indians. There were major differences as well between the New and Academic Lefts. The New Left's hatred of bureaucracy was replaced by an eagerness to manipulate institutions for personal and ideological gain—feminists turning out to be especially good at this. By the time the Movement collapsed most male New Leftists had come to see that sexism was bad form and harmful to the cause. The dragon of male chauvinism having been slain, Academic Leftists of both sexes got along well together as a rule and pursued similar, or at least compatible, ends.

Speech Codes

Speech codes at universities illustrate how much had changed since the sixties. Few episodes in New Left history had resonated more loudly than the Free Speech Movement at Berkeley. By the fall term of 1964, student activists were routinely maintaining literature tables at a strip of sidewalk in front of the main gate of the University of California's flagship campus. This practice violated university rules because *in loco parentis* still held sway, and governing political behavior was among the many controls over student life that existed almost everywhere in higher education. But Berkeley activists believed the sidewalk at issue was off-campus and therefore free territory. In September 1964 the university informed them otherwise and instructed them to remove their tables. On October 1, after the order was defied, campus police arrested Jack Weinburg, a student member of the Congress of Racial Equality. A mass of students then surrounded the police car, holding it hostage overnight. University officials decided not to press the matter, but UC's regents overruled them, bringing charges in November against four student leaders.

This mistake led to further student agitation and a rally before Sproul Hall, the UC administration building, on December 1. Mario Savio, briefly famous as a leader of the Free Speech Movement, gave a fiery address in which he described the university as a machine of which students were the raw material. "It becomes odious, so we must put our bodies against the gears, against the wheels . . . and make the machine stop until we are free." Folk artist Joan Baez sang "We Shall Overcome," and a thousand students occupied Sproul Hall and commenced sitting-in. They were roughly evicted by campus police, who arrested 814 of the protestors. A student strike followed, and the faculty voted that no restrictions be placed on advocacy or the content of speech. This was only an advisory vote but showed where the faculty stood. The Regents fired Berkeley's chancellor, also UC President Clark Kerr, perhaps the best known spokesman for higher education in America. These steps did nothing to curb militancy, which grew ever more extreme—some demanding that obscenity and profanity be included in the definition of protected speech. Soon Berkeley became the foremost symbol of student activism, a heroic one to the New Left, though not to the voters of California who elected the conservative Ronald Reagan as governor partly in the vain hope that he would deradicalize Berkeley.

Given this history, which included successful free speech fights on many other campuses, it might have been supposed that Academic Leftists would bring to the university an unbounded enthusiasm for the First Amendment. Nothing could have been less true, as the speech codes demonstrated. Their origin went back to the mid- to late 1980s when bigotry seemed to be increasing on college campuses. It is unclear whether the incidence of racist and homophobic graffiti, the posting of abusive signs, the distribution of offensive flyers, and other mean-spirited acts actually became more commonplace. It may have been that minority students and their allies were quicker to take offense than they had been in the past. In any event, incidents of bigotry were believed to be on the rise, and numerous universities responded to them by enacting speech codes similar to those in place at Michigan.

A study of 384 campus handbooks and student guides published in 1994 found that 28 percent prohibited advocacy of political causes, the very right that the Berkeley Free Speech Movement had fought to establish. Despite the Michigan court decision, forms of speech considered offensive to minorities were still banned at the University of Michigan. A branch of the State University of New York adopted a rule stipulating that "students found diminishing the dignity of other members of the community through . . . racial, sexual, religious, or ethnic disparagement" would be expelled—although disparagement was a constitutionally protected form of speech and diminished dignity was hard to prove. Speech codes were usually ambiguous. The Fashion Institute of Technology in New York City, for example, prohibited "any behavior that implicitly or explicitly carries messages of racism, sexism, stereotyping, or discrimination of any kind." How a student was expected to know when he or she had implicitly stereotyped someone else was a mystery, given the common practice of referring to certain groups as "dumb jocks" or "blonde bimbos," among other unflattering labels—stereotypes to be sure, and obviously invidious, but impossible to write into speech codes since no one would accept such designations. To complicate matters, 60 percent of the schools had regulations banning harassment, including "verbal abuse," a term so elastic it might be—and in practice was—applied to any negative statement. Forty-seven percent of schools prohibited lewd, indecent, or profane language, which are also constitutionally protected as well as commonly employed in movies, popular music, and the everyday speech of millions of people.

Universities usually justified speech codes on the ground that hate speech was a form of assault. Thus, one Stanford University law professor wrote that racial slurs were so harmful that they constituted acts. "The invective is experienced as a blow, not as a proffered idea." This was a highly subjective criterion, since what one person experienced as a "blow" might to another be little more than an annoyance. Speech codes also raise questions such as the one put forward by the black scholar Henry Louis Gates, Jr., who asked why it was not enough for universities to condemn racist speech; why did they also have to punish the speaker? The universities' usual answer was that written policies condemning racist speech were "mere words." To that one might ask: why were racist expressions acts, but antiracist assertions only words?

Even if, for purposes of argument, hate speech might under some circumstances have the force of a blow, in practice quite innocuous speech could be seen as racist and penalized accordingly. The University of Pennsylvania offered two notorious examples of how this process worked. An early instance was the case of Murray Dolfman, an adjunct professor who taught business law at Penn's Wharton School. In November 1984, finding that no one in his class knew anything about the Thirteenth Amendment, he referred to blacks as ex-slaves (he called himself, as a Jew, an ex-slave also), and asked a black student to read the Amendment aloud several times. This offended at least three of the four black students in his class, who complained to him afterward. Dolfman apologized, conceding that the term "descendants of slaves" would have been more appropriate. Although the incident seemed closed, it was opened again in February 1985 during Black History Month, when Dolfman's offense was recalled and demonstrations held demanding his dismissal. Without taking the time to conduct an investigation, the University Council voted at once to suspend him. Ultimately, Dolfman was forced to write a letter of apology that ran in the student newspaper, compelled to attend re-education classes, and suspended for a year.

Although the Dolfman case brought much unfavorable publicity to Penn, worse lay ahead. On January 13, 1993, an Israeli undergraduate named Eden Jacobowitz, vexed by a group of noisy black female students outside his dormitory, shouted at them to quiet down—as did many other dorm residents. In doing so, however, Jacobowitz called the women "water buffalos," and for this he was charged under Penn's speech code. While perfectly willing to apologize for rudeness, he refused to confess to having employed racial invective, since he did not regard the term *water buffalo* as racist, and neither did a legion of scholars assembled in his defense. It transpired that *water buffalo* was a term often applied to offending students in the Jewish school (*yeshiva*), which Jacobowitz had attended before matriculating at Penn. Nonetheless, it would have gone hard for him had the case not drawn national attention, and Penn's repeated attempts to punish Jacobowitz become so embarrassing to the institution that it dropped its case against him. Conditions at Penn did not really change, however, until in 1995 a new president reversed her predecessor and daringly announced that "the content of student speech is no longer a basis of disciplinary action."

There were literally hundreds of free speech cases in the late 1980s and early 1990s at colleges and universities around the country, so many that the Academic Left was forced to retreat on this issue. After years of complaints and law suits by civil libertarians and

wounded parties the tide began to turn. Some universities revised
or eliminated their speech codes, others stopped enforcing them.
Probably few on the left actually changed their minds on the issue,
but as a practical matter most seem to have come around to the position taken by Professor Gates. He, personally, would have liked
to see hate speech punished, but since doing so inevitably led to
fights over the First Amendment, during which the nature of the
offense tended to be lost, censure was more politic than censorship. If hardly a ringing endorsement of free speech, it represented
a compromise that most people on campus could live with.

Another form of censorship that continued throughout the
nineties consisted of personal rather than institutional retaliation
against individuals and groups who gave offense to minority students. Sometimes, as in the Dolfman case, these were peacefully
delivered, other times not. Penn was one of many schools where
minority students "confiscated" issues of a student newspaper that
contained material displeasing to them. At Berkeley this happened
routinely to the *Daily Californian,* whose office building was frequently defaced as well. In 1991, protestors demanding a greater
minority voice in a University of Massachusetts student newspaper, the *Collegian,* twice invaded its offices, destroying property
and roughing up staff members. No one was punished in this, or in
the numerous similar cases. In practice, speech and conduct codes
applied only to whites, seldom if ever employed against minority
students and teachers.

The fight over speech codes validated a historical point. Critics of the New Left had charged in its glory days that student radicals did not really favor free speech in principle, but sought only
to protect their own right of expression and that of their allies and
favorite victimized groups. Campus speech codes, which were ar-
dently defended by the Academic Left, seemed to reinforce the
point. Stanley Fish, a leading postmodernist who taught both in
the Duke English Department and in its School of Law, did not
even contest it. To the contrary, Fish openly admitted that he had
no interest in the free exchange of ideas, victory being his only
aim. Fish published a book whose title rather awkwardly summed

up his position, *There's No Such Thing As Free Speech And It's a Good Thing, Too* (1993).

The "good thing" to Fish, an English professor unconstrained by grammatical shackles, was not free speech, but rather the lack of it. Further, he meant this in the broadest sense, writing "if you are engaged in some purposive activity in the course of which speech happens to be produced, sooner or later you will come to a point when you decide that some forms of speech do not further but endanger that purpose." Or, lest excessive delicacy blur his point, "free speech principles don't exist except as a component in a bad argument in which such principles are invoked to mask motives that would not withstand close scrutiny." In other words, free speech was the last refuge of the scoundrel. Candor such as this was rare in the free speech fights of the nineties, however, doublespeak being the form of expression preferred by enemies of the First Amendment.

Multiculturalism

Another cause the Academic Left embraced was multiculturalism. The discovery that minorities (and women) possessed a history of their own, one previously neglected by mainstream scholars, was a valuable legacy of the 1950s and 1960s, when formerly marginalized groups became the subjects of extensive study. However, multiculturalism in practice went far beyond the modest claim that the study of American history and culture should be more inclusive. One trend was to invert the study of American history, spending more time and space on minorities and women and less on history as experienced by dead white males (or DWMs). Another trend was to exaggerate the accomplishments of favored groups and individuals by elevating minor black and female writers to the level of Melville and Whitman. The result was a host of textbooks and courses in which previously neglected minorities were overrepresented. There was a certain rough justice to this, achieved at a price, since a student now might learn more about George Washington Carver, for instance, than about his namesake—a DWM to be sure, and yet one whose contributions to America were far from negligible.

But such excesses were hardly major compared to the invention of a fictitious black history by Afrocentrists. This was an odd turn of events since by the 1980s the history of African Americans had been explored, and often celebrated, in a library of scholarly and popular books. That was not good enough for Afrocentrists, who, finding the real history of blacks insufficient, dreamed up one of their own in which Egypt became a black civilization responsible for all that was great in the ancient world. Although scientific evidence went against the idea, they also discovered that blacks had been the first people to discover the Americas. A further stunning revelation, found in a contribution to an Afrocentric book adopted by the Portland, Oregon, school system, was that the ancient Egyptians had supernatural powers and flew about in gliders. For Afrocentrists the wonders never ceased. Nor, as this example suggests, were these intellectual delights confined to a lucky few. While Afrocentrism was produced in colleges and universities, it strongly influenced the curricula of lower schools.

But mainstream multiculturalism was less concerned with antiquity than with the United States, whose history was now found to be a record of persecutions. In 1989 a New York State Task Force on Minorities: Equity and Excellence, which included not a single historian, issued a report on reforming the public school curriculum that began with the following statement: "African-Americans, Asian-Americans, Puerto Ricans/Latinos and Native Americans have all been the victims of an intellectual and educational oppression that has characterized the culture and institutions of the United States and European American world for centuries." The task force's consultant on African American culture and a principal author of the report was Professor Leonard Jeffries of the City College, City University of New York. Jeffries taught in his classes that whites were a cold, materialistic "ice people" who brought "domination, destruction, and death" to the world, as opposed to blacks, who were a warm, humanistic "sun people" mentally and physically superior to whites. It turned out that in addition to his racism, Jeffries was anti-Semitic. Years of bad publicity and legal action finally resulted in Jeffries losing his position as chair of the Department of Black Studies at City College—although he remained a full professor. Despite his fall from grace, multiculturalism was little damaged.

One cannot lay too much of the blame for Afrocentrism at the feet of Academic Leftists. Afrocentrism was an embarrassment to some, and even multiculturalism posed problems—especially for feminists, who found themselves in the awkward position of being expected to defend Third World cultures in which women had few rights and were often brutally treated. Still, the Academic Left went along with these trends as a rule, and multiculturalism fit in nicely with the left's devotion to identity politics, obsession with racial and sexual minorities, and preference for the Third World at the expense of the First. While multiculturalism as a whole went beyond the concerns of the historic New Left, it was a natural extension of New Left beliefs and therefore a part of the Movement's legacy.

To believers in national unity and a common culture, which doubtlessly included a majority of Americans but definitely not the Academic Left, multiculturalism was dangerous precisely because it magnified differences. As a nation of immigrants, America had long struggled with the problem of how to maintain a national identity despite the existence of large minorities. The melting-pot metaphor was never very accurate and fell into disuse. At midcentury liberal intellectuals had rallied behind the idea of cultural pluralism, which, unlike multiculturalism, celebrated diversity. However, cultural pluralism cast the broadest possible net by including all ethnic and racial backgrounds, while at the same time ascribing to them certain core American values such as liberty, democracy, and tolerance. Cultural pluralism aimed to promote assimilation, while multiculturalism was inherently divisive. And division was the last thing America needed during the years of large-scale immigration that began in 1965, when new legislation made it much easier to immigrate—especially for Hispanics and people of color. Fortunately, while everyone paid lip service to multiculturalism, and education at all levels was saturated with propaganda on its behalf, most immigrants understood that, however much they loved their native cultures, the way to get ahead in America was to learn English and give their children the best possible education. This bedrock of common sense usually withstood the onslaught of multiculturalists and saved many children from harm.

Affirmative Action

To the Academic Left, few issues mattered more than affirmative action, even though it had not been an concern in the 1960s. But beginning with the Nixon administration, which lowered standards for minorities because of their educational and other disadvantages, the practice flourished. Universities in particular embraced affirmative action, and by the 1980s most elite institutions of higher learning were routinely admitting minority students—blacks at first and later Hispanics—who would not have qualified previously. This policy was difficult to quarrel with since blacks were unquestionably handicapped by generations of segregation and discrimination. Black students and faculty were grossly underrepresented in most colleges and universities, and, while the civil rights revolution of the sixties was bound to produce better qualified minority students over time, action had to be taken at once to serve the present generation. A double standard for admissions was widely seen as the only way to provide immediate relief. However, this well-intentioned device eventually led to unforeseen problems, and nowhere more so than at UC Berkeley.

Even after the sixties, Berkeley remained the most left-wing university in the country, but because of its academic luster it was also the campus California high school graduates most wanted to attend. However, while the California population grew, largely because of an influx of minorities, Berkeley did not. Thus the campaign for "diversity" through affirmative admissions could only succeed at the expense of whites and Asians—the latter group being numerous in California and having, on average, even better high school records than the former.

Although white applicants to UC Berkeley suffered, too, Asians applicants suffered most because they included a large number of extremely qualified high school graduates, but, as compared to whites, a relatively small number of voters. Berkeley began reducing quotas for Asian admissions as early as 1981, and in 1984 admitted 20 percent fewer Asians than it had the previous year. But the solution proved less than ideal. For one, as late as 1988, despite years of being discriminated against, Asians still made up about one-quarter of the student body. For another, Asian American interest groups proved less tractable than UC had expected. When they learned what was happening, their complaints became loud and frequent. Berkeley first denied, then conceded, that it favored black and Hispanic admissions over white and Asian. But while university admission policy reforms were promised, they never arrived, to the pronounced annoyance of California voters.

Another problem with affirmative action was that it did not have the desired effects. For one, the claim that admitting favored minorities would increase diversity in university life only worked on paper. Once on campus, racial minorities tended to keep to themselves, eating and socializing mainly with others of their own race and demanding separate housing, academic programs, and student centers. Thus, while integrated in the average classroom, students tended to self-segregate elsewhere—a process usually called "Balkanization." But Berkeley administrators did not worry overmuch about Balkanization, as affirmative action's success was measured by the number of "special admits," not by how they behaved after entry. Similarly, the high failure and dropout rates of black and Hispanic students troubled administrators less than it should have. In the late 1980s and early 1990s, whites and Asians had similar dropout rates, between 65 and 75 percent graduating in four years. Fewer than half of Hispanic students did so, and the four-year black graduation rate was below 40 percent. For special admits it was even worse. An internal study at Berkeley found that after five years (increasingly the standard length of time for white students nationwide) only 18 percent of black and 22 percent of Hispanic special admits had graduated. About 30 percent of all black and Hispanic students, whether affirmative action cases or not, dropped out before the end of their freshman year. As the report observed sardonically, they remained in school "only long enough to enhance the admissions statistics."

Despite heavy outside pressure, Berkeley and UCLA, the second most popular UC campus, refused to make significant changes in their admissions policies. The resulting impasse was finally broken as the result of a campaign spearheaded by Ward Connerly, a black friend of Governor Pete Wilson, whom he appointed to the UC Board of Regents in 1994. First Connerly pushed through a policy change requiring the UC system to end affirmative admissions and to end requiring race and gender as factors in hiring and signing contracts. Then he became chairman of a campaign to pass Proposition 209, which banned every kind of affirmative action statewide, an initiative that the voters approved in November 1996 and which went into effect on August 27, 1997—too late to affect admissions for the 1997–98 school year.

At first it looked as if the critics of Prop. 209, who claimed it would mean the end of diversity—such as it was—were going to be proved right. Minority acceptances at UC law schools fell, only one African American joining Berkeley's entering law school class out of seventeen accepted. But the picture changed considerably in 1998, when the first freshman classes chosen under the new rules were admitted to all eight UC campuses. A feature of these new rules was that while race could no longer be a criterion for admission, student essays and a record of having overcome obstacles could enter into the calculation. In theory, essays would allow room for fudging, as evaluating written work was far from an exact science. Minorities might also gain from having done well as other students despite poverty, poor schools, and other liabilities.

In practice, however, the new rules benefitted poor whites and Asians more than it did poor blacks and Hispanics. The director of admissions at UCLA admitted as much. "The fact is that lots of the blacks we admit are middle class, second and third-generation in college while many of the Asian-Americans are poor." Thus, making family income important promoted economic rather than racial diversity, which was not what administrators wanted. Even so, the final results were far less dramatic than had been feared by the friends of affirmative action. Black admissions did fall sharply at the two most desired campuses, Berkeley and UCLA, Berkeley having a decline of 66 percent. But systemwide black admissions fell by only 17.6 percent, while the least popular campuses—excellent schools in their own right—experienced a rise in minority admissions, mostly because more Hispanics now got in. The overall non-Asian minority decline was very small, only 2.4 percent systemwide. And even the fall in black admissions at Berkeley was not entirely a function of merit or the lack of it, since black university administrators there had been urging black high school graduates to avoid Berkeley because of its "hostile environment," as if somehow the university had wanted change instead of having change thrust upon it.

Nonetheless, even alarmists were encouraged by the 1999 figures, for in the spring, "underrepresented" minority admissions for the UC system bounced back to the 1997 level—1997 being the last year of affirmative admissions. Berkeley and UCLA did not return to their old numbers, but systemwide as many blacks, Hispanics, and American Indians were admitted as had been two years previously. Ward Connerly was elated. "The gloom and doom that was being preached by the proponents of preferences was grossly premature," he said. Further, although seldom mentioned in newspaper stories, which tended to focus on raw numbers, most minority students who recently entered UC had gotten in on merit—a little creative rigging of admission requirements notwithstanding. To Connerly, that had been the whole point, as he was deeply offended by the widespread belief that every black UC student was an affirmative admit. And even if minority students had not seen this as particularly stigmatizing, being admitted on the basis of achievement had to promote self-respect. Also, although it was too soon to tell for certain, odds were that the minority failure rates would decline—as was already the case at Berkeley—once UC had a student body chosen to a significant degree on the basis of its ability to succeed.

All else having failed, UC was compelled to face up to its dilemma. If it wanted more "underrepresented" minority students, it would have to help them qualify. Horrifying as this prospect may have been to them, since special admissions had been so easy and inexpensive, UC administrators accepted the inevitable. In 1998 the UC system decided to spend $38.5 million on outreach programs in minority-dominated school systems, beyond the $60 million a year it had already been spending in hopes of warding off Prop. 209. Together with matching funds provided by the public schools, this would double the number of students receiving college preparation assistance. While officials at Berkeley continued to wring their hands over the demise of affirmative action, those at other UC campuses, notably Riverside, responded by enormously increasing their outreach programs. At Riverside the chancellor himself rode the circuit of minority communities, not only to propagandize on behalf of his campus but specifically to tell parents and students what was required for UC admittance. As a result, UC Riverside had not only raised its number of minority students impressively, but even attracted students who had been admitted to higher status institutions by representing itself as more minority-friendly, which, in fact, it was.

Riverside's Chancellor Orbach continued to bemoan, for the record at least, the demise of affirmative admissions, but it was hard to see why, as by dint of honest hard work Riverside was not only winning the numbers game but genuinely benefitting minority students. To all except the ideologically blinkered, this appeared to be a major achievement. Friends of affirmative admission often tried to represent its critics as racists, which may sometimes have been the case. Calling names, however, did not get to the heart of the argument, which was whether minorities benefitted most from a double standard or by efforts to make them eligible for admission on the same basis as other students, which should also make them more likely to graduate. Choosing between the quick fix and lasting results would not seem to be difficult.

The experience of California dramatically pointed up what journalist Michael Lind later called the "diversity scam." Although mountains of propaganda were generated in its defense, there was no real evidence that diversity, as formulated by administrators, did anyone much good. Admitting unqualified students guaranteed that they would underperform whites and Asians almost everywhere, and frequently fail or drop out of public universities. (At elite private universities no one fails, and dropping out is rare.) Why was this better than admitting them to schools where they would have an excellent chance to succeed? And how did it promote diversity when the result of affirmative action was the Balkanized campus, which could call itself diverse on the basis of numbers but was actually self-segregated, as any visitor could readily see?

A peculiar anomaly resulted from how *diversity* was defined. Hispanics constituted a race for affirmative action purposes, but in real life *Hispanic* was only a cultural term, as Latin Americans might be white, black, Indian, or of mixed origins. And unlike African Americans, who experienced centuries of slavery and exploitation in America, few Hispanics can claim to have been similarly victimized here since most of them, or their parents, came to the United States after 1965, when the immigration laws were reformed. The problems of Hispanics are the same as those of most other immigrant groups, who ordinarily are poor, uneducated, and do not speak English fluently. Why should Hispanics, however poor or disadvantaged, get special favors denied to other immigrant groups? Only ideology and interest-group politics could justify what was so patently unfair.

As noted, a further difficulty was that affirmative admissions usually benefitted blacks and Hispanics who were already middle class. It remained very unusual for children of the ghetto or the barrio to gain admission to a UC school. They lived in poverty, went to inferior schools, and lacked access to advanced placement tests (offered by the wealthier school districts) that made it possible to graduate with a grade point average higher than 4.0. In theory a 4.0 was the result of earning straight A's, but in practice, thanks to extra credits gained by doing well on AP tests, graduates of the nation's best high schools routinely had GPA's that exceeded 4.0, even though they might not have received straight A's. Meanwhile students in poor schools, however able, had no chance to attain a GPA higher than 4.0, for the very lack of AP course offerings or examinations. How AP credits were valued varied from state to state, but it remained true across the nation that affirmative admissions benefitted the members of minority groups who least needed help. Thus, Academic Leftists who supported affirmative admissions had eliminated the children of poor and working-class families from their political agenda in favor of the offspring of middle-class minorities. In this manner the great American radical tradition, which had been all about helping the working class and the poor, came to an end. Affirmative admissions, perhaps more than any other issue, gave the lie to professorial pretenses of being revolutionary, or even left-wing.

When it came to ending affirmative admissions, California seemed at first to be the great success story. In other state systems, that of the University of Texas in particular, minority recruitment lagged after the courts banned affirmative admission. But the Texas state legislature, hitherto never known as a bastion of progressive thought, came up with an ingenious answer to the question of how to get more minorities into UT without making race a qualification. Known as the "Ten Percent Solution," the Texas legislature passed a bill guaranteeing admission to UT to everyone in the top tenth of their graduating classes. As most high schools were segregated by race and class, this gave graduates of poor school systems, whose test scores otherwise would have denied them admission, entry to UT. In addition, money was appropriated to help these students stay in college once they matriculated. The Ten Percent Solution was an immediate success, and other state legislatures introduced bills to achieve similar results. Florida adopted a "20 percent solution," which raised minority enrollments statewide by 12 percent in 2000, the first year it took effect.

The beauty of this system was that by not discriminating on the basis of race, it also gave a leg up to poor whites who constituted an absolute majority of all poor people in America and whose high schools were typically as poorly funded as those in the ghettos and barrios. Critics observed that the solution unfairly penalized gifted students from the very best high schools who had not made the top 10 percent because of fierce competition. Yet good students from such schools had plenty of options, and it remained puzzling why any leftist would argue that discrimination against the affluent was a serious national problem. In any case, while the Ten Percent Solution was a great improvement over race-based admissions, the most pressing need was to raise standards at all underperforming lower schools so that every child might have an equal chance at getting into a good college. Until then, race-neutral measures like the Ten Percent Solution would have to do.

A particularly striking feature of the affirmative action debate was that evidence rarely entered into defenses of affirmative admissions. Diversity, while assumed to be beneficial, was really hailed for its own sake, not for its practical effects. Certain universities competed to be the most diverse, regardless of whether this actually promoted integration or mutual respect in the society at large, rating their success in raw numbers and never stopping to ask who was actually profiting from the admission of unqualified students. An apparent exception to this rule was *The Shape of the River* (1998) by William G. Bowen and Derek Bok, which came out after the public had begun to turn against affirmative admissions. Rooted in a huge database consisting of academic and other records of 45,000 students who had attended "selective universities" between the 1970s and the early 1990s, it purported to show that affirmative action worked.

To the credit of the authors—both of whom were former Ivy League university presidents and fairly candid about their methods—what the book actually showed was that students who graduated from elite schools were successful in later life. The twenty-eight colleges and universities chosen for study ranged from Denison to Duke. This list included some very large universities, notably North Carolina and Michigan, but mostly much smaller ones and only a single institution—Pennsylvania State University—representative of the kind of college that most students actually attended. Indeed, twenty-four of the twenty-eight schools considered were private, whereas the great majority of American undergraduates attended public institutions. Nevertheless, Bok and Bowen purportedly proved that the minority students recruited by selective schools had high graduation rates, prospered afterward, and became active in their communities as adults.

This trend was also true, however, of white students—often to a greater degree. Further, there were no control groups in the Bowen and Bok analysis, that is, matched samples that would make it possible to compare, for example, black students admitted to Berkeley under its affirmative admissions policy with a similar group whose members were accepted elsewhere on the same basis as other students. For all that the authors knew, black students admitted on their merits at less selective institutions might have been as successful, or almost as successful, as those in the database. They might also have turned out to be from poorer families, which would mean that the gain to society was greater than that produced by affirmative action. Given the lack of this kind of information, *The Shape of the River* only established that selective institutions, especially private ones, were producing successful graduates of all races. But since everyone already knew this, the study was more than a little redundant.

In the real world of cause and effect, both UT and UC demonstrated that while recruiting minorities on the up and up was anything but easy, it could be done, and, more important, could be done in a way that promised to promote higher retention rates, which ought to have been the goal all along. Admitting poor white and Asian students should also have been a goal, but these were not the demographic groups educators favored and never would have been admitted if affirmative action had not been eliminated. Elsewhere the practice continued, Academic Leftists and administrators—who often were not leftists themselves but nonetheless were attracted by easy and politically correct answers to difficult problems—insisted that affirmative action was essential regardless of evidence to the contrary. But the facts had never really mattered. It had always been politics that determined policy. In most states it continued to do so at century's end, although for how much longer no one could say.

Sexual Harassment

The wrongness of sexual harassment had never been in doubt, nor was there any dispute that it was a long-neglected national as well as campus problem, but it came as a surprise to learn in the 1990s that crusading against it could also have bad effects. Here, as in the struggle over free speech, the witchhunting mentality came into play as the targets were often people whose offenses would, in a less heated environment, not have seemed at all serious. In 1993, J. Donald Silva, a tenured professor of English at the University of New Hampshire, was severely penalized for having offended ten female students. Among his crimes was, in a classroom effort to explain what "simile" meant, to have employed the following example: "Belly dancing is like jello on a plate with a vibrator under the plate." It appears that Silva, an ordained minister, did not realize that vibrators could be used for purposes other than massage. No matter, he had said something dreadful. On two other occasions, outside of class, he made jocose remarks that were not received in the same spirit. Although no one was quite sure what he had actually said, and some had heard nothing, his accusers were sure that he meant to degrade women. On the basis of these flimsy allegations, Silva was convicted of sexual harassment by a kangaroo court composed of two associate professors, a data analyst, and two undergraduate students, and sentenced to a year's suspension and mandatory counseling, to be paid for by himself.

In another incident a few years later, Stephen Dobyns, a novelist, poet, and tenured creative writing professor at Syracuse University, was also suspended for a year after having been convicted of sexual harassment. His sins were that he had splashed a drink in a woman's face at a party and had said something—no one was quite sure what—about her breasts. Then, too, he had been a severe critic of women in his writing classes; he was a severe critic of men, too—not that anyone cared. Of course teachers could not be allowed to throw drinks at people, and making angry remarks to women about their breasts was tasteless and crude. But Dobyns, like Silva, had not touched anyone, had not solicited or received sexual favors, had not coerced anyone, had not, in short, committed any of the acts that ordinarily might be considered forms of harassment. But at his kangaroo court, female students trembled and wept while recollecting his brutish lack of tact and unspeakable offensiveness in critiquing their written work. Dobyns, it was established, did not have a sufficiently tender regard for the sensibilities of the female sex. In accusing him, Syracuse feminists thus put themselves in the awkward position of maintaining both that women were equal to men, but because they were women, should be treated more kindly.

There were many such cases in the 1990s, not of sexual harassment as it was previously understood, but of failing to abide by unwritten standards of behavior—like the neo-Victorian code of etiquette that Dobyns unwittingly violated. Who was charged with harassment and who was not seemed to be governed by the laws of chance. The outcomes of the investigations, too, were arbitrary. Professor Silva went to court, and in a notable decision, Judge Shane Devine ruled that the University of New Hampshire had violated his right of free speech under the First Amendment. Dobyns chose not to sue anyone and endured his suspension. But it scarcely followed that seeking legal redress would have helped him, for in broadly similar cases the courts had gone in different directions.

A case that plumbed the murkiest depths of sexual harassment on campus concerned Professor Jane Gallop. A senior scholar in women's studies, Gallop came to the University of Wisconsin, Milwaukee, in 1991 to teach feminist theory in the Department of English and Comparative Literature. The next year she was charged by two female graduate students with sexual harassment. An investigation resulted in her being cleared on one count, but found her to have violated the university's "consensual amorous relations" policy on the other. Gallop hotly defended herself in print, but did not deny that she had said publicly during the first annual Graduate Student Gay and Lesbian Conference in 1991 that "graduate students are my sexual preference," nor that shortly afterward she had publicly given a deep kiss to the graduate student who later accused her of sexual harassment. But Gallop insisted there was nothing romantic or sexual about these events or in her relationship with the student. "The so-called consensual amorous relation' in question was neither a sexual relation nor even a romantic, dating one;" she wrote, "it was a teaching relation where both parties were interested in writing and talking about the erotic dynamics underpinning the student-teacher relation. Add to that adventuresome topic a teacher and a student whose styles tend toward the pedagogy of shocking performance—and what was never anything but a teaching relation found itself proscribed by university policy."

The real cause for discontent on the part of the student, according to Gallop, was that she had begun to criticize the student's work, hurting her feelings and prompting her charge that Gallop had punished her for rejecting unwanted sexual advances. The university was at fault, Gallop claimed, for failing to recognize that her colorful methods were based on the latest thinking in feminist pedagogy, that teaching should be highly personal. It was outrageous that she, a "recognized feminist theorist," should be found guilty of sexual harassment, since, both as a feminist and a woman, she was by definition incapable of harassing anyone. While Gallop never admitted this, by actually French-kissing her student in public she had gone much further than many male professors charged with sexual harassment. Moreover, her status did protect her, not from censure, but from material harm, as Gallop was not otherwise penalized and remained on the university's faculty. Gallop had brought on herself the embarrassment she suffered with her naive faith that shocking performance as teaching style entailed no risk in the 1990s. Gallop's student, having learned more than she probably wanted to know about feminist pedagogy, transferred out, doubtlessly in hopes of finding a less adventurous mentor.

Postmodernism

Postmodernism was the most explicitly radical aspect of political correctness, so far as language went, and also the hardest to summarize. It first took hold in modern language departments, partly for professional reasons. A perennial concern of language teachers, particularly of English and American literature, is that there is simply not enough great writing to go around. English professors are legion, great writers very rare, forcing Ph.D. candidates to write on ever more narrow topics and devote much attention to the published literature on them. The big advantage of any new approach is that the canon, the recognized body of great books, can be visited without reference to previous scholarship. Conversely, when traditional standards are dropped, little-studied books can be raised from obscurity and proclaimed great, or at least worthy of dissection. The career opportunities are obvious. A large number of previously obscure or marginal authors now become eligible for scholarly attention, and if those authors are women or members of minority groups, all to the better. Further, a Marxist critic could read just about any classic and find power masquerading as literature and philosophy. A feminist could search the canon for misogyny and not be disappointed. A gay scholar could find countless instances of repressed homosexuality, homophobia, or both. Deconstruction, the technique that finds hidden meanings in any text, might possibly be neutral, but in practice was usually employed by leftists to ferret out the shameful values of liberals and conservatives. Thus, the "theorists," as they called themselves—although "dogmatists" would have been more accurate—were not disinterested searchers for truth, but crusading agents of change, which they proposed to bring about by exposing villainy in the canon. How this was supposed to launch a social revolution remained something of a puzzle to civilians.

Actually, except for the theorists themselves and their graduate students, almost nobody believed in this approach to the study of art and literature or was radicalized by it. While postmodernist theorists argued, for example, that Shakespeare, who was constantly being "unmasked," was racist, sexist, imperialistic, and homophobic, most literate people continued to love his work all the same. Undergraduates as well—who are much more difficult to brainwash than is commonly believed—preferred to study literature in terms of itself, rather than as an instrument of power and domination. But postmodernists did not mind their students' lack of acceptance. Despite being self-proclaimed social activists, their real mission was less to transform society than to dominate academia. They controlled the foremost modern language departments, and the Modern Language Association, a huge professional body (32,000 members) whose annual meetings were subjects of much unkind humor owing to paper and session topics such as "Self-Reflectivity, Narrative Strategies, and the Soap Opera as Postmodern Genre." As this example points up, a striking feature of postmodernist tracts was their impenetrable jargon, a special dialect apparently designed to keep the uninitiated—that is, everyone else—in the dark. Postmodernism also extended its reach to the social sciences influencing even historians.

The following is an example of how postmodernist ideas and language inspired a field of history called Subaltern Studies. *Subaltern* means "subordinate to," and the term was chosen by a group of historians to describe their study of the native populations of British India. Other historians of European imperialism became interested in adopting their methods, and in 1994 the prestigious *American Historical Review* published an exchange of views on Subaltern Studies. The following excerpt concludes the essay by Gyan Prakash, an associate professor of history at Princeton University.

Clearly, Subaltern Studies obtains its force as postcolonial criticism from a catachrestic combination of Marxism, poststructuralism, Gramsci and Foucault, the modern West and India, archival research and textual criticism. As this project is translated into other regions and disciplines, the discrepant histories of colonialism, capitalism, and subalternity in different areas would have to be recognized. It is up to the scholars of these fields, including Europeanists, to determine how to use Subaltern Studies' insights on subalternity and its critique of the colonial genealogy of the discourse of modernity. But it is worth bearing in mind that Subaltern Studies itself is an act of translation. Representing a negotiation between South Asian historiography and the discipline of history centered in the West, its insights can be neither limited to South Asia nor globalized. Trafficking between the two, and originating as an ambivalent colonial aftermath, Subaltern Studies demands that its own translation also occur between the lines.

This is not a parody but an exact quotation from "Subaltern Studies as Postcolonial Criticism" (*AHR,* vol. 99, no. 5, December 1994, p. 1490).

Postmodernism was widely, and perhaps even correctly, reviled as a "new barbarianism" by people who believed in accessible scholarship and who were repelled by the cultism and unreadable prose of postmodernists. On the other hand, while hardly anyone outside the university knew about, or had any respect for, these academic sects, it was hard to take them as serious menaces; the stakes were much higher, of course, for graduate students seeking a career in one of the impacted disciplines. Postmodernism certainly had a damaging effect on the careers of scholars, particularly younger ones, who did not endorse the new party line. In hopes of aiding them, as well as to discuss academic subjects in a less partisan way, a number of professional organizations were established in the nineties. Of these, the Association of Literary Scholars and Critics and the Historical Society were two of the most important. And while both attracted a number of distinguished scholars, they were much smaller than the older bodies, such as the MLA and the American Historical Association, which remained largely in the hands of academic leftists. Thus, at the end of the twentieth century, the future of postmodernism seemed secure.

Conclusion

Putting aside careerism and the question of what it means for large parts of higher education to be in the grips of academics with such overtly political agendas, one must ask how harmful in general were the tendencies subsumed under the rubric of political correctness? There is no way to quantify this, but the hundreds of men and women punished for violating speech codes, or charged with sexual harassment in groundless cases like those of Silva and Dobyns, certainly suffered injury—even when they prevailed in court, as many did not. And the white and Asian students who were denied admission to elite public and private institutions of higher learning suffered as well, although probably not excessively since, except for elite institutions, most colleges and universities did not discriminate on the basis of race. Thus, the odds of gifted students being permanently handicapped by not getting into Berkeley were low, even if they and their parents found it hard to view the matter in this sanguine light, Arguably, minority students admitted above their ability who then failed or dropped out of elite institutions suffered more. One of the strongest cases against affirmative action turned on just this point, although, since records were not kept on such students after they left campus, there was no way to be certain of the long-term effects.

Multiculturalism led to unbalanced curricula, pernicious ideas, and unfortunate gaps in learning. It also promoted tribalism, Balkanization, and identity politics. The fad for "black English," sometimes called "Ebonics," briefly popular in the nineties, was potentially very harmful, since the ability to read and write standard English is the skill most needed by minority students. Luckily, Ebonics received such a bad press that it quickly disappeared. On the other hand, bilingual education continued to do serious harm to Hispanic children—the only large minority group that was taught bilingually in many states.

This was demonstrated in 2000, two years after a ballot proposition abolished bilingual education in California, where a million public school children came from Spanish-speaking families. Although the special interests predicted disaster should English-only education prevail, by 2000, children with "limited English" had substantially improved their performance on standardized tests. While the average class size in California had shrunk as well during the interim, the fact that much of the improvement had resulted from ending bilingual education was easily established by comparing school districts. For instance, two neighboring school systems each having about 5,000 Hispanic students in bilingual classes took different approaches. One complied fully with the proposition and ceased bilingualism. The other gave waivers, which were permitted by the law, to half its Hispanic students. Two years later test scores had risen twice as high in the first system as in the second. California's experience made it clear that bilingualism had been holding Hispanic youngsters back for generations, a striking example of how ideology, the desire to create jobs, and interest-group politics combined to sabotage the futures of needy children and was still doing so in other states.

Despite the damage inflicted by the Academic Left, it was preferable to the New Left because there were no casualties. This was not for lack of passion. The pros and cons of each of these tendencies were vigorously debated and strongly felt. But, for the most part, Academic Leftists sought to gain their ends by peaceful means. Postmodernists did not take to the streets in defense of deconstruction or to destroy the intellectual dominance of dead white males. The attack on affirmative admissions, which stirred the strongest feelings, produced some rallies and protests, but the participants were mostly law-abiding adults disinclined to commit violence. It helped that the nineties was a tranquil decade, lacking in major wars and popular movements such as those that had unhinged people's minds in the 1960s.

Yet, links between the New Left and the Academic Left were obvious. This was most apparent in postmodernism and the fight over affirmative admissions. Postmodernism was an ideology, and therefore not subject to proof or the rules of evidence. One would expect, therefore, as indeed was the case, that enthusiasm for postmodernism would be in direct proportion to postmodernists' cultishness, elitism, and unintelligibility. So it had been with New Leftists, whose fever rose even as their numbers dropped and who came to detest the great majority of working Americans for failing to play the roles assigned them by Marx or Mao. At the end, the New Leftists also spoke a language few understood, one salted with jargon and references to obscure leftist writers. Perhaps the major distinction, and a welcome one, was that while the New Left tried to be a revolutionary movement, postmodernists only paid lip service to social change and had little influence off campus.

The greatest difference between the New Left and the Academic Left is that one was a movement of students, the other of professors and administrators. The greatest similarity is that often the participants were the same people. The Academic Left of the 1990s was the New Left grown up, age and success having dulled the fanatical edge that despair and youthfulness whetted. The Academic Left's lack of ambition was another difference. The New Left aimed to change the world; the Academic Left found fulfillment within it. Even its defeats had fewer effects than might have been expected. Affirmative action in college admissions continued to be practiced in most states. Free speech made some real gains, yet it remained harmful to one's career to deviate publicly from the official line at most leading universities. In academia as a whole, political correctness continued to prevail, for even though the media lost interest in it, educators did not. Having failed to change the world, academic "radicals" were content to rule the roost. An old adage is that history repeats itself, first as tragedy, then as farce. The New Left's history was genuinely tragic, a record of death and injury, of lives blighted and careers lost, but the history of the Academic Left was ironic rather than calamitous. At century's end one had to agree with historian John Patrick Diggins that "the New Left is an idea whose time has passed and whose power has come."

BIBLIOGRAPHICAL ESSAY

The first history of Students for a Democratic Society, Kirkpatrick Sale, *SDS* (New York: Random House, 1973), was written shortly after the Movement's collapse by a left-wing journalist who was sympathetic to his subject early on and angry over its later descent into Marxist posturing and violence. Though anything but objective, this remains useful because it is still the most comprehensive chronicle of events and draws heavily on the SDS papers at the Wisconsin State Historical Society in Madison. A less comprehensive but thoughtful book that also came directly out of the New Left experience is Peter Clecak, *Radical Paradoxes: Dilemmas of the American Left, 1945–1970* (New York: Harper & Row, 1973). James Weinstein, a socialist historian, authored an interesting study that also derived from personal experience, *Ambiguous Legacy: The Left in American Politics* (New York: New Viewpoints, 1975). There is much valuable information in James Miller, *"Democracy is in the Streets": From Port Huron to the Siege of Chicago* (New York: Simon & Schuster, 1987). Miller is a strong believer in the two generations theory, that is, that SDS started to go wrong because the second generation of SDS were both younger and crazier than the Old Guard. Maurice Isserman, *If I Had a Hammer: The Death of the Old Left and the Birth of the New Left* (New York: Basic Books, 1987) looks at the Movement from an Old Left perspective. Ron Jacobs, *The Way the Wind Blew: A History of the Weather Underground* (London: Verso, 1997) is brief but informative.

An outstanding history is John Patrick Diggins, *The Rise and Fall of the American Left* (New York: Norton, 1992). Diggins is a distinguished historian of ideas and also eminently readable, a rare combination of talents. His critique of both the New Left and the Academic Left is vigorous but fair, and because his book deals with all the major left-wing movements of the twentieth century, the reader is able see modern leftism in its historical context. On the other hand, Terry H. Anderson, *The Movement and the Sixties* (New York: Oxford University Press, 1995), is one of those single-mindedly partisan works that is closer to cheerleading than to history written by a historian who credits virtually all good features of American life afterward to the Movement and the sixties. A more ambitious effort to show that the New Left and the counterculture greatly improved not just American life but much of Europe's as well is George Katsiaficas, *The Imagination of the New Left: A Global Analysis of 1968* (Boston: South End Press, 1987). An even more ambitious history in the same vein is Arthur Marwick, *The Sixties: Cultural Revolution in Britain, France, Italy, and the United States, c.1958–c.1974* (New York: Oxford, 1998).

Two recent histories that must be read are Doug Rossinow, *The Politics of Authenticity: Liberalism, Christianity, and the New Left in America* (New York: Columbia University Press, 1998) and Richard J. Ellis, *The Dark Side of the Left: Illiberal Egalitarianism in America* (Lawrence, KS: University Press of Kansas, 1998). Both are based on extensive research in primary sources and, in the case of Rossinow, extensive correspondence with, and interviews of, people associated with the Movement. His book also contains a good bibliography, making it exceptionally valuable for interested students. Rossinow paid a great deal of attention to events at the University of Texas, Austin. In part this seems to have been because leftism at UT had a strong religious base, which supports his ideas about the importance of such factors as existentialism, authenticity, and anxiety to the New Left. One need not agree with his ideas to find much that is worthwhile in this thoughtful study. Ellis, too, has a hobby horse—the pernicious effect of illiberal egalitarianism in society from the antislavery movement to the present. But his book is based on good scholarship and serious thinking, and, like Rossinow's, will benefit the reader.

Because so many New Leftists were highly literate the biographical and autobiographical literature is rich. Interviews with a broad range of former New Leftists conducted in the early nineties can be found in Ron Chepesiuk, *Sixties Radicals Then and Now: Candid Conversations with Those Who Shaped the Era* (Jefferson, NC: McFarland & Company, 1995). Sara Evans, *Personal Politics: The Roots of Women's Liberation in the Civil Rights Movement & the New Left* (New York: Random House, 1979), is a good account by one who was there. Todd Gitlin, a past president of SDS, is the author of *The Sixties: Years of Hope Days of Rage* (New York: Bantam, 1993), an autobiography that, while defensive in tone, contains a great deal of information. Helpful in the same way is Tom Hayden, *Reunion: A Memoir* (New York: Random House, 1988), by another past president of SDS. Not to be missed is the exuberant Jerry Rubin, *Do It!* (New York: Ballentine, 1970). Free (Abbie Hoffman), *Revolution For the Hell of It* (New York: Pocket Books, 1970) is the second edition of this popular memoir, which fully captures the Yippie spirit. Among the biographies of Hoffman is one coauthored by his brother, Jack Hoffman, and Daniel Simon, *Run Run Run: The Lives of Abbie Hoffman* (New York: Putnam's, 1994). See also Jonah Raskin, *For the Hell of It: The Life and Times of Abbie Hoffman* (Berkeley, CA: University of California Press, 1996). There is also a film about him, suitably titled *Steal This Movie* (2000).

Although the New Left was strong on many campuses, the University of California, Berkeley, and the University of Wisconsin, Madison, had the strongest radical traditions extending back into the 1950s and forward into the 1970s. Not surprisingly, both campuses generated a great deal of literature in addition to radical actions. David Horowitz, *Student* (New York: Ballentine, 1962), written when the Movement was very young, establishes the origins of Berkeley activism in earlier student campaigns such as those against HUAC and to save Caryl Chessman, and also discusses the student political party SLATE. Hal Draper also discusses SLATE in *Berkeley: The New Student Revolt* (New York: Grove Press, 1965). Draper was an Old Leftist on campus reenergized by the Movement. Quite a few books were written and/or edited by scholars and social scientists who were at Berkeley during the Free Speech Movement period. These include Lewis S. Feuer, *The Conflict of Generations: The Character and Significance of Student Movements* (New York: Basic Books, 1969); Nathan Glazer, *Remembering the Answers: Essays on the Student Revolt* (New York: Basic Books, 1970); Seymour Martin Lipset, *Rebellion in the University* (Boston: Little Brown, 1971); Seymour Martin Lipset and Sheldon S. Wolin, eds., *The Berkeley Student Revolt: Facts and Interpretations* (New York: Anchor Books, 1965); Michael V. Miller and Susan Gilmore, eds., *Revolution at Berkeley: The Crisis in American Education* (New York: Dell, 1965); and Sheldon S. Wolin and John H. Schaar, *The Berkeley Rebellion and Beyond* (New York: New York Review, 1970).

On leftism at Wisconsin see Tom Bates, *Rads: The 1970 Bombing of the Army Math Research Center at the University of Wisconsin and Its Aftermath* (New York: HarperCollins, 1992). This is a very detailed rendering of a central event with a good deal of background and context. More than most writers, Bates succeeds in giving something of the flavor of life on campus during the New Left's revolutionary days. See also Paul Buhle, ed., *History and the New Left: Madison, Wisconsin, 1950–1970* (Philadelphia: Temple University Press, 1990). This collection of essays, many of them autobiographical and often celebratory, does make clear the importance to sixties activists of the University of Wisconsin history department and the intellectual foundation laid down for them in the fifties, especially by a group revolving around University of Wisconsin historian William A. Williams. He founded the revisionist school of American diplomatic history which discovered imperialism everywhere in American life, not just in the nation's foreign policy. Williams's book, *The Tragedy of American Diplomacy* (New York: Dell, 1962), a revised and expanded version of the 1959 first edition, was widely read by New Leftists and exercised considerable infuence.

Much has been written about the ideas of the New Left, but the intellectual who made far and away the greatest impression on them was C. Wright Mills, a sociologist at Columbia University who died in the early sixties. His most influential book was *The Power Elite* (New York: Columbia University Press, 1956), which argued that America had fallen into the malign hands of three elite groups— politicians, business leaders, and the military. He was not a Marxist and deliberately avoided terms like "ruling class," which was part of his appeal to SDS in its early days when it was trying to steer clear of Marxist analyses. Curiously, Arthur Lothstein, ed., *"All We Are Saying": The Philosophy of the New Left* (New York: Putnam's, 1970), has no essay on Mills, favoring those who were more fashionable figures at the end of the sixties like Herbert Marcuse and Jean-Paul Sartre. Mills is also omitted by Theodor Roszak, *The Making of a Counter Culture: Reflections on the Technocratic Society and its Youthful Opposition* (Garden City, Long Island, NY: Doubleday, 1969), which is concerned with Timothy Leary, the Beat Generation, and such intellectuals as Marcuse and Norman Brown.

Among the many works that attribute all that was wrong with America in later years to the New Left and the counterculture are L. H. Gann and Peter Duignan, *The New Left and the Cultural Revolution of the 1960s: A Reevaluation* (Stanford, CA: Hoover Institution, 1995); and Peter Collier and David Horowitz, *Destructive Generation: Second Thoughts About the Sixties* (New York : Summit Books, 1989). The insightful and well-balanced essay by John B. Judis, "The Spirit of '68," *The New Republic,* (August 31, 1998), 20–27, links the sixties to the nineties in a variety of ways and places the New Left and the counterculture in a broad historical context.

Although the Academic Left has been the subject of many articles, most of them polemical, there are few useful books that deal with it and fewer still by historians. John Patrick Diggins, *The*

Rise and Fall of the American Left, cited above is a rare exception. Lawrence W. Levine is a distinguished historian, but his *The Opening of the American Mind* (Boston: Beacon Press, 1996) is a celebration of the Academic Left's rise to power, not a work of history. Although the Academic Left and political correctness are not quite the same, the latter being more inclusive, political correctness originated on campus and remained closely tied to it. A good example of the PC controversy in the early nineties is Paul Berman, ed., *Debating P.C.: The Controversy Over Political Correctness on College Campuses* (Boston: Beacon Press, 1992). A fascinating contribution is Christopher Lasch, *The Revolt of the Elites and the Betrayal of Democracy* (New York: Norton, 1995). Lasch made his name as a left-wing historian in the 1960s but in later years developed a position unique to himself. In this book he is critical of both PC and the Academic Left, among other targets. Arthur M. Schlesinger, Jr., the dean of American historians, has written *The Disuniting of America: Reflections on a Multicultural Society* (New York: Norton, 1998), which views multiculturalism in terms of the broad sweep of American history and the search for a national identity. Much of the material in my chapter on the Academic Left comes from contemporary newspaper and magazine accounts that would take many pages to list. A superb example of the journalist as critic is Michael Lind, "The Diversity Scam, *The New Leader* (July/August 2000), 9–12. A fine survey of the end of affirmative admissions at the University of California is James Traub, "The Class of Prop. 209," *New York Times Magazine* (May 2, 1999), 44+. On Jane Gallop see Daphne Patai, "Galloping Contradictions: Sexual Harassment in Academe," *Gender Issues* (Winter/Spring 1998), 86–106. A splendid critique of postmodernism is John M. Ellis, *Literature Lost: Social Agendas and the Corruption of the Humanities* (New Haven: Yale University Press, 1997).

There are Web sites devoted not only to figures from the sixties such as Tom Hayden and Bob Dylan who were still active at the time of this writing, but to some of the dead, including Timothy Leary, Abbie Hoffman, and even Jerry Rubin.

INDEX

The New Left: A History
Copy editor and production editor: Lucy Herz
Indexer: Fred Leise
Printer: McNaughton & Gunn, Inc.

since oil exports are more lucrative than natural gas exports,
the government may move to subsitute domestic oil consumption
with natural gas consumption. But increased domestic natural
gas use need not preclude the development of exports. Iran's
vast reserves can easily support domestic as well as export
projects.

Nuclear Power

Iran's posture towards nuclear power will be watched closely,
in part because a decision to resume construction of two
nearly completed reactors may be prompted by a desire to
acquire an "Islamic bomb"--an outcome that, however impracti-
cal, would be sure to send strategic shock waves throughout
the Middle East and beyond, and would be sure to revive the
debate over the relationship between the spread of civilian
nuclear power and nuclear weapons proliferation.

Even if the decision to complete the reactors is made on
non-weapons considerations, the implications may be the same
ultimately.

It is, of course, recognized that there are serious dis-
advantages--in security, political, and economic terms--which
outweigh the incentives for going nuclear in most developing
countries. But a civilian nuclear program could increase the
potential to build weapons, both on shorter notice and at
little extra cost.

Already, a number of additional countries have, by starting up civilian nuclear power programs, moved down the path to
nuclear weapons capability without having decided to do so in
advance. For those countries, the "distance remaining will be
shorter, less arduous, and much more rapidly covered. It need
take only a smaller impulse to carry them the rest of the
way."[9] That impulse could come in the wake of a failure of
nuclear reactors either to meet exaggerated performance
standards or to provide competitively priced electric power.
Indeed, if nuclear reactors do prove to be a major technical
or financial fiasco--and this likelihood cannot be ruled out--
a frustrated developing country could be prompted to consider
a weapons program to justify its substantial investment in
civilian reactors and human resources.

The international nuclear regime of the past 20 years has
been built on an a priori judgement that civilian nuclear
power should not only be made accessible but actively and
indiscriminately promoted in the developing countries. This
vulgarization of nuclear power was stepped up in the 1970s
by the major nuclear manufacturers, who, faced with dim
prospects for domestic sales in the industrial countries,
increasingly turned to untapped and more lucrative export
markets in the developing world. These nuclear vendors

approached Iran, Brazil, South Korea, and the Philippines, among others, initially offering not only reactors but the full range of related fuel cycle services including uranium enrichment, fuel fabrication, and spent fuel reprocessing. Dozens of orders worth tens of billions of dollars were placed in quick succession. Dozens more seemed imminent.

But even as developing countries were breaking ground for their nuclear facilities, debate was shaping up over the desirability of this development.

On the one hand, some of the industrial countries, par- ticularly the United States, expressed concern that the indiscriminate sale of nuclear technology was contributing to worldwide proliferation of nuclear weapons, and sought means to check the trend. What triggered this concern was the underground explosion by India in 1974 of a small nuclear device reportedly built with plutonium extracted from the spent fuel of a Canada-supplied research reactor, apparently without literally violating its existing safeguards agreement. Alarm over the spread of similar nuclear weapons capability was further intensified by the proposed sale of sensitive nuclear fuel cycle (uranium enrichment and spent fuel repro- cessing) facilities to Brazil, South Korea, and Pakistan.

On the other hand, energy planners in those developing countries having nuclear power hopes and plans--notably Iran-- had begun to question the desirability of proceeding down the nuclear power route. Debate focused not on nuclear weapons proliferation, but on the economic, technical, and environ- mental viability of nuclear reactors, especially for those countries with access to alternative, preferably indigenous, sources of energy.

As a result of these misgivings among both sellers and buyers, prospects for significant nuclear sales dimmed between 1978 and 1980. Important cutbacks have been contemplated in several developing countries having sizable nuclear programs; today, prospects for nuclear power appear no brighter in the developing countries than in the industrial countries them- selves.

Iran's cancellation of its nuclear power program is perhaps the most dramatic reversal of all. Although the immediate cause was the change in government, internal pres- sures for a reassessment of the Iranian program had been building for some time, and the original goal would in all likelihood have been cut back anyway, based on a serious reappraisal of the pros and cons of this option for Iran.

The considerations that enter into nuclear power deci- sion-making in the developing countries are highly complex and varied. Some countries see a civilian nuclear power program from the start as a means of developing a capacity to build nuclear weapons. Others acquire nuclear reactors to enhance national prestige. Still others hope that access to nuclear

technology and training will place them on the nuclear technology learning curve. For such countries, the short-lived
Iranian experience with nuclear power provides few insights
on how or whether to proceed. But for those countries who
seek nuclear reactors out of a serious interest in commercial
electric power generation, the Iranian experiment provides a
valuable lesson: with perhaps a few exceptions, nuclear power
is not practical in the developing countries, based on economic, technical, infrastructural, and safety considerations.

Petrochemicals

Iran's decision to scale down its once ambitious petrochemical
program will affect not only the future course of its own
industrialization but its potential petrochemical customers
and competitors. The decision will also be studied by other
OPEC countries engaged in or contemplating similar programs.

The OPEC countries have long believed that there is
significant value added in the refining, transportation, and
distribution of oil (as well as in the processing of petrochemicals) that is rightfully theirs to capture. Moreover,
they view such industries as an integral part of their development strategy. Not only would local production of petrochemicals replace costly imports, for example, but excess
production could be exported, thereby helping to break free
from dependence on export of a single raw material--oil. The
development of a larger petrochemical industry would lead to
the birth of supporting secondary industries and to the growth
of the end-product sector. Finally, owing to the skilled
labor required, many new training opportunities and jobs would
be created.

Based on this logic, and on the vast availability of
cheap and secure supplies of petrochemical feedstocks, i.e.,
oil, natural gas, and natural gas liquids (NGL), some OPEC
countries launched petrochemical industries in the 1960s and
1970s. Major projects are currently planned or under construction in Saudi Arabia, Iran, Kuwait, Iraq, Venezuela, and
Indonesia. Yet previous targets have been modified by rapidly
escalating construction costs on the one hand, and economic
slowdown and existing excess capacity on the other. The total
number of petrochemical plants proposed, planned, or under
construction in the OPEC countries in 1978 totaled an estimated 86, compared to 750 worldwide.

Development of these petrochemical projects presupposed
that the plants would be competitive internationally and that
substantial export markets for their products exist, particularly in the industrial countries. But the Iranian experience
with petrochemicals has cast a long shadow of doubt on both of
these premises. Construction costs for new plants in Iran and

elsewhere in the Middle East have been running substantially
higher than costs in Europe and North America. Even with
cheap feedstocks, the products from these plants may not be
sufficiently competitive to make the plants economically
practical. Furthermore, even if the products could be priced
competitively, these projects would come on stream at a time
when the industrial countries face considerable surplus capacities in their own petrochemical industries and have therefore
resisted opening up their markets to OPEC petrochemicals.

OPEC's entry into downstream markets generally, and
petrochemicals specifically--even on a limited scale--will not
be smooth, as shown in Iran. Protectionist attitudes are
likely to complicate relations between the industrial countries and the oil exporters, particularly when products from
the new plants enter the market in the 1980s. Already, OPEC
officials are complaining about their predicament. They note
that while at the beginning of 1980, they held 68 percent
of estimated worldwide proven reserves of oil and produced
and exported 49 percent and 84 percent of the world totals,
respectively, their share of refinery capacity was only
6.6 percent, their share of tanker tonnage only 3.5 percent,
and their share of petrochemicals a meagre 3.2 percent. OPEC
countries have been encouraged, they say, to import equipment
and technical services from the industrial countries in
order to build petrochemical plants, only to be barred from
selling their products to western markets.

Some OPEC countries have threatened to tie sales of
petrochemicals to oil sales, a solution that would be disrup-
tive and could lead to confrontation. Clearly, it would be in
the interest of both sides if some accommodation were worked
out based on market sharing for existing production and
complementary investments for future projects.

                                NOTES

1. For a detailed discussion, see Edwin A. Deagle, Jr., Bijan
    Mossavar-Rahmani, and Richard Huff, Energy in the 1980s:
    An Analysis of Recent Studies, Group of Thirty, New York,
    1981.
2. See International Energy Agency, Energy Policies and
    Programmes of IEA Countries: 1980 Review, Organization
    for Economic Cooperation and Development, Paris, 1981.
3. This discussion is from Deagle et. al.
4. While most of the OPEC countries stepped up a reassess-
    ment of national oil strategies after 1978, no two coun-
    tries will proceed in an identical fashion. Indeed it
    should be noted that there is no single OPEC policy as

such; only a mosaic of individual interests of 13 countries separated not only by geography, language, and
religion, but also by resource base, population size, and
form of government.

5. Additionally, as of mid-1979, there were some 23,000
producing oil wells in the OPEC countries, half of them
in Venezuela, compared to 582,200 such wells in the
entire free world. Thus, four percent of the free
world's wells were producing a staggering 65 percent of
its oil.

6. In 1975, total OPEC domestic oil consumption was 1.3
million b/d; by 1980, this figure had reached 2.5 million
b/d and was expected to grow to 4.0 million b/d by
1985.

7. Detailed statistics on OPEC oil consumption are available
in Organization of the Petroleum Exporting Countries,
OPEC Annual Report 1979, OPEC, Vienna, 1980.

8. Gross production was about 19,845 million cf/d, which
was 11 percent of the world total. About half of this
gas was flared.

9. Albert Wohlstetter, "Spreading the Bomb Without Quite
Breaking the Rules," Foreign Policy, No. 25, Winter 1976,
p. 148.

II

Energy Demand

2 Economic Framework for Long-Range Policy

Iran is the second largest country (after Saudi Arabia) in the Middle East but it is by far the most populated. The total area is 1,648,000 square kilometers; its population, 37 million. It is bordered on the north by the Soviet Union and the Caspian Sea; on the east by Afghanistan and Pakistan; on the south by the Persian Gulf and the Gulf of Oman; and on the west by Turkey and Iraq.

The terrain consists of a vast central plateau (altitude over 1,000 meters) rimmed by mountain ranges, most notably the Alborz mountains in the north and the Zagros mountains in the west. In the central and eastern parts of the plateau there are vast deserts. Narrow coastal plains are located along the shore of the Caspian Sea, the Persian Gulf, and the Gulf of Oman.

Temperature and precipitation vary with elevation. Except for the Caspian littoral (the most fertile in Iran), which receives relatively high average annual rainfall, precipitation occurs mainly in the winter and diminishes from southwest to southeast.

For administrative purposes Iran is divided into 23 provinces. Khuzestan in the southwest is the province with the largest area of potentially arable land; it also contains most of the country's proven oil and associated natural gas reserves, as well as its only navigable river. In addition to hydrocarbons, Khuzestan has important deposits of iron ore, copper, lead, salt, manganese and chromium. About 85 percent of the country's installed hydropower capacity and about one-third of its installed electric power generating capacity are

25

located in Khuzestan, making this province the single most important region in Iran, in terms of energy supply.

POPULATION

Unlike many in the Middle East oil-producing countries, the population of Iran is not homogeneous although it is Persian at its core. The migrant Kurdish, Lur, Qashqai, and Bakhtiari tribes trace their origins to the early Iranians of Indo-European descent. In the northern provinces, Turkic and Tatar influences are evident while Arab strains predominate in the southeast.

Iran's population grew at a rate of almost 3 percent throughout the 1960s and into the mid-70s--most rapidly in the urban areas, reflecting migration to the cities. Markazi Province, which includes Tehran, has the largest urban concentration in the country. Recently, however, the rate of overall population growth has been slower; it is expected to decline to 2.4 percent a year between 1977 and 1982, and to just over 1 percent by the turn of the century. In absolute terms, Iran's population is projected to grow from 34.7 million in 1977 to 55 million by 2002.

ECONOMY

As one of the world's most important producers and exporters of oil, Iran has been and in all likelihood, will again become inextricably linked to the world economy.

A Glance Back at the 1970s

Because of the extent of its dependence on oil for purchasing power, Iran's economy has been unable to escape the effect of changes in world oil prices and of international demand for Iranian oil. Both factors shaped economic conditions in the country in the mid-1970s and helped to precipitate the political discontent which ultimately led to the 1978-79 revolution.

In the decade preceding the 1973-74 oil price increases, Iran had achieved a moderately high rate of growth and relative price stability, but the pace of its economic expansion accelerated rapidly when world oil prices quadrupled, causing concurrent increases in its earnings (see table 2.1). The spending spree that followed was complicated by two important and inter-related problems--infrastructural bottlenecks and inflation.

Table 2.1. Iran's Oil Revenues: 1973-80

(million U.S. dollars)

Year	Revenue
1973	5,716
1974	20,902
1975	19,161
1976	22,753
1977	23,557
1978	21,735
1979	19,079
1980	13,005

Source: International Monetary Fund (1981) and author's estimates.

Iran's infrastructural facilities were not sufficient to
accommodate the increasing demand for goods and services
generated by the large-scale infusion of oil wealth. Since
these facilities could not be expanded quickly enough, bottlenecks developed that were first felt in the congestions of
Iranian ports, which delayed offloading of imported cargo;
delays in internal distribution due to an antiquated and
inadequate transportation system; and shortfalls in electric
power generation with frequent brownouts and blackouts in the
large cities and industrial areas after 1974. Losses to the
economy were tremendous. In 1974 alone, Iran paid a reported
$1 billion in demurrage charges as a consequence of port
congestion--an addition of more than 15 percent to the value
of imported merchandise.
    Other problems arose from shortages of skilled and semi-
skilled labor. Aggregate supply could not rise rapidly
enough to meet aggregate demand and the resulting disequilib-
rium exerted considerable inflationary pressure on the
economy. The problem of inflation was compounded by rapid
increases in the cost of a wide range of imports.

The government failed to design appropriate monetary and fiscal measures to cope with these stresses, which, in fact, were compounded by a 1974 decision drastically increasing government outlays and doubling goals for the Fifth Development Plan--only a year after its commencement--without proper consideration given to the country's overall ability to absorb the infusion of these larger sums.

Poor planning led to further sharp price increases and to misappropriation and wastage of resources. Mishandling of the economy by the Pahlavi regime played a major role in creating the social tensions and the general atmosphere of political discontent which preceded its overthrow.

The conduct of agricultural policies was particularly significant. In the 1960s, the government moved to break up large private agricultural estates and to grant land to small farmers; but soon thereafter, it reversed itself, and opted instead for establishing large government-controlled farmers' cooperatives into which the more productive villages were assimilated. Those villages not considered sufficiently productive were allowed to collapse economically.

At about the same time, the government began to encourage private domestic and foreign investors to set up new agri-business complexes on choice lands, moving in with heavy direct and indirect assistance, including subsidized fertilizers, price supports, guaranteed purchases, and attractive credits to support these ventures. Small farmers could hardly compete under these circumstances, and village after village was deserted as inhabitants headed for the cities in search of work.

Although for the most part the agri-business complexes operated profitably, the government-administered cooperatives did poorly; the net result of the overall agricultural policies of the 1960s and 1970s was disastrous. Agricultural production stagnated, dependence on imported foodstuffs grew steadily, and the internal migration of a large percentage of the rural labor force to urban areas aggravated the already serious problems of congestion in cities such as Tehran.

Looking Ahead

Oil will continue to be Iran's principal source of foreign exchange earnings at least through the 1990s. Future governments in Tehran will thus face the same fundamental question: how to transform oil in the ground into economic development in anticipation of the day when demand for or supply of Iranian oil dries up?

Before the revolution, industrialization, supported by maximum oil production, was the cornerstone of the government's development effort; but the odds for creating an

efficient industrial structure, capable of competing internationally and earning sufficient foreign exchange to replace
oil, were considered almost nil for reasons which included the
general climate and conditions in which industrial enterprise
operated.

Whether this picture will now change in the wake of the
revolution is uncertain. For the next several years and
perhaps longer, the country will be xenophobic in its commercial relations and nationalistic in its economic planning.
Imports will be restricted to such basic staples as foodstuffs. Self-reliance will be emphasized. Ventures with
foreign companies, in and outside Iran, will be few. The role
of the state in the economy will become larger still, reducing
that of the private sector, particularly in industry.

Beyond these broad changes, it is not known what new
development strategies, if any, may be adopted by the present
government. Obviously, there will have to be growth and
diversification as well as self-reliance. In practice, this
would mean channeling substantial resources into the agricultural and manufacturing sectors, aiming first to reduce
dependence on massive importation of foodstuffs and second, to
develop viable export industries.

Agriculture has long been the slowest growing sector in
Iran with only minimal productivity increases. This is partly
due to the scarcity of irrigation water in relation to land--a
shortage that limits the expansion of cultivated land and the
yield of the area already under cultivation--and to unfavorable climatic conditions; key to the stagnation has been the
government's neglect and its damaging agricultural policies.

While it is unrealistic to expect that Iran can become
agriculturally self-sufficient in the foreseeable future--
except perhaps for certain grains--much can be done to reverse
negative trends. Direct government support is needed in this
sector as well as attention to such measures as providing
incentives, developing better production techniques, and supporting education and skill learning.

It remains to be seen whether such a campaign, if successfully carried out, could deal with even part of the
greater demand for food that will accompany economic growth
and/or improvements in the distribution of national income,
and perhaps even reduce Iran's dependence on imported foodstuffs. It is certain that, at best, large-scale development
of the agricultural sector can result only in import substitution and that Iran cannot expect to become a net exporter of
agricultural products. Nonetheless, development of this
sector would have important spillover effects, making it
critical in the overall national development picture. For
example, the steady migration of rural workers and their
families to congested urban areas can be slowed down, even
reversed, if agriculture is once again made attractive to the

small farmer-owner-operator or even to the absentee-owner, and if electric power, schools and health services are brought to rural areas.

Manufacturing on the other hand, is promising as a source of foreign exchange earnings. Huge oil revenues provide opportunities for rapid industrialization in Iran; foreign exchange earnings permit importation of plant and equipment, and growing incomes provide the demand base for the output.

In the past, the course of Iran's industrialization was determined either in terms of prestige/national interest considerations (the distinction was not always clear), as with steel and petrochemicals; or in terms of import substitution. The import substitution industries, many owned by businessmen close to the government or to the royal family—if not by the royal family itself—enjoyed substantial protection from outside competitors. As a result, domestic prices for most products manufactured in Iran were relatively high and quality very low. For most, handsome profits precluded any real incentive to improve efficiency and quality, while at the same time, the government did little to encourage exports, especially of industrial products that could be internationally competitive. All of this should be changed and export-oriented manufacturing encouraged in Iran; a reborn, truly private sector has a very important role to play in the reconstruction of the Iranian economy.

Iran's economic development strategy, if designed around an efficient industrial sector and a renewed agricultural one, and fueled, at least initially—by oil revenues, can attain its objectives. The other precondition to economic growth is, of course, political stability and security.

High economic growth in Iran, as elsewhere, will continue to depend upon ever increasing amounts of energy. The historical pattern of energy use in Iran is examined next before looking at how different assumptions about rates of economic growth can be expected to affect energy demand and inter-fuel mixes during the next 20 years.

3 Historical Patterns

PRIMARY ENERGY

In 1977, the last year for which aggregate national figures are available, oil products supplied nearly 77 percent of all primary energy consumed in Iran.[1]   Natural gas contributed another 14.8 percent, followed by solid fuels and hydropower, which supplied 5.9 percent and 2.2 percent of Iran's total consumption, respectively (see table 3.1).

During the Fifth Development Plan, primary energy consumption grew at an average annual rate of 17.5 percent, from 0.61 quad per year in 1972 to 1.35 quads per year in 1977. During this same period, consumption of commercial primary energy (oil, natural gas, hydropower and coal) grew at an average annual rate of 17.3 percent, rising from 0.59 quad per year in 1972 to 1.32 quads per year, while consumption of non-commercial primary energy (fuel wood, charcoal, coal and animal wastes) grew from 0.02 quad per year to nearly 0.03 quad per year, registering an average annual rate of growth of 8.8 percent. The share of commercial primary energy thus rose from 96.7 to 97.8 percent, while the share of non-commercial primary energy dropped correspondingly, from 3.3 to 2.2 percent of the total.

Per capita primary energy consumption during this five-year period grew at an annual average rate of 14.0 percent from 19.84 million btus (mm btus) per year in 1972 to 38.90 mm btus per year in 1977.

Total primary energy consumption in 1977 by end-use sector was: industry, 41.5 percent; residential and commercial use, 20.7 percent; transportation, 21.4 percent; electric power generation, 13.3 percent; and agriculture, 3.0 percent (see table 3.2).

31

Table 3.1.   Composition of 1977 Primary Energy
Consumption by Type of Fuel[a]

	Quads[b]	Percent of Total
Oil Products[c]	1.04	77.0
Natural Gas[d]	0.20	14.8
Solid fuels	0.08	5.9
Hydropower	0.03	2.2
Total	1.35	99.9

[a]Primary energy consumption figures for Iran include oil and natural gas feedstocks into the petrochemical sector. Excluding these feedstock uses, the total annual primary energy consumption figure for 1977 would be 1.34 quads.

[b]Data for Iran were originally denoted in kilocalories and converted into British Thermal Units (btus) for the purpose of this study using the following conversion factor: one kilocalorie equals 3.9682 btus. One quad (or one quadrillion btus) equals 10^{15} btus.

[c]Includes refinery use and loss but excludes bunker fuel oil.

[d]Excludes natural gas used in the oil fields as producers' fuel and flaring.

(Percentage totals to the nearest round number.)

Source: Plan and Budget Organization of Iran (1978).

Table 3.2.   Primary Energy Consumption by End-Use in 1977[a]

	Quads	Percent of Total
Industrial	0.56	41.5
Transportation	0.29	21.4
Residential and Commercial	0.28	20.7
Electric Power Generation	0.18	13.3
Agricultural	0.04	3.0
Total	1.35	99.9

(Percentage totals to the nearest round number.)

Source: Plan and Budget Organization of Iran (1978).

Oil Products

Oil has historically been the single most important source of primary energy in Iran, supplying over three-quarters of the total in 1977.

Table 3.3 shows 1977 sales of major oil products in Iran. Total sales of domestic oil products climbed at an average annual rate of nearly 17 percent, from 230,000 b/d to 500,000 b/d, reflecting, in part, high rate of gross national product (GNP) growth during this period.

Table 3.3. Composition of 1977 Domestic Oil Sales by Type of Product[a]

	B/d	Percent of Total
Gas oil	155,888	30.5
Fuel oil	109,221	21.4
Kerosene	102,294	20.0
Motor Gasoline	79,615	15.6
Bitumen, lubes, waxes	25,711	5.0
Jet fuel, aviation gas	22,764	4.4
Propane, butane	15,640	3.0
Total	511,133	99.9

[a]Excludes refinery use and loss.

(Percentage totals to the nearest round number.)

Source: National Iranian Oil Company (1978) and Plan and Budget Organization of Iran (1978).

In 1977, transportation accounted for the largest proportion of total oil product use in Iran, with about 153,400 b/d (30.2 percent of the total), followed by residential and commercial use (26.1 percent), non-energy intensive industries (12.2 percent), energy intensive industries (12.2 percent), agriculture (4.7 percent), and petrochemical feedstocks (0.7 percent).

Miscellaneous use accounted for nearly 71,000 b/d or 13.9 percent of the total (see table 3.4).

Three products--gas oil, fuel oil and kerosene--accounted for a disproportionately high 75 percent of all oil products consumed in Iran in 1977.

Table 3.4. Oil Products Consumption by End-Use in 1977

	B/d	Percent of Total
Transportation	153,400	30.2
Residential and Commercial	132,700	26.1
Energy Intensive Industries[a]	62,000	12.2
Non-energy Intensive Industries	62,000	12.2
Agriculture	24,100	4.7
Petrochemical Feedstock	3,400	0.7
Miscellaneous	70,700	13.9
Total	508,000	100.0

[a]Includes petrochemicals, oil refining, cement, steel, sugar, and brick industries.

Source: Plan and Budget Organization of Iran (1978).

Gas Oil

Gas oil alone represented 30.5 percent of all oil products sold in the country that year. The gas oil category includes diesel fuel, used primarily in transportation and agriculture, and light fuel oil. Diesel fuel for transportation represents almost half of all gas oil sales; most of it is used for high-way transportation and the remainder for rail and marine transport. In agriculture diesel fuel is used to operate tractors, irrigation pumps, and other farm machinery. Light fuel oil is used principally in non-energy intensive industries, for commercial and residential heating, and for electric power generation. In each of these applications, gas oil is a competitive fuel with other oil products and with natural gas.

Fuel Oil

Fuel oil ranks second among oil products in volume of sales. Two grades are sold in Iran: light fuel oil with a viscosity of 600, and a heavier fuel oil, mazout, with a viscosity of 2000. The biggest users of fuel oil are industrial customers, especially the cement, sugar, and brick industries. Output of fuel oil from Iranian refineries has traditionally exceeded domestic needs by a large margin.

Kerosene

In 1977, kerosene represented 20 percent of domestic oil product sales. Used almost exclusively in the residential and
commercial sectors, kerosene is, in Iran as in other developing countries, a key source of rural fuel supply. Kerosene
demand was somewhat moderated in the 1970s by the use of
alternative fuels, mainly liquefied petrolem gas (LPG) and
natural gas, in urban areas.

Motor Gasoline

Motor gasoline use in Iran stood at nearly 80,000 b/d, or
nearly 16 percent of all oil product sales in 1977. But use
of motor gasoline has been rising faster than any other oil
product due to the increasing rise in personal income and in
automobile purchases during the 1970s.

Bitumen, Lubes, and Waxes

Bitumen, lube oils, greases, and waxes made up 5 percent of
all domestic oil product sales in 1977; on a volume basis,
bitumen accounted for over half.

Jet Fuel and Aviation Gas

Two types of jet fuel are consumed in Iran: ATK is a kerosene
fuel used for commercial aircraft; JP4 is a 75/25 blend of
gasoline and kerosene, used primarily for military aircraft.
Sales of both products rose at a rapid rate in the 1970s to
almost 23,000 b/d, reflecting the growth in both commercial
air travel and Iranian air force activity.

Liquefied Petroleum Gas

Sales of LPG, a mixture of propane and butane, totaled 15,640
b/d in 1977, most of it to the residential and commercial
sectors for cooking and water heating; some was used in industrial applications. On a volume basis, LPG represented
3 percent of all oil products consumed in Iran in 1977.

Natural Gas

Natural gas consumption in Iran in 1977 is shown by
end-use in table 3.5.
Historically the petrochemical industry has been the
single largest domestic consumer of natural gas in Iran, for
both fuel and feedstock. Oil refineries, especially the

Table 3.5. Natural Gas Consumption by End-Use in 1977[a]

	Million Cf/d	Percent of Total
Energy Intensive Industries	344.4	66.9
Electric Power Generation	147.3	28.6
Non-energy Intensive Industries	16.7	3.2
Residential and Commercial Use	6.3	1.2
	514.7	99.9

[a]Figures include natural gas used as petrochemical feedstock but exclude natural gas used in the oil fields as producers' fuel or flared.

(Percentage totals to the nearest round number.)

Source: Plan and Budget Organization of Iran (1978).

Abadan Refinery, have accounted for a large proportion of total use. Consumption of natural gas for electric power generation has also been rising rapidly, together with other industrial, residential, and commercial uses. Large quantities of natural gas produced in association with crude oil continue to be flared at the wellhead; flaring in 1977 stood at just under half of the total.

Solid Fuels

In 1977, solid fuels supplied about 6 percent of the total primary energy consumed in Iran. The use of fuel wood, charcoal, and animal wastes in the residential and commercial sectors will continue to diminish as personal income rises and remote areas are linked to electric power, natural gas, and oil supply systems. Coal is the principal solid fuel in the industrial sector, used primarily in the Isfahan steel mill.

Hydropower

Hydropower supplied 2.2 percent of Iran's total primary energy consumption in 1977 from two large and six smaller dams. No separate breakdown for end-use consumption of energy from hydropower plants is available since the bulk of the electric power generated is fed into the national grid along with supplies from other sources.

ELECTRICITY

Total 1977 consumption of electric power in Iran amounted to 17.51 billion kilowatt hours (KWh), representing an average increase of 20 percent during the Fifth Development Plan. That year, Ministry of Energy facilities accounted for 14.21 billion KWh or over 80 percent of the total nationwide consumption, with the balance supplied by privately operated facilities; the Ministry of Energy supplied close to 70 percent of all electric power used in industry, and almost all of that used in other sectors.

Industry was the largest consumer of government-supplied electric power in 1977 with 47.1 percent of the total, followed by the residential and commercial sectors, each with 22.5 percent; street lighting, 3.6 percent; agriculture, 3.2 percent, and miscellaneous use, 1.0 percent (see table 3.6).

Table 3.6. Electricity Consumption by End-Use in 1977[a]

	Billion KWh	Percent of Total
Industrial	6.70	47.1
Residential	3.20	22.5
Commercial	3.20	22.5
Street Lighting	0.51	3.6
Agriculture	0.46	3.2
Miscellaneous	0.14	1.0
Total	14.20	99.9

[a]Figures represent Ministry of Energy-supplied electricity only. In 1977, another 3.3 billion KWh of electric power was produced from non-Ministry of Energy facilities and roughly the same volume consumed. Transmission losses are minimal in the private sector, since generating facilities are usually located at or very near the points of consumption.

(Percentage totals to the nearest round number.)

Source: Plan and Budget Organization of Iran (1978).

NOTES

1. Primary energy denotes energy contained in fossil fuels
    such as coal and oil, and energy derived from renewable
    sources such as the sun and wind, as distinct from
    secondary fuels such as electric power and synthetic or
    manufactured gas. Primary energy data for Iran include
    oil and natural gas used as feedstocks in the petro-
    chemical sector.

4 Energy Demand Projections

Two comprehensive attempts were made in the two years before the revolution to project long-term domestic energy demand in Iran--a study prepared by the SRI International in 1977 and a second study prepared a year later by Iran's Plan and Budget Organization.[1] They were intended as internal planning documents and never made public; in fact, circulation of the studies was restricted, even in the upper echelons of government.

The SRI study projected domestic demand for energy in Iran by energy type, end-use sector, and province, up to the year 1997. SRI's forecasting was based on empirical relationships between energy consumption and economic, demographic, industrial output and price parameters in each end-use sector. The relationships were derived from an analysis of historical patterns of energy consumption in Iran and elsewhere.

Seven energy demand scenarios were analyzed by SRI to determine the effect of economic growth, natural gas use, energy prices, and nuclear power growth on energy demand. SRI's base case scenarios reflected the consultant's best judgment at the time about the most likely rate of economic growth (averaging about 9 percent annually over the 20-year study period); a relatively high increase in natural gas use, especially in the early years; and rapid expansion of nuclear power use.[2]

In mid-1978, several months before the revolution, the P&BO study modified and updated the SRI study to develop a 25-year energy plan based on a single scenario for energy demand.[3]

No new official study of Iran's energy future has been prepared. The new leadership is absorbed in an internal power struggle and the Iran-Iraq war; it has not turned its attention to long-term economic and energy planning. Bureaucratic function is disrupted--at times paralyzed--and the general revolutionary fervor, reaching into nearly all segments of the society has left little time for such esoteric concerns as data collection and analysis that are key to the planning process. The period since the revolution has seen a significant turnover in government officials; many young experts have left the country and it seems unlikely that the government can bring together the expertise to study long-term energy options, at present.

FORECASTING METHODOLOGY

This book has drawn on both the SRI and P&BO studies for projections of domestic energy demand in Iran until the turn of the century. The SRI study's low economic growth scenario is used to demonstrate a high growth case, since its assumption that annual GNP growth would average nearly 8 percent over the period of the study was believed to be high, though not entirely beyond attainment.

Iran is part of a world economy in which projected long-term annual economic growth rates for the industrial countries have dropped from 4.0-4.5 percent to 2.5-3.0 percent or less in the last several years. This is expected to result in less economic growth in the developing countries as well, perhaps lowering the long-term economic growth rate in Iran by several percentage points a year. The disruptions to the Iranian economy resulting from the revolution and the Iran-Iraq war will also contribute to the reduction in long-term economic growth rates.

In order to more accurately reflect the changes in Iran's economic prospects, a second scenario was drawn up based on an assumption of no real GNP or energy demand growth between 1977 and 1982. This low growth scenario further assumes that GNP growth will average 7 percent annually between 1982 and 1987 as the economy recovers in the wake of a return to political stability. After 1987, economic growth rates are assumed to settle at about 5 percent annually. Table 4.1 lists the projected annual GNP growth rates for the two scenarios on a five-year interval basis, as well as population size at the end of each period.

The low growth scenario was developed on the basis of energy/economy relationships and primary fuel consumption patterns implicit in the P&BO study. While the methodology

Table 4.1. Economic Growth Parameters for
Energy Demand Scenarios

| Year | Population (millions) | GNP Growth Rate (percent per year) | |
		High Growth	Low Growth
1977	34.7		
		7	0
1982	39.0		
		7	7
1987	43.5		
		8	5
1992	48.2		
		9	5
1997	52.0		

Sources: SRI International (1977) and author's estimates.

developed here is admittedly rudimentary, it is nonetheless
designed to provide projections of energy demand as useful
guides for long-term energy planning and formulation of
broader economic policy. These projections reflect orders of
magnitude and trends rather than precise figures. Moreover,
no attempt has been made to accurately predict short-term
fluctuations caused by temporary supply/demand imbalances and
lags as a response to sudden changes in economic conditions.
The projections represent, instead, equilibrium values based
on the average long-term trend of year-by-year demand variations.

Both the high growth and the low growth projections are
premised on an overall national economic policy of intensive
industrialization with priority for investment in heavy
industry and infrastructure and for the development of export
industries.

Both studies assume that the government will pursue the
following broad guidelines and objectives within the energy
sector:

- Curtailment of domestic consumption of oil products to
  the extent possible, given high capital costs of building
  refineries on the one hand, and the continuing need for
  foreign exchange from exports of oil, on the other.
- Stepped-up natural gas use, particularly as a substitute
  for middle-distillate oil products.
- Development of hydropower potential where feasible.
- Use of coal primarily for coking in the steel industry,
  and for power generation only if substantial low-cost
  reserves were discovered.

● Conservation of energy use principally through public
   education, government regulation, and research and
   development.

One important difference exists between the two scenarios. The SRI study's scenario (high growth scenario here) has
not been modified to take into account the post-revolution
cancellation of Iran's once ambitious nuclear power program
(see nuclear power section). The latter scenario thus projects installation of 2,400 MW_e of nuclear capacity by 1982,
growing to 5,400 MW_e by 1992 and 9,000 MW_e by 1997. These
projections are still considerably below the original government target of 23,000 MW_e by 1994. The low growth scenario
projects no role for nuclear power in Iran over the next two
decades, and assumes, instead, that the cancelled nuclear
reactors will be replaced by natural gas- and oil-fired
plants.

PRIMARY ENERGY CONSUMPTION: HIGH GROWTH VERSUS LOW GROWTH

Table 4.2 gives a detailed comparison between projected primary energy demand by energy type for the high economic growth
and the low economic growth scenarios used for study here.
   Domestic consumption of primary energy in Iran is projected to grow from 1.35 quads in 1977 to 6.98 quads in 1997
in the high growth scenario and to 4.37 quads in the low
growth scenario.
   Per capita primary energy consumption during this 20-year
period is projected to grow from 38.90 mm btus in 1977 to
134.23 mm btus in 1997 in the high growth scenario, and to
84.04 mm btus in the low growth scenario. Both projections
are based on an average annual population growth of 1.8 percent.
   Moreover, between 1977 and 1997, the composition of
primary energy consumption in Iran is projected in the scenarios to change as follows:
1. Domestic oil consumption would grow from 1.04 quads to
   3.77 quads in absolute terms in the high growth scenario,
   while dropping back from 77 percent of total primary
   energy consumption to 54 percent of the total in 1997.
   In the low growth scenario, domestic oil consumption
   would grow to 2.53 quads, but its share of the total
   would drop back to only 58 percent, in part, reflecting
   cancellation of the nuclear power program. In both
   scenarios, oil would retain its place as Iran's single
   most important source of primary energy.
2. Natural gas consumption would gain substantially in
   both absolute and relative terms in both scenarios. In

Table 4.2. Comparison Between Projected Primary Energy Consumption for High Economic Growth and Low Economic Growth Scenarios

	Annual Demand (quads)					Percent of Total				
	1977	1982	1987	1992	1997	1977	1982	1987	1992	1997
Oila										
High Growth	1.04	1.76	2.50	3.11	3.77	77	68	63	56	54
Low Growth	1.04	1.04	1.70	2.18	2.53	77	77	66	61	58
Natural Gas										
High Growth	0.20	0.61	1.13	1.73	2.30	15	23	29	31	33
Low Growth	0.20	0.20	0.74	1.12	1.56	15	15	29	31	36
Hydropower										
High Growth	0.03	0.07	0.08	0.14	0.18	2	3	2	2	3
Low Growth	0.03	0.03	0.06	0.08	0.10	2	2	2	2	2
Solid and Misc. Fuels										
High Growth	0.08	0.07	0.10	0.26	0.26	6	3	2	5	4
Low Growth	0.08	0.08	0.09	0.19	0.18	6	6	3	5	4
Nuclear Power										
High Growth	--	0.08	0.13	0.28	0.47	--	2	3	5	7
Low Growth	--	--	--	--	--	--	--	--	--	--
Total Domestic Demand										
High Growth	1.35	2.59	3.94	5.52	6.98	100	100	99	99	101
Low Growth	1.35	1.35	2.59	3.57	4.37	100	100	99	99	100
Per Capita Primary Energy Consumption (million btus/year)										
High Growth	38.90	66.41	90.58	115.00	134.23					
Low Growth	38.90	34.62	59.54	74.07	84.04					

aExcludes bunker but includes petrochemical feedstocks.

(Percentage totals to nearest round number.)

Sources: SRI International (1977), Plan and Budget Organization of Iran (1978), and author's projections.

the high growth scenario, natural gas consumption would grow from 0.20 quad to 2.30 quads in absolute terms, and in relative terms, from 15 percent of the total to 33 percent in 1997. In the low growth case, natural gas consumption would grow to 1.56 quads, while its share of the total would increase rapidly to 36 percent, again reflecting in large part, the substitution of natural gas-fired electric power plants for nuclear ones.

3.   In the high growth scenario, hydropower would grow from 0.03 quad to 0.18 quad, although its share of the total would inch up to 3 percent. In the low growth scenario, hydropower would grow somewhat less rapidly to 0.10 quad but its share would remain unchanged at 2 percent.

4.   Consumption of solid and miscellaneous fuels, notably coal, would grow from 0.08 quad to 0.26 quad in the high growth scenario, while dropping from 6 percent of the total primary energy consumed in 1977 to 4 percent in 1997. In the low growth scenario, consumption of solid and miscellaneous fuels would grow to 0.18 quad in 1997, but again, the share would drop from 6 percent to 4 percent of the total.

5.   Nuclear power would supply 0.47 quad or a 7 percent share in 1997 in the high growth scenario. There is no development of a nuclear power program in the low growth scenario.

Oil

In both scenarios, oil will make the largest contribution to total supplies of primary energy in Iran between 1977 and 1997, growing from about 500,000 b/d in 1977 to 1.82 million b/d in 1997 in the high growth scenario, and to a more modest 1.22 million b/d expectation in the low growth scenario (see table 4.3).

Table 4.3. Comparison Between Projected Oil Demand for High Economic Growth and Low Economic Growth Scenarios

(thousand b/d)

	1977	1982	1987	1992	1997
High Growth	502.9	851.1	1,208.9	1,503.9	1,823.0
Low Growth	502.9	502.9	822.1	1,054.2	1,223.4

The low growth projections for oil consumption for 1977-82 more accurately reflect the situation as of mid-1981, but only because oil consumption has not increased noticeably in the three years since the revolution due to the economic slowdown and damage to the country's refineries--most notably the Abadan Refinery--as a result of the war with Iraq. However, once the country's refining capacity is restored, the rate of domestic oil consumption may again rise rapidly with economic recovery or with a focused government effort to make more oil products available to users in poor urban and rural areas.

Domestic consumption of oil may also be pushed up if goals for development of alternative energy sources are not met and the government is forced to fall back on oil products to satisfy rising demand for energy. In fact, the level of natural gas use in domestic markets is the single most important factor in determining future oil product requirements in Iran. The interrelatedness of these two fuels--particularly with regard to their roles in meeting Iran's domestic energy requirements--cannot be overemphasized.

Natural Gas

Natural gas consumption is projected to register the fastest growth in both scenarios--more than twelvefold between 1977 and 1997 in the high growth scenario, and eightfold in the low growth one. Domestic use of natural gas is projected to increase from 514.7 million cf/d to 6,301.4 million cf/d in the high growth scenario, and to 4,274.0 million cf/d in the low growth scenario (see table 4.4).

These figures, however, exclude the large quantities of natural gas used as producers' fuel and for reinjection in the oil fields themselves, or the share of gross production of natural gas which is still flared. The distinction should be kept in mind when comparing figures for domestic consumption of natural gas as fuel and gross production figures.

Hydropower

Both high and low growth scenarios project a growing role for hydropower in Iran, with more rapid growth from 1,804 megawatts-electric (MW_e) in installed capacity in 1977 to 7,800 MW_e in 1997 in the high growth scenario, and more moderate growth to 3,700 MW_e in 1997 in the low growth scenario (see table 4.5). Both scenarios greatly understate the country's vast hydropower potential, as will be discussed in Chapter 7.

Table 4.4. Comparison Between Projected Natural
Gas Demand for High Economic Growth and Low
Economic Growth Scenarios[a]

(million cf/d)

	1977	1982	1987	1992	1997
High Growth	514.7	1,671.2	3,095.9	4,739.7	6,301.4
Low Growth	514.7	514.7	2,027.4	3,068.5	4,274.0

[a]Includes petrochemical feedstocks but excludes producers'
fuel used in oil fields, reinjection, and flaring.

Table 4.5. Comparison Between Projected Hydropower
Installed Capacity for High Economic Growth
and Low Economic Growth Scenarios

Installed Capacity (MW_e)

	1977	1982	1987	1992	1997
High Growth	1,804	1,990	2,800	4,800	7,800
Low Growth	1,804	1,804	2,400	3,000	3,700

Nuclear Power

Table 4.6 shows the pace of development of nuclear power in
Iran under the high growth scenario which assumes that the
pre-revolution goals will be met, albeit on a reduced scale.
As will be explained in detail later, this assumption is
highly unrealistic but it was retained to demonstrate the
impact of the nuclear power program on changes in demand for
other primary energy supplies. The low growth scenario, of
course, projects no role for nuclear power in Iran at least
until 2000.

Electricity

Finally, table 4.7 compares electric power consumption in five-year intervals between 1977 and 1997 in the high and low growth scenarios.

In the high growth scenario, electric power consumption in Iran is expected to grow from 14.20 million kilowatt hours (KWh) in 1977 to 122.49 million KWh in 1997. The low growth scenario projects a much lower growth of electric power consumption, primarily due to reduced industrial activity; total nationwide consumption is projected to reach only 67.22 million KWh in 1997.

Table 4.6. Comparison Between Projected Nuclear
Installed Capacity for High Economic Growth
and Low Economic Growth Scenarios

Installed Capacity (MW_e)

	1977	1982	1987	1992	1997
High Growth	0	2,400	2,400	5,400	9,000
Low Growth	0	0	0	0	0

Table 4.7. Comparison Between Projected Electric
Power Demand for High Economic Growth and Low
Economic Growth Scenarios

(million KWh)

	1977	1982	1987	1992	1997
High Growth	14.20	31.71	53.66	85.96	122.49
Low Growth	14.20	14.20	34.34	49.88	67.22

NOTES

1. SRI International and Yekom Consultants, A Long-Range
    Energy Plan for Iran, study prepared for the government of
    Iran, Tehran, May 1977 (unpublished), and Plan and Budget
    Organization of Iran, "Twenty-Five Year Energy Plan" (and
    addendum), Tehran, 1978 (unpublished).
2. Specifically, in its base case scenario, SRI projected an-
    nual GNP growth rates of 9 percent between 1977 and 1982,
    8 percent between 1982 and 1987, 9 percent between 1987
    and 1992, and 10 percent between 1992 and 1997. SRI
    projected that 3,300 MW_e of nuclear power capacity would
    be installed by 1982, rising to 6,600 MW_e by 1987, 15,000
    MW_e by 1992, and 24,600 by 1992. Finally, SRI projected a
    more than sevenfold increase in overall energy consumption
    between 1977 and 1997 to 10.01 quads.
3. P&BO projected a GNP growth rate of 9 percent annually be-
    tween 1977 and 1992, rising to 10 percent between 1992 and
    1997. P&BO's projections of 1997 nuclear power installed
    capacity (24,600 MW_e) and overall energy consumption
    (10.24 quads) were nearly identical to those of SRI.

III

Energy Sources and Strategies

5 Oil

Iran's proven oil reserves, estimated at 58.0 billion barrels as of January 1, 1980, represent nearly 10 percent of the world total.[1] At high pre-revolution production rates, the reserves-to-production ratio was about 30:1; in mid-1981, it was more than 100:1. If Iran produces at the current target level of 4.0 million b/d, its proven reserves will last about 40 years. Table 5.1 shows how reserves-to-production ratios have changed during the past several years.

Table 5.1. Oil Proven Reserves, Production, and Reserve Life

Year	Proven Reserves (billion barrels)	Production (billion barrels/year)	Reserve Life (years)
1977	63.0	2.1	30
1978	62.0	1.9	33
1979	59.0	1.2	49
1980	58.0	0.6	97

Source: American Petroleum Institute, Basic Petroleum Data Book, API, Washington D.C., 1980 and author's estimates.

These figures are intended only to show an order of magnitude, and should be used carefully however, as production levels and proven reserves estimates change periodically in Iran, as they do in nearly every major oil-producing country.

In Iran, current estimates of proven oil reserves are probably far too conservative. It should be recalled that proven reserves represent only that percentage of oil-in-place (in Iran's case, about 17 percent) that can be recovered from already developed fields using existing production facilities and--significantly--at current oil prices. Very little weight is given to extensions of new and therefore poorly defined fields, to known reserves within existing fields that have not yet been exploited, and to possible deeper and more difficult reservoirs. Virtually no weight is given to potential discoveries or to oil that might be recovered through secondary or tertiary methods.

Thus, proven reserves represent an estimation, under a rather limited definition, of what may be called a current inventory of recoverable oil underlying existing wells within a specific geographic and geological area. Proven reserves do not reflect the reasonable expectations of experts concerning the amount of oil that will ultimately be recovered from known fields. For this purpose, a broader, more speculative estimate of probable reserves is made, based on geological knowledge and evidence. Beyond that, an even more speculative estimate is made of possible reserves.[2]

In Iran's case, for example, additional oil from secondary recovery, and from reserves that were considered uneconomic when proven reserves were last estimated years ago--but which are now recoverable at much higher world prices--may increase Iran's proven reserves by one-half or more. For example, the secondary recovery program drawn up in the mid-1970s based on large-scale injection of natural gas into the oil fields was, alone, expected by officials to raise recovery factors by at least 5 percent, or an additional 20 billion barrels, which is equivalent to two-thirds of total U.S. proven reserves of oil.

To understand how this secondary recovery program was expected to work, one should briefly recall how oil is recovered. An oil reservoir should not be thought of as a pool, although it is often referred to as such. Rather, within a given reservoir, droplets of oil saturate pores and cracks in permeable rock, much like water in a sponge. The oil in these structures is generally covered over by a large dome of trapped natural gas, and sits, in turn, on a layer of water and brine. Once a well is drilled into this reservoir, pressure from the overlying natural gas and the underlying trapped water begins to wash out the pores and drives the oil into the well and ultimately to the surface.

As oil is produced from the reservoir, this natural drive gradually declines until it ends, invariably leaving some of the oil unrecovered. The amount of oil recovered by natural drive depends, of course, on reservoir conditions such as rock porosity, oil viscosity, and type of drive. But the recoverable percentage of oil-in-place is also sensitive to the rate of production. For natural drive to be most effective, the production of oil should be slow enough to permit uniform advance of either water or natural gas to invade and flush out oil droplets from tight sections of rock. Otherwise, at higher production rates, the more mobile water or natural gas will tend to form flow channels to the well, bypassing the oil and leaving a large portion of it trapped in the reservoir.

Thus, there is some rate of production for any reservoir in a given state of depletion at which maximum effective use can be made of natural drive to increase the ultimate recovery from that reservoir. A higher--or lower--rate of production, it follows, will result in some reduction in ultimate recovery.

Throughout much of the history of the Iranian oil industry, little consideration was given to this notion of maximum efficient rate of recovery. The government, faced with low and often falling oil prices on the one hand, and rising development needs on the other, thought only of increasing total revenues by pressing for increased production. Meanwhile, the international oil companies which operated the oil fields shared these same short-term interests in producing as much from each reservoir and each country as the market would bear, usually by methods now considered wasteful.

As a result, a larger-than-desirable proportion of the available natural drive was used up and unduly large quantities of oil which could have been obtained still remain trapped underground.

Furthermore, under these circumstances, excessive amounts of associated natural gas produced together with the oil were flared by the companies and wasted for lack of any economic interest in harnessing the gas. As a consequence of such haphazard development, the ultimate recovery from fields such as Gach Saran, is believed to have been seriously reduced.

The first phase of this secondary recovery program was based on the gathering and treatment of associated natural gas, produced unavoidably with oil and hitherto flared, from the Khuzestan oil fields, for reinjection into the aging fields themselves. This process was expected not only to improve the ultimate recovery of oil from the fields but also to maintain production capacity at a level of 6.2 million b/d for a minimum of five years--scaled down from the earlier target of 7.3 million b/d. The next phase of this multibillion dollar program would have required the use of additional

quantities of natural gas from Iran's largest non-associated
natural gas field, Pars, located offshore in the Persian Gulf.
Ultimately, the massive program would have used 8,000 million
cf/d to 15,000 million cf/d of natural gas. A small pilot
project involving reinjection of relatively small quantities
of dome gas into the Haft Kel reservoir was completed in 1976.
But the rest of the reinjection program is largely in abey-
ance, pending a reassessment of its overall desirability in
the context of the country's changing oil production goals.

It should be noted that while there is general consensus
regarding the need for some form of enhanced oil recovery in
Iran, some experts question whether natural gas reinjection
will, in fact, bring about the best results. The decision in
the mid-1970s to proceed with a natural gas reinjection program was based only on laboratory tests. While those tests
did indicate significantly greater success for this procedure
than for water flooding in most of the Khuzestan oil fields,
they add, it remains to be seen whether pilot tests in the
fields themselves will confirm those findings.

PRODUCTION

For years, Iran's oil production represented a staggering
10 percent of the world total, giving it a special role in
the world oil market. In the three years since the 1978-79
revolution, Iran's output has dropped dramatically, yet the
country remains--and will continue to be--a significant force
in world oil affairs, not only for geopolitical reasons, but
because even at lower output, Iran is potentially a significant producer of oil, particularly in a tight market.

The modern oil industry in Iran dates back to the sweep-
ing concession obtained on 1901 by the British financier,
William Knox D'Arcy, granting him the right of oil exploration
and exploitation throughout most of the country. Seven years
later, oil well number 1 at Naftun struck oil at a depth of
less than 1,200 feet and the giant Masjid-i-Suleiman reservoir
was discovered.

In 1909, the D'Arcy group founded the Anglo-Persian Oil
Co., Ltd. and the first shipments of oil from the Middle East
were made in 1912 from Abadan, where a refinery had been
completed that year.

With the outbreak of World War I, Iranian oil production
assumed increased importance as a secure source of fuel oil
for the British Navy. At the urging of Winston Churchill,
then First Lord of the Admiralty, the British government in
1914 organized a majority interest in Anglo-Persian Oil Co.
(the company's name was later changed to Anglo-Iranian and

finally in 1954 to British Petroleum). Production and refining capacity tripled during the war.

In 1923, the Naft-i-Shah field was discovered. Haft Kel, Pazanun, Gach Saran, Naft-i-Sefid and Agha Jari fields followed.

Production expanded after World War II, rising to more than 700,000 b/d at the beginning of 1951. That was nearly half of the total for the Middle East, but operations were disrupted that year because of a prolonged dispute between the Anglo-Iranian Oil Co. and the Iranian government over a revision of the concession terms, which were outdated and heavily weighted in the company's favor.

Efforts had begun several years earlier to secure for Iran a fairer share of revenues accruing from oil production and a greater say in the operation of the industry. Anglo-Iranian at first refused to consider a renegotiation of a 1933 revised version of the original concession, but after lengthy talks, the company offered to increase its royalty payments to Iran from four to six shillings per barrel, to guarantee a minimum royalty payment of £4 million and to settle certain outstanding claims. This token offer was not accepted and in April 1951, the Iranian parliament formally approved a proposal by the popular nationalist leader, Dr. Mohammad Mossadeq, to nationalize Iran's oil industry.

Following nationalization, the government set up the National Iranian Oil Co. (NIOC) and took steps to dispossess Anglo-Iranian. Great Britain, meanwhile, moved to exert economic and political pressures on Iran. Oil operations were shut down. Tankers were instructed not to accept Iranian oil for shipment. The cruiser, Mauritius, was anchored off Abadan, ostensibly to "protect the life of British citizens." Later, as negotiations failed to yield results, paratroopers were moved to Cyprus, Iran's sterling balances in England were frozen and British licenses for export of "scarce materials" to Iran were revoked.

The British government also took its case to the United Nations Security Council and the International Court of Justice at the Hague. In both forums, Britain suffered setbacks. The U.N. Security Council voted to postpone any action until after the World Court delivered its opinion. When the Court finally did so, it ruled--as Iran had contended--that it had no jurisdiction over the case. Several other attempts at a negotiated settlement failed. Meanwhile, the economic and political situation in Iran deteriorated rapidly. In mid-August 1952, Shah Mohammed Reza Pahlavi fled the country, only to return days later, after a coup d'etat organized and largely financed by the U.S. Central Intelligence Agency had overthrown Premier Mossadeq and restored the monarchy in Iran for another 27 years.

Following the coup d'etat, oil negotiations were resumed, this time between Iran and a consortium of foreign companies which included U.S. oil interests, in recognition of the latter's role in restoring the Pahlavi regime. In October 1954, a new agreement was signed under which this consortium would manage operation of the oil fields and the refinery at Abadan for a 25-year period. British Petroleum held 40 percent of the consortium share; five major American companies including Exxon, Texaco, Gulf, Mobil, and Standard Oil of California, each held 7 percent, and a group of six smaller independent American companies known as Iricon (Aminoil, Atlantic Richfield, Continental Oil, Getty Oil, Charter Oil, and Standard Oil of Ohio) held a total of 5 percent; Royal Dutch Shell held 14 percent and the remaining 6 percent was held by Compagnie Française des Pétroles.

Other companies also showed interest in the Iranian oil industry. Beginning in 1957, Iran entered into agreements with private and government-owned companies in the United States, Europe and Japan covering exploration and development of uncommitted territory, both onshore and in the Persian Gulf. These agreements were structured as either 75-25 profit sharing agreements, in which Iran secured 50 percent of the profits and the right to apply a further 50 percent income tax on the foreign concessionary company's profits in Iran; or as service contracts, in which the outside party acted strictly as a contractor for NIOC. Important discoveries were made, particularly offshore, of which several are currently producing.

In July 1973, Iran and the consortium arrived at a new 20-year agreement to replace that of 1954. Under the new agreement, referred to as the 1973 Sales and Purchase Agreement, NIOC assumed operational control of the oil producing areas that it had owned since 1954 but which had been operated by the consortium; and the consortium established the Oil Service Company of Iran (OSCO) to act as contractor for exploration and production activities in the agreement areas, charging NIOC for all exploration, development, and production costs. The consortium companies, which thereafter became legally known as Iran Oil Participants, Ltd., were given exclusive long-term rights to purchase at favorable prices all the crude oil produced in this area, except for some quantities refined for internal consumption and small quantities of crude earmarked for export by Iran itself. Although the provisions of the 1973 agreement differed in form from participation agreements between the oil companies and other governments in the Persian Gulf area, the net effect for both sides was comparable. However, because of operating and fiscal changes that occurred since its writing, NIOC and the companies were in the process of modifying the 1973 agreement at the time of the 1978-79 revolution.

Table 5.2 lists the service contractors and other foreign oil companies active in Iran before the revolution.

Thus, before the revolution, oil production in Iran was handled in three ways: (a) by foreign service contractors who performed specific activities on behalf of NIOC in return for fees or other incentives, the most important of these contractors being OSCO; (b) by joint ventures between NIOC and foreign oil interests set up on the basis of prearranged profit sharing formulae; and (c) by NIOC itself.

OSCO produced about 90 percent of all Iranian oil, or about 5 million b/d on average. Another 500,000 b/d were produced by four joint venture companies in which NIOC owned a 50 percent share. The four, which operated offshore oil fields, were the Société Irano-Italienne des Pétroles (SIRIP) which was formed in 1957 with Italy's AGIP; the Iran-Pan American Co. (IPAC) formed in 1958 with the Pan American Petroleum Corporation; the Lavan Petroleum Co. (LAPCO) formed in 1965 with four American companies; and finally, the Iran-Marine International Oil Co. (IMINOCO) formed in 1965 with American, Indian and Italian interests. NIOC itself produced another 20,000 b/d on average from the Naft-i-Shah oil field. In the summer of 1978, SOFIRAN, a service contractor to NIOC, began production from the Sirri fields at an average rate of 7,800 b/d, with an ultimate capacity of 75,000 b/d. Table 5.3 details Iran's 1978 oil production.

There were, in addition, two other joint ventures, the Iran-Nippon Petroleum Co. (INPECO) set up with American and Japanese interests, and the Hormuz Petroleum Co. (HOPECO) with American and Brazilian interests. Both ventures realized only limited exploration success.

Since the revolution, the Iranian government has unilaterally severed its relationship with the consortium companies, taking over the assets and functions of OSCO and setting up a new corporate division, NIOC Fields, to replace it. NIOC has also taken over the foreign shareholdings of the four joint offshore producing ventures. Instead, a new company has been formed to operate the offshore fields. The company, known as Continental Shelf Oil Company of the Islamic Republic of Iran, formally assumed control in the summer of 1980.

A third company, the National Iranian Drilling Co. (NIDC) was formed after the revolution to take over responsibility for most drilling operations.

NIOC has negotiated intermittently with all the foreign companies to arrange compensation and establish conditions for possible future relations. The consortium has claimed several hundred million dollars in compensation, mostly for equipment left behind in Iran and for contracted payments. The question of compensation for the joint ventures and for the service contractors, who have also left equipment behind in Iran, has yet to be resolved.

Table 5.2. Foreign Oil Companies Active in Iran Prior to the 1978-79 Revolution

Company	Owners	Percentage Share
Companies Associated with NIOC		
Iran Oil Participants, Ltd. (i.e. the consortium)	British Petroleum	40
	Royal Dutch Shell	14
	Compagnie Française des Pétroles	6
	Exxon	7
	Gulf	7
	Mobil	7
	Standard Oil of California	7
	Texaco	7
	Iricon Agency Ltd., consisting of	1-2/3
	Atlantic Richfield	5/6
	Aminoil	5/6
	Getty Oil	5/6
	Charter Oil	5/12
	Continental Oil	5/12
	Standard Oil of Ohio	
Service Contractors to NIOC		
Oil Service Company of Iran	Iran Oil Participants	100
AGIP Iran Petroleum Co.	AGIP	100
DEMINEX Iran Oil Co. (two contracts, each for a different area, signed July 30, 1974)	Deutsche Erdolversorgunsgesellschaft m.g.H. (DEMINEX)	100
EGOCO (European Group of Oil Companies) (contract effective June 26, 1969)	ERAP	32
	Hispanica de Petroleos S.a. (Hispanoil)	20
	Petrofina	15
	Oesterreichischt Mineraloeverwaltung (O.e.m.v.)	
LAR EXPLORATION CO. (LARES) (contract signed August 20, 1974)	Ashland Oil Company	5
	Pan Canadian	N/A
		N/A
Philiran (Phillips Oil Co. of Iran) (contract effective September 29, 1969)	Phillips Petroleum Co.	50
	Continental Oil Co.	25
	Cities Service	25

Table 5.2--Continued

Company	Owners	Percentage Share
Service Contractors to NIOC--Continued		
SOFIRAN (contract effective December 13, 1966)	Entreprise de Recherches et d/Activitées Pétrolières (ERAP)	40
	Mitsubishi Oil Development Company	40
	Société Nationale de Pétroles d'Aquitaine	20
TOTAL Iran	Compagnie Françaises des Pétroles	100
Ultramar Iran Oil Co. (contract signed August 7, 1974)	American Ultramar Ltd. (Wholly owned by Ultramar Co., Ltd. of the U.K.)	100
NIOC Joint Ventures		
SIRIP (Société Irano-Italienne des Pétroles) (agreement effective August 27, 1957)	NIOC	50
	AGIP	50
IPAC (Iran-Pan American Company) (agreement effective June 5, 1958)	NIOC	50
	AMOCO Iran Oil Co.	50
IMINOCO (Iran Marine International Oil Co.) (agreement effective February 13, 1965)	NIOC	50
	AGIP	16-2/3
	Phillips Petroleum	16-2/3
	Oil & Natural Gas Commission of India	16-2/3
LAPCO (Lavan Petroleum Co.) (agreement effective February 13, 1965)	NIOC	50
	Atlantic Richfield	12-1/2
	Murphy Oil	12-1/2
	Sun Oil	12-1/2
	Union Oil	12-1/2
INPECO (Iran-Nippon Petroleum Co.) (agreement effective January 5, 1972)	NIOC	50
	IRAPEC (Owned by Teijin Ltd., North Sumatra Oil Development Corp. and other firms)	33-1/3
	Mobil	16-2/3
HOPECO (Hormoz Petroleum Co.) (agreement effective January 5, 1972)	NIOC	50
	Petrobras	25
	Mobil	25

Table 5.3. Crude Oil Production by Company in 1978[a]

(thousand b/d)

	Volume	Percent of Total
NIOC Khuzestan Fields	4,626.4	88.5
NIOC Naft-i-Shah	15.1	0.3
IPAC	325.4	6.2
LAPCO	172.1	3.3
IMINOCO	40.9	0.8
SIRIP	39.3	0.8
SOFIRAN[b]	7.8	0.2
Total	5,227.0	100.1

[a]The 1978 figures do not accurately represent average pre-revolution production rates due to the oil workers' strike in the last quarter of the year.

[b]SOFIRAN started commercial production in July 1978.

(Percentage total to nearest round number.)

Source: National Iranian Oil Company (1978).

EXPORTS

In the six years preceding the revolution, 1973 through 1977, Iran was exporting 5.0 million b/d of oil on average, a rate second in the world only to that of Saudi Arabia. Of the total Iranian figure, 60 to 70 percent was exported by the trading companies of the consortium; about 25 percent by NIOC from its 50 percent share of the four joint ventures and from its share of the oil produced by OSCO; and the rest by the joint venture companies themselves. Table 5.4 details the channels through which Iranian oil was exported in 1978.

Table 5.4. Crude Oil Exports by Company in 1978

(thousand b/d)

	Volume	Percent of Total
NIOC[a]	1,184.6	26.5
Trading Companies[b]	2,709.7	60.6
IPAC	321.5	7.2
LAPCO	166.4	3.7
IMINOCO	41.6	0.9
SIRIP	40.5	0.9
SOFIRAN	6.0	0.1
Total	4,470.3	99.9

[a]NIOC exported an additional 135,800 b/d of refined oil products from the Abadan Refinery.

[b]Representing the consortium companies.

(Percentage total to nearest round number.)

Source: National Iranian Oil Company (1978).

The largest importer of Iranian oil before the revolution was Japan, followed by the United States, Great Britain, and the Netherlands. Iran also exported smaller quantities of oil to Canada, other Western European countries, and many Third World countries.

After the revolution, Iran's oil exports dropped substantially but the direction of exports remained the same for some time. Almost half of Iran's contract sales reportedly went to the major international oil companies which were part of the original consortium, and Japan remained a major importer. Of course, the Iran-U.S. crisis and consequent embargoes on Iranian oil imports by the U.S. and its allies radically changed the situation. In mid-1980, Iran's contract and spot sales averaged less than 800,000 b/d, that oil going mostly to Rumania, Poland, Bulgaria, Czechoslovakia, Yugoslavia, East Germany, Spain, Sweden and Finland, and to some Third World countries such as India, Brazil, South Korea, North Korea, Turkey, and Sri Lanka. With the outbreak of the war with Iraq, exports fell to a trickle by year-end.

Exports picked up once again in 1981 but did not exceed the average daily mark of one million barrels during the first half of the year. Given the continuing supply glut in the market, and the continuing perception of Iran as an unstable and insecure trading partner, few buyers rushed to increase their imports from Iran.

Export-Related Activities and
Overseas Investments

In the mid-1970s, NIOC launched a modest program in oil exploration and development outside of Iran and in downstream operations involving refining, transportation, and distribution of oil in foreign markets.

Upstream Activities

The first upstream activity outside Iran involved the formation of a joint venture in the early 1970s with British Petroleum. Exploration and production rights were obtained for a North Sea block off Scotland and although initial drilling showed some signs of oil and natural gas, no commercial fields were discovered.

The second such activity included NIOC, British Petroleum, Standard Oil of California, and SAGA of Norway, each with a 25 percent share. Exploration and production rights were granted for ten blocks in three areas of the continental shelf off western Greenland. No significant finds have been reported.

NIOC also participated in a broad range of downstream activities abroad. The oldest is the Madras Refinery in India in which NIOC has held a 13 percent share; the refinery was established in the 1960s with a capacity of 58,000 b/d. Iran also has held a 24.5 percent share in Madras Fertilizers, Ltd., which has a capacity of 500,000 tonnes per year of various fertilizers.[3]

Another joint venture was established in 1971 to operate the Sassolberg Refinery in South Africa. NIOC took a 17.5 percent share in the refinery, which has a capacity of 75,000 b/d. More recently, a 50-50 venture was formed between NIOC and Sang Yong, a private South Korean firm, to construct and operate a 60,000 b/d refinery in Onsan, South Korea. This refinery came on stream some months after the Iranian revolution. Under an agreement signed in 1976 NIOC contracted to supply Onsan Refinery with 60,000 b/d of crude oil.

NIOC also joined with the Senegalese Oil Co., IRASENCO, to purchase the marketing interests of Shell Senegal. At the time, NIOC expressed its intention to construct and operate a new refinery, a phosphate mine, port facilities, and a fertilizer plant in Senegal.

Since the revolution, Iran has retained its interests in the Madras Refinery and the fertilizer company; however, its position with respect to some of the other joint ventures is somewhat uncertain. Following Iran's embargo of oil exports to South Africa despite its earlier commitment to supply the refinery, the South African government took over Iran's interests in the venture. Moreover, Iran has shown no interest in IRASENCO. As for NIOC's involvement in the Onsan Refinery, its share has been sold to the Korean partners for a reported $20 million.

In addition to investments in overseas refineries, Iran had reached a provisional agreement with Japan in 1976 for the construction of a refinery in Bushehr in southern Iran to refine products solely for export to the Japanese market. The target date for completion of this refinery was 1983, and the capacity was expected to range between 125,000 b/d and 250,000 b/d. This project appears unlikely to go ahead in the near future.

Downstream Activities

Iran's participation in export-related downstream activities is limited to a fleet of seven crude oil and oil product tankers with a combined capacity of about 970 thousand dead weight tons (dwt). The fleet, owned and managed by National Iranian Tanker Co. (NITC)--a wholly owned subsidiary of NIOC--originally included three small vessels, the first of which was launched in 1959 and scrapped in 1977, and the other two launched in 1960 and 1961 and scrapped in 1978. Of the remaining seven tankers, two very large crude carriers (VLCC) of 228,054 dwt and 230,095 dwt were launched in 1975 and are under long-term charter to Sanko Lines of Japan; two VLCC of 222,745 dwt and 215,140 dwt, launched in 1972 and 1971 respectively, were acquired by NITC in 1976 along with three product carriers, each with a capacity just over 25,000 dwt. NITC bought these five carriers from the British Shipping Co. to be used in a 50-50 joint venture with the British Tanker Co. The two parties formed three joint companies: the Irano-British Shipping Co. which is the legal owner of the five NITC carriers and the five others (two VLCCs and three product carriers) contributed by the British Tanker Co.; the Irano-British Management Co., responsible for operations; and the Irano-British Shipping Service Co., a temporary company that will operate the vessels until the management company is established. Earlier plans envisaged the expansion of the tanker fleet from just under 1 million dwt to 10 million dwt over a period of 15 years.

Iran also has some smaller privately owned product tankers which carry middle-distillate oil products between the pipeline terminal at Bandar Mahshahr and Bandar Abbas. A

Table 5.5.   NIOC Tankers

Name of Tanker	Year Commissioned	Size (dwt)
Azarpad	1975	230,095
Kharg	1975	228,054
Shush	1972	222,745
Simond	1971	215,140
Marun	1974	25,245
Mokran	1974	25,244
Minab	1974	25,244
Total		971,767

Source: National Iranian Oil Company (1978).

product pipeline, however, is planned between the two points.
Table 5.5 lists Iran's tanker fleet.

DOMESTIC CONSUMPTION

Keeping pace with the growing thirst for oil products at home,
Iran has been forced to invest a considerable amount of money
and effort in boosting its internal refining capacity.   The
name-plate capacity of its refineries was increased from
685,000 b/d in 1972 to almost 1.0 million b/d by 1978; with
the completion of two new refineries at Tabriz and Isfahan,
total capacity was slated to reach 1.2 million b/d (see
table 5.6).
    According to the high growth projections scenarios dis-
cussed earlier, at least 100,000 b/d in new refinery capacity
will be needed every other year merely to keep pace with
growing domestic demand for middle-distillate products in the
1980s and 1990s, even with stepped-up efforts to substitute
natural gas for oil products.
    Large quantities of residual heavy products, notably fuel
oil, would be left over, reflecting the historical mismatch
between Iran's demand for various oil products and the natural
composition or mix of these products in crude oil; only two

Table 5.6. Capacity of Existing Refineries

(b/d)

Tehran I	125,000
Tehran II	100,000
Shiraz	45,000
Lavan Topping Plant	20,000
Kermanshah	18,500
Abadan[a]	630,000
Isfahan	200,000
Tabriz	80,000
Total	1,218,500

[a]While the Abadan Refinery has been damaged as a result of continuous shelling during the Iran-Iraq war, there are conflicting reports about the extent of the damages inflicted so far. But even if the refinery escapes total destruction, it would be advisable to replace it with a number of inland smaller refineries, given the now-evident vulnerability of the Abadan location.

Source: National Iranian Oil Company (1978).

middle-distillates, kerosene and gas oil, account for a disproportionately high one-half of all oil products consumed in the country. For years, Iran has had to export large volumes of leftover products, sometimes with great difficulty and at a loss owing to slack markets for such residual products, and, in turn, has had to import kerosene and gas oil.

The country's middle distillate problem can be at least partly corrected through the steady importation of additional quantities of kerosene or gas oil, through price and other kinds of penalties to reduce the demand for such products, through the installation of hydrocracking or isomax units in existing or planned refineries to treat heavy residuum, or through stepped-up substitution of natural gas, particularly to replace kerosene in commercial and residential use. This latter course is perhaps the most efficient and politically the most acceptable solution.

PROSPECTS FOR OIL

In the five years before the revolution, Iran was producing an average of just over 5.5 million b/d--about 1.0 million b/d short of its then sustainable capacity--although production had climbed to as much as 6.0 million b/d in September 1978. A month later, the country's oil workers began a slowdown, and soon a total strike, in an effort to help bring down the Shah. Production slipped to 5.5 million b/d in October, 3.4 million b/d in November, and 2.4 million b/d in December. By January and February 1979, Iran's oil production barely sufficed to meet internal requirements. After March, production began to climb slowly, leveling off at about 3.8 million b/d for the rest of the year.

The new Islamic government set a 4.0 million b/d level as its production target for 1980 but was unable to reach it because its traditional buyers turned away for a combination of political and commercial reasons. Following the deterioration of U.S.-Iranian relations in 1979, the United States barred imports of oil from Iran and pressured its allies to do the same; some followed suit to show political solidarity, but most did so because the softening of the world oil market would not support the high prices Iran was demanding.

Demand for Iranian oil will eventually pick up again but when it does, the 4.0 million b/d level is expected to remain as a self-imposed ceiling on production through the 1980s; actual production will depend on a host of political, economic, technical, and market factors, and, given Iran's present difficulties, will probably remain below the ceiling at least over the next year or two.

It should be noted that even if the Iranian government were economically pressed and politically prepared to lift its ceiling, it would probably be unable to produce at pre-revolution levels on a sustained basis under any reasonable set of assumptions. Difficulties arising from falling reservoir pressure, excessive salt contamination, and poor maintenance have mandated a shutting-in of an increasing number of oil wells; production capacity may be further restricted by damage to the oil infrastructure resulting from the war with Iraq.

Relief is unlikely from exploration for new oil fields or development of existing ones in view of several factors: political reluctance to open up new areas to foreign oil companies on terms that might attract foreign expertise and risk capital; massive capital requirements (perhaps over $10 billion for a modest exploration and secondary recovery program) and the ensuing risks to be borne by Iran if it chose to go ahead on its own, a move that would require the return of large numbers of skilled foreign technicians; an apparent lack of pressure to make the decision in light of the adequacy of government earnings even at low production levels; and, finally, the continuing administrative disorder in the country.

Exploratory drilling already had been declining before the revolution, largely because of the general reduction in foreign operations in Iran and the (unsuccessful) completion of the previous exploratory programs by existing joint venture companies and service contractors; it has since ground to a near halt. Between 1973 and 1978, only 139 exploratory oil and natural gas wells were drilled throughout Iran, while over 10,000 such wildcat wells were drilled in the United States in 1978 alone (see table 5.7).

Even with an intensified exploration program, it is unlikely that many new super-giant oil fields, defined as containing more than 5 billion barrels of reserves, like the Agha Jari and Gach Saran (which together supply nearly one-third of Iran's total proven reserves) will be discovered in Iran (see table 5.8).

The potential for discovery of giant fields (containing at least 500 million barrels of oil reserves) and for reserve growth in known fields from extensions, new pool discoveries and full development is nonetheless very promising.[4]

Even if a decision could be made quickly to resume a secondary recovery program, for example, the long lead times mean that no significant results could be expected before the late 1980s. Thus, while even conservative estimates indicate that Iran holds some 10 percent of the world's total published proven reserves of oil, its ability to lift this oil out of the ground for shipment to the world market is expected to remain limited in the near future.

As long as Iran is unable to increase its oil production capacity, the amount of oil it can export will diminish steadily, for a substantial portion of its domestic energy consumption has traditionally been--and will continue to be--supplied by oil products. In 1977, as noted earlier, some 77 percent of all primary energy consumed consisted of oil products; even if this share declines, the actual volume of domestic oil consumption will continue to rise steeply.

In view of the significant export value of oil, on the one hand, and the physical constraints on oil production relative to such alternative sources of energy as natural gas, on the other, Iran has long sought, for the most part unsuccessfully, to limit the use of oil at home. Continuing failure to do so will have serious implications for Iran's foreign exchange earnings position--and hence for its development effort--as well as for the world oil market generally.

Table 5.7. Wildcat Wells Drilled Between 1973 and 1978

	1973	1974	1975	1976	1976	1978
Number	18	27	26	26	25	17
Percentage of OPEC	4.8	6.8	7.1	8.2	8.2	4.6
Percentage of World	0.2	0.2	0.2	0.2	0.2	0.1

Source: Petro-Canada and Petroleos de Venezuela, World Oil
Supply Prospects, Vol. I, Feb. 1980.

Table 5.8. Giant Oil Fields

Field (by rank)	Discovery Date	Reserves (billion barrels)
Agha Jari	1936	9.5
Gach Saran	1937	8.0
Ahwaz	1958	6.0
Marun	1963	6.0
Bibi Hakimeh	1961	4.5
Paris	1964	3.0
Haft Kel	1927	2.0
Sassan*	1965	1.5
Karanj	1963	1.3
Rostam*	1966	1.0
Total		42.8

*Offshore fields.

Source: Mehdi Parsi, "Energy Problems in Iran in Relation to
Discovery and Production of Oil and Gas," National Iranian Oil
Company, Tehran, April 1980 (in Farsi), and International
Petroleum Enyclopedia 1980, PennWell Publishing Co., Tulsa,
1980.

NOTES

1. These estimates are released annually by the trade press; Iran has never officially accepted or rejected the published estimates, and at least until the 1978-79 revolution, such estimates were used as working estimates for planning purposes within the country itself.

2. For a more detailed discussion, see Bijan Mossavar-Rahmani and Jesse C. Denton, "On the Theory of Crude Oil Prices- II. Price Elasticity of Crude Oil Reserves," in Energy Conversion, vol. 17, no. 2-3, Oxford, 1977.

3. The tonne or metric ton is equivalent to 1,000 kilograms, or 2,204.62 pounds.

4. For a more detailed discussion of the known and ultimately recoverable oil resources of the world, see Richard Nehring, Giant Oil Fields and World Oil Resources, Rand Corporation, Santa Monica, 1978.

6 Natural Gas

Iran's proven reserves of natural gas, estimated at 490 tcf as of January 1, 1980, rank second in the world only to those of the Soviet Union, and exceed the proven reserves of all the other Middle East countries combined. Table 6.1 shows Iran's reserves and production statistics for recent years and the corresponding computed reserves-to-production ratios.

Table 6.1. Natural Gas Proven Reserves,
Production, and Reserve Life

Year	Proven Reserves (tcf)	Gross Production (tcf/year)	Reserve Life (years)
1977	330	2.0	165
1978	500	2.0	250
1979	500	1.4	357
1980	490	n.a.	n.a.

Sources: American Petroleum Institute, Basic Petroleum Data Book (update), API, Washington, D.C., 1980, and Organization of the Petroleum Exporting Countries, Annual Statistical Bulletin: 1979, OPEC, Vienna, 1980.

On the basis of current reserves estimates and generous projections of domestic consumption, exports, and reinjection, Iran's natural gas reserves are expected to last well into the next century. Thus, the problems of natural gas supply in Iran do not concern physical availability but rather location of natural gas reserves and their efficient utilization.

The last comprehensive analysis of Iran's natural gas reserves by field was released by the National Iranian Gas Company (NIGC) in mid-1977 (see table 6.2). Those figures placed proven reserves at about 375 tcf, of which 210 tcf, about 53 percent, was of the associated kind, found dissolved in and produced unavoidably with oil from the major fields in Khuzestan.

Iran also has huge non-associated natural gas fields, many discovered only recently, whose potential is at least equal to, and perhaps twice as much as, that of the associated reserves. Important non-associated natural gas fields are located in Khuzestan, Qeshm Island, Kangan, Khangiran and offshore in the Persian Gulf.

Four of the offshore discoveries (known as the C, B, F, and G fields) are considered particularly promising. The C field, later named Pars, was chosen for development first because of its proximity to shore. Test wells indicate that this field is one of the largest in the world, holding as much as 75 tcf, according to Iranian estimates. Officials expect that as more information is gained through similar drilling in other non-associated fields, estimates of Iran's proven reserves of natural gas will be revised, ultimately reaching 600 tcf, a figure equivalent in calorific content to more than 100 billion barrels of oil--much higher than Iran's present proven reserves of oil.

PRODUCTION AND UTILIZATION

To date, nearly all of Iran's natural gas production has been in association with oil produced from the Khuzestan and offshore oil fields. Small amounts of dome gas are also produced in the Khuzestan oil fields. Minor quantities of non-associated natural gas are produced in the Khangiran field of the Sarakhs area to supply the city of Mashad, as well as in the Gavarzin field on Qeshm Island to supply Bandar Abbas.

Until the late 1960s, most of the associated natural gas produced in Iran was flared, vented, and wasted; by 1979, the last year for which figures are available, flaring had been reduced to less than half of total production.[1] Pre-revolution plans called for reducing flaring to a bare minimum through an ambitious natural gas gathering and utilization program.

Table 6.2. Estimated Natural Gas Reserves by Field

(tcf)

	Proven	Probable	Possible
Associated			
Khuzestan Oil Fields	210.0	210.0	210.0
Nonassociated			
Khangiran	18.0	18.0	18.0
Tang-e-Bijar	0.5	0.6	0.6
Sarajeh	0.3	0.4	0.4
Qeshm	4.0	6.0	8.0
Kangan	11.0	15.0	21.0
Nar	14.0	17.0	21.0
Aqar	10.0	12.0	15.0
Pars (C Structure)	54.0	65.0	75.0
B Structure	25.0	50.0	89.0
F Structure	9.0	17.0	66.0
G Structure	7.0	15.0	39.0
Sarkhun	5.0	7.0	10.0
Kashu	5.0	10.0	15.0
Babaqir	2.0	2.0	5.0
Total	374.8	445.0	593.0

Source: National Iranian Gas Company (1977).

Table 6.3 shows production, flaring, exports and domestic utilization of natural gas in Iran in recent years.[2] Between 1973 and 1978, natural gas production rose from 4,660.3 million cf/d to 5,336.9 cf/d at the same time that flaring was cut back from 2,753.4 million cf/d (59.1 percent of total production) to 2,490.4 million cf/d (46.7 percent of total production). Exports remained more or less unchanged during this period, while domestic utilization rose from 1,065.8 million cf/d or 22.9 percent of total production to 2,145.1 or 40.2 percent of total production between 1973 and 1978. The stepped-up reinjection program accounted for the bulk of these increases. The entries for 1979 reflect reductions in natural gas output resulting from the disruptions to the oil sector during the revolution. Iran's natural gas output continued to decline in 1980 and 1981, according to preliminary estimates, and will only recover when oil production begins to climb from current depressed levels.

Exports

IGAT Project

The first and most important attempt to utilize associated natural gas in Iran was the completion, in 1970, of the Iran Gas Trunkline (IGAT) to export associated natural gas from the large Ahwaz, Agha Jari, and Marun oil fields in Khuzestan. The 42/40 inch, 1,100 kilometer cross-country trunkline has a capacity of 1,600 million cf/d of which 968 million cf/d was originally earmarked for export and 632 million cf/d for domestic consumption via spur lines feeding several cities en route, notably Tehran, Qom, Kashan, Shiraz and Isfahan.

After the start-up period, exports stabilized at an average of about 880 million cf/d between 1973 and 1977, before dropping to slightly over 700 million cf/d in 1978 following the reduction in Iran's oil production during the last quarter of the year as a result of the oil workers' strikes.

The IGAT natural gas exports were never attractive from an economic standpoint. The original price was set at a low $0.17 per thousand cubic feet at the delivery point in Astara on the Irano-Soviet border, payable in rubles.

Since rubles could only be used in the Soviet Union itself, the transaction was effectively limited to barter between the two countries. Iran used its credits against Soviet assistance in the construction of a steel mill in Isfahan, a machine tools plant in Arak, and other projects.

With increased world oil prices, Iran negotiated for higher natural gas prices and the last agreed-upon price for IGAT sales was $0.75 per thousand cubic feet. Even though the higher price was a considerable improvement, it stood below

Table 6.3. Production and Utilization of Natural Gas

(million cf/d)

	1973	1974	1975	1976	1977	1978	1979
Flaring							
Volume	2,753.4	2,682.2	2,279.4	2,698.6	2,553.4	2,490.4	1,528.0
Percentage	59.1	55.5	51.9	55.4	46.5	46.7	39.8
Exports							
Volume	841.1	879.4	926.0	898.6	895.9	701.4	376.0a
Percentage	18.1	18.2	21.8	18.4	16.3	13.1	9.8
Domestic Utilization[b]							
Volume	1,065.8	1,274.0	1,186.3	1,276.8	2,041.0	2,145.1	1,935.0
Percentage	22.9	26.4	27.0	26.2	37.2	40.2	50.4
Total Production	4,660.3	4,835.6	4,391.7	4,874.0	5,490.3	5,336.9	3,839.0

aEstimate.

bIncludes petrochemical feedstocks, reinjected gas, producers' fuel, and transmission losses.

Source: Organization of the Petroleum Exporting Countries, Annual Statistical Bulletin 1979, OPEC, Vienna, 1980, and Organization of the Petroleum Exporting Countries, Annual Report 1979, OPEC, Vienna, 1980.

the market value then for natural gas, translating into the equivalent of only $4.35 per barrel of oil. Still, Iran could not spend all of its credits against imports from the Soviet Union; by 1978, it had accumulated unused credits equal to several hundred million dollars.

Immediately after the revolution, Iran asked the Soviet Union to pay substantially higher prices for its natural gas, "retroactive to the first day of the revolution," partially in hard currencies. Negotiations between the two countries broke down in the spring of 1980 and exports were cut soon thereafter; at first, Iran reportedly claimed that damage to the trunkline by a landslide in the south forced the cut-off. Even if exports are resumed, Iran will probably not renew the present sales contract when it terminates in 1985 because of financial considerations and the need to divert additional volumes of natural gas to domestic users along the pipeline route.

IGAT-II Project

In addition to the IGAT project, three other natural gas export projects were planned or under construction before the revolution, whose fate is now uncertain. The first and most advanced of these involved the construction of a second and larger cross-country trunkline dubbed IGAT-II. Based on its discoveries of non-associated natural gas, Iran concluded a 20-year trilateral sales agreement in 1975 with Sojuzgasexport of the Soviet Union, Ruhrgas of West Germany, Gaz de France, and OMV of Austria. Under the terms of this switch deal, Iran was to supply 1,300 million cf/d of natural gas to the three Western European companies at the Irano-Soviet border. They were to hand this natural gas over to the Soviet Union and would, in turn, receive somewhat reduced volumes (with deductions made for transit payments) delivered at the Czech-West German and Czech-Austrian borders. The Iranian natural gas would thus be consumed in the southwestern regions of the Soviet Union where it is needed, while the Western European companies would receive natural gas from the Soviet Union's Orenburg and western Siberian natural gas fields.[3]

Of the natural gas delivered to Western Europe, Ruhrgas was to receive 50 percent, Gaz de France 33.33 percent, and OMV 16.67 percent. Czechoslovakia later negotiated with Iran to buy another 150 million cf/d of natural gas under the trilateral agreement, thus bringing Iran's total deliveries at the Irano-Soviet border to 1,450 million cf/d with payment in hard currencies by the four end-use buyers.

Natural gas for this project was to be supplied from the onshore Kangan and Nar natural gas fields southeast of Bushehr, and transmitted via a new 56/48 inch, 1,358 kilometer trunkline running parallel to IGAT. The new trunkline was also intended to distribute 970 million cf/d of natural gas to users along its route within Iran itself, bringing its total capacity to 2,420 million cf/d.

The IGAT-II project came under criticism at home since its inception, again because the contract price for the natural gas was considered too low. Although the IGAT-II price was initially set at nearly $1.00 per thousand cubic feet—somewhat higher than natural gas sold under the terms of the existing IGAT project—this time the natural gas came from non-associated fields slated for development for this specific purpose, and not from previously flared associated natural gas. Even a minimal intrinsic value for the non-associated natural gas, it was argued, would yield a negative net return (or back) at the wellhead, given the high cost of producing and delivering to the Soviet Union.

In light of such criticism, the post-revolutionary government in 1979 cancelled—or, at least, postponed indefinitely—the IGAT-II project. Since substantial construction work is already finished on the second trunkline, it may eventually be completed and used solely for domestic natural gas distribution.

Kalingas Project

A second aborted Iranian natural gas export project was the Kangan Liquefied Natural Gas (Kalingas) project, set up in 1972 as a joint venture between NIGC (50 percent) and a consortium of European, American, and Japanese companies to produce and export 1,200 million cf/d of gas from the Pars field in liquefied natural gas (LNG) form. At first, the foreign partners included International Systems and Control Corp., Nissho-Iwai Co., Ltd.; Chicago Bridge and Iron Co.; Halfden-Ditler-Simonson and Co.; and Lone Star Co. By 1978, faced with financing problems, all the foreign partners except Japan Kalingas—a group of Japanese companies which held a 15 percent share—and Chicago Bridge and Iron Co.—which held a 2.5 percent share—dropped out of the project and assigned their shares to NIGC.

Kalingas was slated for completion in three phases of 400 million cf/d each, with the first deliveries earmarked for Japan. NIGC officials put total capital costs of the project at about $2 billion; a more realistic estimate, including investments in sea transport, would have exceeded $5 billion. Even at the lower estimate, the Kalingas project would have been marginally profitable, at best.

Columbia-Moss Rosenberg Project

A third aborted natural gas export project involved the export of LNG to the United States. Under the terms of the

preliminary agreement signed in 1978 between NIGC, Columbia
Gas Systems of the United States, and Moss-Rosenberg of
Norway, Moss-Rosenberg was to build a barge-mounted floating
liquefaction plant in Norway to be towed and placed in the
Persian Gulf; Columbia Gas Systems was to ship some 400 million cf/d of Iranian natural gas processed at this plant,
to its LNG terminal at Cove Point, Maryland. The project
never got off the ground because of problems involving technology, financing, and U.S. regulatory procedures.

El Paso-Distrigaz Project

Another LNG export project which never moved beyond a memorandum of intent was the El Paso-Distrigaz project. According
to the memorandum signed in 1974, NIGC (50 percent shareholding), El Paso Natural Gas Co. of the United States (25
percent shareholding), and Distrigaz S.A. of Belgium (25 percent shareholding), were to form a joint venture for the production and export of LNG, at first 2,000 million cf/d of
natural gas, with a possibility of raising this volume to
3,000 cf/d. Half of the LNG produced by this venture was to
be exported to the U.S. East Coast and the rest to Western
Europe.

The three partners also planned to form another company
under similar terms for transportation of the LNG. Two modes
of transportation were considered. Under the first option,
natural gas would be transmitted via pipeline across Iran to
Iskanderun in Turkey, where it would be liquefied and shipped
to the European and American markets. The other alternative
called for liquefaction of the natural gas near Kangan on the
Persian Gulf for shipment via the Suez Canal. Natural gas was
to be supplied from the Pars field and the project was to be
operational in the early 1980s.

The El Paso-Distrigaz project was the largest of its kind
planned anywhere. Correspondingly, the investment requirements were considerable. The project encountered major
difficulties in financing and was abandoned as unrealistic a
few years later.

Domestic Utilization

In addition to export, Iran's associated and non-associated
natural gas is earmarked for use internally as producers' fuel
in the oil fields; for reinjection into the fields to increase
recovery; for general residential, commercial, and industrial consumption; and for petrochemical feedstocks. Table 6.4
shows a breakdown of field use of natural gas in Iran for
1977.

Table 6.4.   Field Use of Natural Gas in 1977

(million cf/d)

Producers' Fuel	203.2
Reinjection	906.9
Total	1,110.1

Source: National Iranian Gas Company (1978).

Producers' Fuel

A significant portion of associated natural gas is consumed
in the oil fields for power recovery through the use of expansion turbines or as direct fuel.[4] In 1977, for example,
203.2 million cf/d or almost 10 percent of all natural gas
used domestically in Iran was consumed as producers' fuel.

Reinjection

Iran's plans for massive gas reinjection into the Khuzestan
oil fields to maintain reservoir pressure and increase the
ultimate recovery of oil have already been discussed.   The
reinjection program had a high priority insofar as natural gas
use was concerned and was expected to consume a large part of
all natural gas used domestically in Iran in the 1980s and
1990s.   Unofficial estimates of natural gas use for secondary
recovery ranged between 8,000 million cf/d to 15,000 million
cf/d.   About 85 percent of the reinjected natural gas was
expected to be recovered eventually, however.   The reinjection program was started in 1976 and, within two years,
accounted for 907 million cf/d or 44 percent of all natural
gas utilized domestically.

Industrial, Commercial, and Residential Use

Most of the natural gas used by the industrial, commercial,
and residential sectors in Iran comes from the Khuzestan oil
fields and is supplied to the users through the IGAT distribution network.   However, given the limited availability of
associated natural gas and capacity of the existing trunkline
on the one hand, and the discovery of non-associated natural
gas in other parts of the country and growing demand for
energy on the other, Iran launched several new projects in the
mid-1970s to develop its natural gas reserves for domestic
consumption.

The first such project was Qeshm Island. Qeshm Island off Bandar Abbas has sizable non-associated natural gas reserves under development to provide fuel for a large section of the country's southeastern region. The first phase of the development plan was completed in early 1980 and involves the transmission of 35 million cf/d of sweet or desulfurized natural gas from the Gavarzin field (proven reserves of 1.4 tcf) on Qeshm Island to a large, recently completed electric power plant at Bandar Abbas via a 70 kilometer pipeline. Transmission of natural gas to the power plant is expected to increase to 75 million cf/d after an initial buildup period; another 25 million cf/d of natural gas is planned for other uses in Bandar Abbas, bringing the total transmission to 100 million cf/d under this phase of the project. The second phase of the project, not yet advanced beyond the initial engineering and planning stages, is to carry another 500 million cf/d of natural gas from the Sarkhun field (proven reserves of 5 tcf) to a planned gas reduction steel mill in Bandar Abbas, to the giant copper complex at Sar Cheshmeh, and to other industrial users in the region.

Another major domestic natural gas project involves the Khangiran non-associated field discovered near Sarakhs in northeastern Iran in 1968. Its proven reserves of natural gas are estimated at 18 tcf. Natural gas from Khangiran will be used for the industrial development of the Khorasan and Mazandaran provinces. The first phase of this project involves the transmission of 57 million cf/d to the city of Mashad by 1981. The second phase calls for construction of a pipeline from Sarakhs to Neka in Mazandaran to supply fuel for a new 1,400 MW_e electric power generating plant. This phase, in turn, is planned for completion in stages. The first step is the drilling of 12 wells and installation of a natural gas gathering system and a treatment plant; an 850 kilometer pipeline will supply towns en route via small spur lines. Initial capacity of the treatment plant is 750 million cf/d. Stage two involves drilling another 12 wells, increasing the capacity of the treatment plant to 1,250 million cf/d, and installation of compressor stations.

The third major project for domestic utilization of natural gas is the expansion of the Ahwaz-Haft-Tapeh project. Its purpose is to supply associated natural gas from the Khuzestan fields to industrial, commercial, and residential users in the Ahwaz and Haft-Tapeh region; at start-up in 1971 its capacity was about 34 million cf/d; after expansion, the capacity will increase to 260 million cf/d.

PROSPECTS FOR NATURAL GAS

Exports

In the fall of 1976, Iran announced that while its existing natural gas export commitments would be honored, no new
such projects would be considered because of unattractive
market conditions. Prices of natural gas imported into the
industrial countries were just beginning to be tied to prices
of imported residual oil products, which, while representing a
substantial improvement over the past, still resulted in
significantly lower net-back to the exporting countries due to
higher transmission costs. Iran, it was reasoned, risked
reducing its total foreign exchange earnings by exporting
natural gas, as customers for its high net-back oil would
shift to low net-back natural gas, which is a cleaner and
hence more desirable fuel at an equivalent price.

The economics of natural gas exports were even more
questionable where intercontinental LNG trade was concerned
because the rising cost of liquefaction and transportation
threatened to wipe out any positive net-back on such sales.

The OPEC Gas Pricing Committee, which bears responsibility for monitoring the situation in the world natural gas
market on behalf of the OPEC member countries, used a net-back
calculation to determine the economics of LNG projects in a
January 1980 study.[5] First, the committee determined the
closest alternative fuels to LNG in the major consuming markets and assigned a weighting to each fuel based on its
substitutability. Next, based on the market price of each
alternative, the committee calculated the weighted average
calorific equivalent price of these alternatives (measured in
mm btus) to determine competitive prices of LNG delivered to
end-use markets. The example below illustrates OPEC's price
calculations for a hypothetical Persian Gulf LNG project
destined for the European market in late 1979.

The OPEC Gas Pricing Committee determined the substitutability of LNG in Western Europe as follows: 30 percent low
sulfur fuel oil, 30 percent high sulfur fuel oil, 30 percent
gas oil, and 10 percent naphtha.

Based on oil product prices in the Rotterdam market in
December 1979, the committee calculated the competitive fuels
price for Persian Gulf LNG at the point of consumption in
Western Europe at $5.96 per mm btu.

From this $5.96 per mm btu LNG price, the committee sub-
tracted regasification costs at the receiving terminal of
$0.40 per mm btu. Thus the price of LNG delivered to the
hypothetical receiving terminal, i.e., the cif (costs, insur-
ance, and freight) price in Western Europe was computed at
$5.56 per mm btu. To derive a net-back price at the point of

loading, or the fob (free on board) price in the Persian Gulf, the committee subtracted transportation costs of $1.75 per mm btu (based on costs incurred by transporting half of the LNG on a 40,000 cubic meter carrier and the rest on a 125,000 cubic meter carrier).

The fob price of Persian Gulf LNG delivered to Western Europe was thus estimated as follows:

LNG fob price (in the Persian Gulf)=
    cif price (or competitive fuels price minus regasifi-
    cation costs) minus transportation costs
                    or
LNG fob price (in the Persian Gulf)=
    $5.56 (or $5.96 - $0.40) - $1.74 = $3.82 per mm btu.

The net-back at the wellhead itself is of course lower since production, gathering costs, pipeline transportation from the associated or non-associated natural gas fields to liquefaction plants, and liquefaction costs have to be deducted from the fob price as well; these costs were recently estimated by Iranian officials at $2.00 per mm btu. Thus the natural gas wellhead value based on the above calculations is an estimated $1.82 per mm btu for a Persian Gulf-Western Europe LNG project. This figure is equivalent to about $10.50 a barrel of oil. The average wellhead price of Persian Gulf oil at the time of this calculation in late 1979 exceeded $30 a barrel.

While natural gas prices at the wellhead in these hypothetical calculations (which nonetheless realistically reflect actual prices and cost patterns) are still about one-third of the price of an equivalent amount of oil, they represent a considerable improvement in the net-back price for natural gas over previous years. Similar calculations for 1978 yielded negative net-backs at the wellhead for hypothetical Persian Gulf LNG sold to the United States and Western Europe, and a positive net-back of merely $0.02 per mm btu for LNG sold to Japan.

With the recent rise in crude oil prices, the economics of Persian Gulf LNG export projects has, perhaps for the first time, become favorable for those exporting countries who have been able to negotiate for increased prices. In January 1980, for example, Abu Dhabi's cif price for LNG sold to Japan rose to $5.39 per mm btu from $2.36 only a year earlier. But since the revolution, Iranian officials argue that natural gas prices should rise even higher to provide sufficient incentives for large scale export development.

In 1980, Iran proposed a new formula to replace the one under study by the OPEC Gas Pricing Committee. Rather than set cif prices for natural gas on the basis of competitive fuels prices in each market and then work back to a wellhead price, Iran is advocating a uniform wellhead intrinsic value for all OPEC natural gas, to be set at 80 percent of fob fuel

oil prices on an energy equivalent basis, or $3.78 per mm btu.
The 80 percent fuel oil equivalency is to be taken as a minimum and gradually increased to a 100 percent crude oil equivalency, according to the proposal. To this price would then
be added production, gathering, and pipeline transportation
costs to the liquefaction plants, and liquefaction costs
themselves--a total of $1.97 per mm btu--bringing the fob
price to $5.75.

According to this proposal the cif price of Persian Gulf
LNG delivered to Western Europe was estimated as follows:
LNG cif price (in Western Europe)=
    fob price (or natural gas intrinsic value plus produc-
    tion, gathering, pipeline, transportation costs to the
    liquefaction plants, and liquefaction costs) plus
    transportation costs

                              or

LNG cif price (in Western Europe)=
$5.75 (or $3.78 + $1.97) + $1.74 = $7.49 per mm btu.
If the cif price is adjusted to account for another $0.40
per mm btu in regasification costs, the total price of Persian
Gulf natural gas in Western Europe is $7.89 per mm btu in this
hypothetical case.

It is unlikely at this time that potential importers of
LNG would be willing to accept such a formula and the ensuing
high natural gas prices. Moreover, as long as political
uncertainties continue, few buyers would be willing to share
in the investments or to build a dependency on LNG imports
from Iran.

Similar barriers exist to the development of a large new
Iranian cross-country trunkline for export purposes.

Domestic Utilization

Considering the vast Iranian supplies of natural gas, the low
production costs, and the relatively limited export prospects
as compared with those for oil, Iran should pursue a vigorous
policy of rapid natural gas development. Every effort should
be made to resolve existing bottlenecks and to accelerate expansion of natural gas transmission and distribution systems.
The economics of stepped-up natural gas utilization on a
national level are extremely favorable, and the savings in
annual oil refining and pipeline costs, plus the export value
of the oil saved, far outweigh the cost of any expanded system
over the long run. Industrial users will probably be quick
to switch to natural gas once it is made available. Penetration into the residential and commercial market, however, may
be slow unless natural gas use is actively promoted and economic incentives are offered to encourage consumers to switch
from liquid-fueled to gas-fueled appliances.

As noted earlier, domestic consumption of natural gas
in Iran is projected to grow to 4,274.0 million cf/d in 1997
in a low economic growth scenario and to 6,301.4 million c/fd
in a high economic growth scenario. These figures represent substantial increases over 1977 consumption levels of
514.7 million cf/d, and can be met through some combination
of: (a) resumption of high levels of oil production to
increase associated natural gas output, or alternatively,
maintenance of lower oil production levels and reduction in
natural gas reinjection targets, which ranged from 8,000
million cf/d to 15,000 million cf/d in the 1980s; (b) reduction in flaring of associated natural gas (1,528.0 million
cf/d in 1979) to the extent possible; and (c) stepped-up
development of Iran's non-associated natural gas resources
which are still largely untapped.

LPG

As natural gas utilization increases, larger quantities of
NGL will also become available because natural gas must be
processed before it can be compressed for reinjection or
transported through pipelines. This NGL can then be fraction-
ated to yield ethane, natural gasoline and LPG consisting of
propane and butane.

LPG--35 to 40 percent of all NGL produced on a volume
basis--is also produced in oil refineries, and is an excellent
feedstock for petrochemicals as well as a clean and versatile
premium fuel. In 1977, some 15,600 b/d of LPG were consumed
internally in Iran, although substantially larger quantities
of recoverable NGL were lost in flared natural gas and in
pipelines.

The future availability of LPG in Iran will depend on the
size and scope of the natural gas gathering program. In all
likelihood, the internal supply of LPG will exceed its demand.
The economics of LPG use in Iran are similar to those of
natural gas use. Rather than export any surplus LPG, Iran can
use its output to displace kerosene, gas oil and even gasoline
in existing markets, and as an incremental fuel in new ones.
LPG, which can be transported as bottled gas or in bulk by
road tankers, is a particularly attractive substitute for
kerosene and gas oil in residential and commercial uses in
areas that cannot be quickly and cheaply served by a natural
gas pipeline distribution network. Once the natural gas
network is extended to these areas, substitution should be
rapid since only simple modifications would be required to
convert from LPG to natural gas use. Thus, prior conversion
to LPG should help increase the rate of penetration of natural
gas into some residential and commercial markets.

Diesel fuel and motor gasoline could also be replaced
with LPG, where available, with only minor modifications to

convert trucks, buses, taxis, and private automobiles to LPG use.

In this way, the rate of increase in the domestic demand for oil products would be slowed down, saving oil for export or for future use. Additionally, by substituting LPG for middle-distillates, the complexity, the number, and the cost of future refineries can be reduced.

The substitutions described above are technically feasible but would require a major restructuring of the LPG industry. For significant market penetration, LPG would have to be widely and readily available at a price competitive with that of other fuels, distribution facilities would have to be greatly expanded, and other economic incentives offered to encourage the use of LPG.

NOTES

1. Most of the flaring occurs directly at the wellhead. Additional natural gas is flared after partial utilization. The Kharg Petrochemical Company and the NGL plants, for example, flare large amounts of natural gas after removal of NGL and sulfur.
2. Domestic consumption figures used in Table 6.3 and the rest of this section do not correspond exactly to figures in the earlier section of this book because of differences in sources--which affect use of conversion factors and choice of Iranian or Gregorian calendars--and perhaps more importantly, because these entries include transmission losses and reinjected natural gas whereas the earlier ones do not.
3. For a detailed study of the Soviet natural gas industry, see Jonathan P. Stern, Soviet Natural Gas Development to 1990, Lexington, D. C. Heath and Co., 1980.
4. An expansion turbine is any form of turbine, excluding steam turbines and gas turbines, that extracts mechanical power from a gas stream by allowing the gas to expand in a controlled fashion.
5. Organization of the Petroleum Exporting Countries Energy Studies Department, "Pricing of Gas: Updating of Background Information," OPEC, Vienna, 1980, and Organization of the Petroleum Exporting Countries Gas Pricing Committee, "Report of the 10th Meeting of the Gas Pricing Committee: January 28-29, 1980," OPEC, Vienna, 1980.

7 Hydropower

INTRODUCTION

Iran possesses a fairly large hydropower potential at sites
located almost exclusively in its mountainous western and
northwestern regions. The largest concentration--over two-
thirds--lies in the rivers flowing southward from the Zagros
mountains of Khuzestan into the Persian Gulf, and particularly
in the Karun River and its tributaries. The balance of the
known hydropower resources are principally in the Alborz
mountain range along the Caspian Sea and along the northwestern borders of the country. Studies point to possibili-
ties for power development of smaller magnitude, in combination with water supply development for irrigation, in other
parts of the country.

DEVELOPED RESOURCES

Iran's developed hydropower capacity currently totals some
1,804 MW$_e$ (see table 7.1). The largest single concentration
is in the 1,000 MW$_e$ Karun Dam (formerly known as the Reza Shah
Kabir Dam). The balance is distributed among another large
plant--the 520 MW$_e$ Dez Dam--and some smaller irrigation and
water supply projects.

Several hundred megawatts of additional installed hydropower capacity are expected to come on stream soon as plants
already in advanced construction are completed, notably the
120 MW$_e$ Lar-Kalan-Lavarak Dam at Lar and the 30 MW$_e$ Jiroft Dam
at Halilrud.

Table 7.1. Existing Hydropower Facilities

Plant/River	Installed Capacity (MW$_e$)	Completion Date
Karun	1,000	1976
Dez	520	1962
Karaj	91	1961
Sefid Rud	88	1961
Zayandeh Rud	55	1970
Jaje Rud	22	1967
Aras	22	1970
Mahabad	6	1970
Total	1,804	

Source: Iranian Ministry of Energy (1978).

Before the revolution, the Iranian government had projected the growth of installed hydropower capacity to nearly 3,000 MW$_e$ by the early-1980s, but it is now doubtful whether this goal will be met because the ongoing political turmoil has caused a substantial slow-down of industrial projects.

UNDEVELOPED RESOURCES

Iran has significant, as yet undeveloped, hydropower resources. The 1975 Monenco study estimated Iran's known conventional hydropower potential at about 14,700 MW$_e$ (14,000 MW$_e$ in dependable capacity) with another 3,750 MW$_e$ in pumped storage capacity in the Alborz mountains in the north[1] (see table 7.2). Another study (by SRI) estimated total conventional hydropower potential in Iran at nearly 13,000 MW$_e$, with an additional 2,400 MW$_e$ in pumped storage capacity. Of the total conventional hydropower potential, SRI estimated that 7,590 MW$_e$ of capacity would be competitive with fossil fuel plants at a cost for fuel of $0.40 per mm btus, and another 2,575 MW$_e$ of capacity at fuel costs of $1.50 per mm btus. The pumped storage potential would, of course, be

Table 7.2.   Undeveloped Hydropower Resources[a]

(sites developed or under construction excluded)

Region	Capacity (MW_e)	
	Installed	Dependable
Khuzestan		
Karun River	9,260	9,100
Dez River and Others	3,385	2,968
Azarbayjan		
Aras River	624	561
Lake Rezayeh	48	36
Little Zab	522	460
Tehran Region	67	51
Alborz Mountains	754	754
Interior Basins	31	25
Total	14,691	13,955

[a]Excludes another 3,750 MW_e in pumped storage capacity.

Source: Monenco (1975).

economical only in large integrated power systems where the energy necessary to pump water from the lower to the upper reservoirs would be supplied by continuously operated nuclear and/or large fossil-fired power plants during off-peak demand periods.

Iran's conventional hydropeaking potential (i.e., sites usable for generation of electricity during periods of high demand only rather than on a sustained basis) has still been only partially investigated.   For example, the Monenco study estimated that at least 10,000 MW_e of dependable conventional peaking capacity can ultimately be developed along the Karun River alone, which, even in dry years, can provide such capacity for up to four hours daily.   This may ultimately

prove more favorable than pumped storage, as the large number
of nuclear reactors required for off-peak pumping will probably not be built. Some limited use of pumped storage,
however, may become necessary in the future, particularly
as a means of providing peaking service to the Tehran area
since major pumped storage sites are located along the Alborz
mountain range, closer to Tehran than are the conventional
hydropower sites.

PLANNING THE FUTURE

A number of promising hydropower sites have already been
identified and subjected to some engineering analysis, ranging
from preliminary map studies to excellent reconnaisance-grade
studies, including the following: the Karun, Dez, Bakhtiari,
Karkheh, and Quzel Owzan rivers, and the Alborz mountain
range rivers.

Before decisions can be made on construction, however,
the proposed sites should be subjected to systematic feasi-
bility studies and additional cost estimates prepared. Moreover, the trade-offs between developing potential sites for
power generation and adapting them for irrigation--where
applicable--must be carefully assessed, recognizing the need
to develop Iran's agriculture more fully.

NOTES

1. Pumped storage is increasingly utilized as a source of
   peaking capacity, particularly in large, integrated power
   grids where the base-load is met by nuclear-generated
   power. A pumped storage system consists of an upper and a
   lower reservoir connected by tunnels with a power installation consisting of a reversible generating pumping unit.
   During periods of excess power supply, water from the
   lower reservoir is pumped to the higher one; the flow is
   reversed during periods of peak demand to generate power.

8 Solid and Miscellaneous Fuels

COAL

Iran's coal resources are estimated at about 6 billion tonnes (roughly equivalent to 20 billion barrels of oil on an energy basis) of which approximately 3.7 billion tonnes consist of high grade coal suitable for coking or metallurgical use and 2.3 billion tonnes of lower grade product for use as steam coal (see table 8.1).

Of the total resources, only one-tenth is judged commercially accessible at this time and included in proven reserves estimates; most of Iran's coal is located in deep, thin seams that are difficult and expensive to mine.

Iran's coal production is concentrated in the Kerman region and the output is used primarily as coking coal at the Isfahan steel mill. Five mines, Sangerud, Karmozd, Shahrud, Pabedana-Upper, and Babnizu-Upper supply an average of 550,000 tonnes per year to the steel mill. In addition to the coking coal mined in Iran, some high quality coking coal has been imported from West Germany, amounting in the late 1970s to less than 15 percent of total requirements.

The cost of producing steam coal is substantially higher in Iran than that of natural gas, on an energy equivalent basis. Furthermore, the environmental problems associated with coal production and use make it less desirable a fuel than natural gas or even residual fuel oil. Larger quantities of steam coal are expected to become available eventually as a by-product of coking coal in the Kerman area, especially if the planned program for expansion of the Isfahan steel mill is implemented.[1] But even though this steam coal will have no value unless it is burned, it remains to be determined whether the relative capital cost of new coal-fired power plants and

Table 8.1.   Estimated Coal Resources

(million tonnes)

Coal Regions	Coal Type		
	Coking	Steam	Total
Central Iran			
Kerman	1,071.6	458.3	1,529.9
Tabass, Niband	234.4	756.4	990.8
Subtotal	1,306.0	1,214.7	2,520.7
Alborz Range			
Gheshlagh	231.3	–	231.3
Shahrod	207.6	–	207.6
Damghan	239.0	200.5	439.5
Alasht	750.0	–	750.0
Glandrood	250.0	630.0	880.0
Norood	120.0	200.0	320.0
West Alborz	200.0	50.0	250.0
North Khorassan	450.0	–	450.0
Subtotal	2,447.9	1,080.5	3,528.4
Total Iran	3,753.9	2,295.2	6,049.1

Source: National Iranian Steel Company (1976).

the cost of transporting the coal from the mine to the pro-
spective plant would justify an expansion of coal-generated
electric power capacity in Iran at this time.   Clearly,
however, a modest exploration program should be continued to
locate and identify coal reserves, generating sound decisions
about coal use in the future should the economics of coal
production, transportation, and consumption change in relation
to other fuels.

ADVANCED ENERGY TECHNOLOGIES

At present, the abundance and relatively low cost of fossil
fuels in Iran, particularly natural gas, preclude the need for

any major program to develop alternative sources of energy.
Given the current early stage of development, complex technology, and high cost, alternative energy sources should
not be expected to make a substantial contribution in Iran in
the 1980s.

Solar

Perhaps the only alternative energy potential may lie in the
small-scale application of existing solar energy technologies
in remote towns, villages, and nomadic areas, including water
heaters for communal bath houses, milk heaters for milk processing and pasteurization, coolers for storing food and
medical supplies, home space and water heaters, crop drying,
small-scale water pumping, and desalination equipment.
    A proposal was submitted to the Iranian government in
the mid-1970s by Sofretes, a French company, to set up a
pilot program involving ten solar stations to be distributed
throughout the country at a cost of 215 million French francs
(about $40 million). This project appears unlikely to go
ahead, since official interest in large-scale solar programs
seems to have waned considerably.
    The siting potential for solar energy in Iran is, none-
theless, considered very favorable. Some 60 percent of the
country is classified as arid or semi-arid and Iran has one of
the highest factors for insolation in the world. A large
portion of the population is distributed in small and remote
villages--60,000 villages have a population of under 2,000.
The high cost of distributing fossil fuels and transmitting
electricity to these scattered villages enhances the relative
attraction of solar energy. Consequently, solar heating and
solar electric conversion using thermal or photovoltaic
systems are expected to have large-scale applications in Iran,
perhaps by the turn of the century.

    Solar Heating. There are a number of ways to use solar
energy for heating purposes. The simplest, passive solar systems, use architectural design to provide modest solar assist
in heating buildings. These include small northern windows,
large southern windows, and large southern overhang to shade
high summer sun and admit low winter sun. A more complex system uses electrically driven heat pumps to draw thermal energy
from a solar-heated reservoir. Between these two concepts
lies a range of alternatives, most of which use water-cooled,
metallic, flat plate, and non-tracking collectors.
    The potential for solar heating application depends on
the coincidence in time of the energy required (degree day
heating requirement) and the energy available (insolation).
To obtain a quantitative measure of this potential in Iran,

the SRI study used the following procedure: the average monthly hours of sunshine during the six coldest months (November
to April) were calculated from monthly insolation data for
17 weather stations located throughout Iran. The averages
were then normalized to give the sunniest station a rating of
1.0. Total degree days [degree days = (18° C - Average Daily
Temperature, ° C) X (number of days)] were also calculated
for the same six-month period, and the results were again
normalized to give the highest degree day station a rating of
1.0. The solar heating rating was then derived as the simple
product of the normalized insolation and degree day ratings
(see table 8.2).

According to these calculations, the greatest potential
for solar heating application lies along the Zagros mountains
from the province of Fars in the south and northward through
Hamadan, Kurdestan, and Azarbayjan Sharghi. The coastal
regions along the Persian Gulf and the Caspian Sea are the
least favored areas for solar heating. The Caspian region has
the lowest insolation in the country combined with a moderate
heating requirement. At the opposite extreme, the Persian
Gulf region has excellent insolation, but very low heating
requirements.

Solar Electric Power

The generation of electricity from sunlight can be accomplished in several ways but the two greatest potential applications in Iran are solar thermal power plants and photovoltaic or solar cells.

In solar thermal processes, sunlight is collected by a
reflective surface and concentrated at a highly absorptive
receiver. Complex control systems continuously track the sun
to keep the sunlight focused on the receiver. Very high
concentration ratios produce temperatures of over 1,000° C at
the receiver. Heat from the receiver is passed to a fluid
such as water, helium, or air for use in conventional heat
engines.

Photovoltaic cells, on the other hand, generate electricity directly from the sunlight by separating charges in
specially treated semiconductors. Such cells are the main
source of electric power for spacecraft but high cost has not
permitted large-scale application. If the cost of producing
these systems can be reduced, photovoltaic cells will become
extremely attractive because this type of conversion requires
no moving parts, making it operationally very attractive.

The potential for solar electric power applications is a
function of total annual insolation. The average hours of
sunshine per month for 19 weather stations throughout Iran are
shown in table 8.3. The solar electric power rating is
determined by normalizing the average hours of sunshine on the

Table 8.2. Potential for Solar Heating

Weather Station	Province	Average Hours of Sunshine per Month[a]	Total Degree Centigrade Days[b]	Relative Degree Days	Relative Hours of Sunshine	Solar Heating Rating
Hamadan	Hamadan	163	2770	1.00	0.66	0.66
Isfahan	Isfahan	227	1843	0.67	0.92	0.62
Sanandaj	Kurdestan	175	2369	0.86	0.71	0.61
Tabriz	Azarbayjan Sharghi	153	2662	0.96	0.62	0.60
Kermanshah	Kermanshahan	189	2082	0.75	0.76	0.57
Rezaiyeh	Azarbayjan Gharbi	145	2625	0.95	0.58	0.55
Shiraz	Fars	234	1557	0.56	0.94	0.53
Mashad	Khorassan	171	2094	0.76	0.69	0.52
Kerman	Kerman	222	1528	0.55	0.90	0.50
Tehran	Markazi	200	1676	0.60	0.81	0.49
Semnan	Semnan	198	1652	0.60	0.80	0.48
Zahedan	Sistan and Baluchestan	218	1167	0.42	0.88	0.37
Khorramabad	Lorestan	191	1227	0.44	0.77	0.34
Rasht	Guilan	91	1489	0.54	0.37	0.20
Ahwaz	Khuzestan	190	480	0.17	0.77	0.13
Bushehr	Bushehr	224	225	0.08	0.90	0.07
Bandas Abbas	Saheli-Jonoob	248	15	0.005	1.00	0.005

aData for six coldest months, November to April, based on a five-year average: 1966-71.

bBased on 18°C. Ten-year average: 1963-73.

Source: SRI International (1977).

93

Table 8.3. Potential for Solar Electric Power

Weather Station	Province	Annual Average Sunshine per Month[a] (hours)	Maximum Hours of Sunshine per Month[a] (percent of annual average)	Minimum Hours of Sunshine per Month[a] (percent of annual average)	Solar Electric Power Rating
Shiraz	Fars	285	127	71	1.00
Isfahan	Isfahan	275	126	73	0.96
Bandar Abbas	Saheli-Jonoob	270	122	84	0.95
Bushehr	Bushehr	269	125	82	0.94
Khorramabad	Lorestan	267	136	66	0.94
Tehran	Markazi	261	136	71	0.92
Zahaden	Sistan and Baluchestan	260	127	72	0.91
Shahr-Kord	Chahar-Mohal Bakhtyari	259	141	67	0.91
Kerman	Kerman	258	126	76	0.91
Semnan	Semnan	253	138	67	0.89
Sanandaj	Kordestan	250	147	48	0.88
Kermanshah	Kermanshahan	250	138	66	0.88
Mashad	Khorassan	246	150	60	0.86
Rezaiyeh	Azarbayjan Gharbi	244	151	48	0.86
Ahwaz	Khuzestan	244	135	63	0.86
Hamadan	Hamadan	236	154	57	0.83
Tabriz	Azarbayjan Sharghi	234	157	46	0.82
Babolsar	Mazandaran	172	141	70	0.60
Rasht	Guilan	127[b]	225	38	0.45

[a]Five-year average: 1966-71.
[b]Data for one year only.
Source: SRI International (1977).

94

basis of the station with the highest insolation--Shiraz. The
potential for solar power is highest in the central, south-
central and southeastern regions of Iran, while the poorest
prospects are in the Caspian region.

Wind

The most important factor in determining the potential for
wind energy is its characteristics--speed and pattern--at the
site. The energy in the wind increases with the cube of wind
velocity so it is desirable to locate a wind energy conversion
system where wind velocity is high and naturally increased by
local terrain. Even-flowing wind over gradually sloping hills
yields substantially more power than turbulent winds over
rough country, for example. Wind pattern is important because
the more uniform the wind speed, the higher the capacity
factor achieved.

Average annual wind speed at 15 weather stations throughout Iran are shown on table 8.4. Highest average wind veloci-
ties are in Kerman, Sistan and Baluchistan, and Azarbayjan
Sharghi, but still considerably lower than the mean wind speed
of 15.6 knots (29 kilometers per hour) which is the basis for
the design of many wind turbines currently considered economically promising for electric power generation.

Wind speed is often influenced by topographical features
and more information is needed to specify sites in Iran with
average wind speeds greater than those occurring at the established weather stations, because cities and airports, where
many weather stations are located, are usually low-wind sites.

Geothermal Energy

Geothermal energy is broadly defined as heat emitted from
within the earth's crust, usually as hot water or steam.
Specifically, there are at least four broad types of geothermal resources: hot water fields, dry steam fields, hot
brine (wet steam) fields, and hot dry rocks. Of these, the
first three have been exploited for electric power generation
or as a source of direct heat, although hot brine has serious
drawbacks for power generation such as corrosion, pollution,
and disposal of waste water. A reconnaissance study of the
general geothermal potential in northwestern Iran undertaken
in the 1970s identified four geothermally promising zones--
Sabalan, Damavand, Maku-Khoy, and Sahand--covering a total
surface area of 31,000 square kilometers.[2] However, additional surveys and exploration drilling are needed to define
the nature and extent of Iran's geothermal resources.

Table 8.4. Average Wind Speed

Weather Station	Province	Yearly Average Wind Speed[a] (knots)	Maximum Average Wind Speed per Month[a] (percent of annual average)	Minimum Average Wind Speed per Month[a] (percent of annual average)
Kerman	Kerman	9.4	142	64
Zahedan	Sistan and Baluchistan	8.0	142	70
Tabriz	Azarbayjan Sharghi	7.8	131	69
Bushehr	Bushehr	6.4	125	81
Bandar Abbas	Saheli-Jonoob	6.0	124	86
Ahwaz	Khuzestan	5.5	138	78
Shiraz	Fars	5.2	136	69
Isfahan	Isfahan	5.1	176	62
Tehran	Markazi	4.9	146	71
Mashad	Khorasan	4.8	143	68
Bandar Enzeli	Guilan	4.6	126	78
Khorammabad	Lorestan	4.6	127	59
Semnan	Semnan	3.1	150	42
Rezaiyeh	Azarbayjan Gharbi	2.9	125	78
Babolsar	Mazandaran	2.4	125	74

[a]Five-year average: 1961-66.

Source: SRI International (1977).

NOTES

1. The first phase of the expansion will produce enough steam coal to supply a nearly 60 MW_e power plant (Zarand) that can burn either coal or fuel oil but currently burns fuel oil.
2. Ente Nazional per L'Energia Elettrica, "Geothermal Power Development Studies in Iran," Report prepared for the Ministry of Energy of Iran, February, 1976.

9 Electricity

GENERATING FACILITIES

The electric power supply system in Iran consists of facilities managed by the Ministry of Energy, as well as others owned and operated by the private sector and several semi-autonomous government agencies. Most existing and planned facilities, however, are under the Ministry of Energy; this government system accounted for 79.1 percent of the installed generating capacity and 81.2 percent of the electric power consumed in the country in 1977, and it is likely that this proportion will continue to increase.

As of 1977, generating facilities managed by the Ministry of Energy had a total name-plate capacity of 6,093 MW_e, of which 1,722 MW_e (28.3 percent) was fossil steam; 1,997 MW_e (32.8 percent) gas turbine and combined cycle; 1,804 MW_e (29.6 percent) hydropower; and 570 MW_e (9.3 percent) diesel (see table 9.1). This represents nearly threefold an increase from the 1972 total of 2,094 MW_e. The effective capacity of the system was much less, however, because it has always been plagued by poor maintenance, shut-in capacity, and lack of spare parts and skilled technicians.[1]

During the period between 1972 and 1977, the largest gains in new installed capacity were made by gas turbines and combined cycle facilities, which jumped from 172 MW_e in 1972 to 1,997 MW_e in 1977, thereby shifting rank from lowest to highest in terms of contribution to the overall system. The share of diesel units dropped from 17.8 percent to 9.3 percent of the total system.

In 1977, the installed name-plate capacity of non-Ministry of Energy facilities totaled 1,607 MW_e, mostly consisting of fossil steam and diesel facilities.

Table 9.1. Ministry of Energy Installed Power Generating Capacity by Type[a]

	1972		1977		1982[b]	
	MW_e	Percentage of Total	MW_e	Percentage of Total	MW_e	Percentage of Total
Fossil Steam (Oil and Gas)	746	35.6	1,722	28.3	8,622	55.5
Gas Turbine and Combined Cycle	172	8.2	1,997	32.8	3,161	20.4
Hydropower	804	38.4	1,804	29.6	2,919	18.8
Diesel	372	17.8	570	9.3	820	5.3
Total	2,094	100.0	6,093	100.0	15,522	100.0

[a]These figures do not include privately owned or other non-Ministry of Energy facilities. In-stalled capacity of all such non-Ministry facilities totaled 1,607 MW_e in 1977.

[b]Adjusted to reflect cancellation of 2,400 MW_e installed in nuclear capacity but otherwise includes all plants in operation, under construction or commissioned prior to the revolution. As a result of the disruptions caused by the revolution and the Iran-Iraq war, construction work on a number of the new projects has been slowed down or altogether halted. Therefore actual installed power generating capacity is expected to be substantially lower in 1982.

Source: Plan and Budget Organization of Iran (1978).

Government estimates prepared in 1978 anticipated another near tripling of the Ministry of Energy system to 17,922 MW_e by 1982. It is an unlikely target to reach, however, due to the cancellation of two nuclear reactors which were to have 2,400 MW_e of capacity on line in 1982 and the delays in planning and construction of other power plants since the revolution. Excluding the nuclear reactors, the capacity in 1982 of all generating facilities in operation or under construction or commissioned as of 1977 was to have totaled 15,522 MW_e. The government further estimated that total Ministry of Energy capacity would reach 23,976 MW_e by 1987. This schedule will probably not be met either unless a concerted effort is begun soon to plan and construct the necessary facilities, considering the long lead times involved.

Fossil Steam

As of 1978, construction was under way for several thousand megawatts of fossil steam power generating capacity throughout the country, including two large natural gas-fired units being built at Neka and Bandar Abbas. Earlier cost estimates for these plants, which did not anticipate delays resulting from the revolution, ranged between $350 and $400 per kilowatts-electric (KW_e) of installed capacity.

These fossil steam plants, like others already operating in Iran, will provide chiefly base-load power supply and, like their smaller predecessors, they have been designed to burn more than one kind of fuel--that is, either natural gas, gas oil, or residual fuel oil. This flexibility in power plant fuel offers substantial advantages in Iran's overall allocation of fossil fuels. For example, an increasing number of plants now burning oil derivatives can be converted to cheaper and more plentiful natural gas as it becomes more widely available.

With the cancellation or indefinite postponement of the nuclear power program, additional fossil steam plants will have to be built to provide base-load electric power supply. These plants can operate most efficiently on natural gas although some may alternate between natural gas and excess fuel oil from the country's existing and planned inland refineries. Because it is uneconomical to transport fuel oil by pipeline from such refineries to coastal loading terminals for export or for sale as bunker fuel to tankers operating out of the Persian Gulf, fuel oil produced in excess of regional demand can be used as power plant fuel even where natural gas is available. Such dual-fuel power plants can therefore balance regional fuel oil consumption with fuel oil production from a nearby inland refinery.

Diesel

The relative importance of diesel generation, which in the past has been used extensively in Iran, will diminish rapidly, except in towns and villages remaining isolated from the main transmission system. Although diesel power plants are versatile and relatively efficient, their initial capital cost is very high; they require premium diesel fuel which is in short supply in Iran; and they do not offer the opportunity for economies that are available with fossil steam generation in a large, integrated system.

Installed diesel capacity rose from 372 MW_e to 570 MW_e between 1972 and 1977 but dropped back as a percentage of total generating capacity from 18 percent to just over 9 percent during this period.

Hydropower

Iran's hydropower plants had an installed capacity of 804 MW_e in 1972, rising to 1,804 MW_e in 1977 with the commissioning of the giant Karun Dam. While additional hydropower capacity is under construction, earlier targets for 2,919 MW_e of installed hydropower by 1982 will not be met. Nevertheless, Iran has substantial undeveloped hydropower resources. Iran's hydropower plants have annual capacity factors as high as those of its fossil steam plants, and like the fossil steam plants, they are currently used principally for base-load supply.

Gas Turbine and Combined Cycle

Meanwhile, intermediate- and peak-load supply can be met by new combustion gas turbines and combined cycle plants, as well as by conventional hydropeaking and pumped storage facilities, as discussed earlier.

Development of combustion gas turbines in recent years has led to improved performance characteristics, and increasing numbers of such plants have been installed in Iran. The units, basically combining a jet aircraft-type gas turbine and a power generator, burn either natural gas or a range of oil products. Their capital investment costs are lower than for other types of power plants owing to the inherent simplicity, and they do not require boilers, cooling equipment, or other auxiliaries that are standard features of fossil steam plants. In Iran, installed costs have averaged several hundred dollars per KW_e installed. Moreover, combustion gas turbines do not require much cooling water, a fact that allows greater

flexibility--in a country like Iran with its uneven distribution of water--to site close to load centers and minimize
transmission costs and losses. They can be started up in
minutes, making them ideal for peaking purposes. Finally,
their simplicity substantially lowers installation time (and
lowers the cost of interest during construction). The Monenco
study estimated that lead time for construction of such plants
will range between 15 and 30 months versus 54 to 66 months for
fossil steam, 36 to 60 months for expansion of existing
hydropower facilities, 96 months for new hydropower and pumped
storage, and 102 months for nuclear facilities.

The principal disadvantages of combustion gas turbines
are lower thermal efficiency relative to fossil steam plants
and higher operating and maintenance costs. The lower efficiency factor has a less pronounced economic effect in
Iran, where natural gas is both abundant and relatively cheap
compared with most alternative sources of fuel. Non-fuel
operating and maintenance expenses are only a small part of
the delivered cost of electricity, so this disadvantage,
too, is not significant.

Combustion gas turbines, therefore, offer Iran an attractive choice for supplying peak-load and even some intermediate-load requirements.

Improvements in combustion turbine design and performance
have led to increased worldwide commercial application of
so-called combined cycle units in recent years. A combined
cycle unit has a combustion gas turbine topping cycle and a
steam turbine bottoming cycle. Thus the combustion turbine's
hot exhaust gases are used to produce steam for the steam
turbine, with the combustion turbine typically accounting for
about two-thirds of the total unit's output. The principal
advantages of this type of power plant are high efficiency,
moderate capital costs, and relatively low water requirements
for condenser cooling. Unit sizes are increasing and some
manufacturers offer modular units that can be easily transported and quickly installed. Projected advances in the
design of system components--especially materials and designs
that will increase the maximum turbine inlet temperature,
for example--are expected to produce continuing efficiency
improvement and operating economy.

Capital costs of combined cycle power plants range between 50 and 100 percent more than those of simple combustion
gas turbines, although fuel costs are effectively lower
because the plants operate at higher efficiency. The actual
operating cost of these plants, however, has yet to be determined, mostly because it is uncertain what price should be
assigned to the fuel. While there is a consensus that
the price of natural gas used in power plants should reflect
its opportunity cost, it is still undecided whether the opportunity cost of natural gas in Iran is best represented by the

cost of gathering and delivering currently flared or wasted associated natural gas; the net-back in petrochemical uses; the net-back from exports; or the value of the gas in rein-jection into oil fields to increase ultimate oil recovery. But any of these opportunity cost figures is likely to be below the cost of alternative fossil fuels. Thus, all factors considered, combustion cycle plants compare favorably with fossil steam plants for base- and intermediate-load operations in Iran.

TRANSMISSION SYSTEM

Iran's electric power transmission system is not yet fully interconnected. The main system extends through Khuzestan, Lorestan, Kermanshahan, Azarbayjan, Zanjan, Guilan, Markazi, and Mazandaran provinces only. Power supply facilities in other provinces are not only isolated from the main system, but are, for the most part, isolated from each other as well.

In 1977, a total of about 8,000 circuit kilometers of high voltage transmission lines were operating in Iran. A breakdown of these lines by voltage class and the historical expansion of the system is given in table 9.2.

The 230 kilovolt (KV) lines comprise the backbone of Iran's transmission system, with 132 KV lines serving to supplement the bulk of transmission requirements. However, it is expected that 132 KV will rapidly evolve into the role of regional transmission--or subtransmission--with higher voltage lines providing the bulk transmission capacity. A new voltage level--400 KV--was introduced with the commissioning of the Karun Dam, and additional 400 KV lines have been planned to integrate most of the Ministry of Energy's power supply sys-tem. The present interconnected system will then be extended to Isfahan, Yazd, Kerman, Fars, Bushehr, and Saheli Jonoob provinces. After this major expansion of the bulk transmis-sion is completed, power transfers over long distances will be possible.

CONCLUSION

Iran's power supply system is one of its basic industries and part of the infrastructure upon which the growth of other sectors of the economy depends. Demand for electric power will continue to rise rapidly in the residential, commercial, and industrial sectors, requiring a larger, more aggressive program of power facility construction each year. Moreover, there is now and will continue to be a need for a major expansion of the country's bulk transmission system to achieve greater economy of operation by integrating most facilities into a single system, and because, in some instances at least, new generating facilities will be much more remote from load centers than in the past.

Table 9.2.   Ministry of Energy High Voltage
Transmission System

(circuit kilometers)

Voltage Class (KV)	1972	Percentage of Total	1977	Percentage of Total
132	1,320	31.7	2,800	35.0
230	2,984	69.3	4,381	54.8
440	-	-	820	10.2
Total	4,304	100.0	8,001	100.0

Source: Plan and Budget Organization of Iran (1978).

NOTES

1. The P&BO study estimated system losses in 1977 at 16.4 percent, load factor at 57.8 percent, and reserve margin at 81.5 percent.

10 Nuclear Power

INTRODUCTION

Iran has made a dramatic turnabout in its commitment to nuclear power. Only six years after the Pahlavi regime announced what was certainly one of the world's most ambitious nuclear power programs--installation of 23,000 MW_e by 1994--the new Iranian government appears to have totally eliminated the nuclear program.

The decision to drop the original goal was, of course, prompted by the revolution. Pledging to restructure the country's social, political and economic policies and institutions prevalent under the former regime, the new government moved rapidly to reverse what had long been regarded as excesses in the acquisition of arms and industrial hardware. Accordingly, the once grandiose but now highly unpopular nuclear program was among the first and hardest hit.

It is, however, important to note that as much as four years ago, a year and a half before the revolution dethroned the Pahlavi regime, the Iranian nuclear program had already come under criticism at home as unrealistic and indeed unsound for economic, political and infrastructural reasons. Based on a preliminary assessment of the benefits and the associated costs and risks of the nuclear power option in the Iranian context, pressure had been mounting since the fall of 1977 to downgrade the 23,000 MW_e target substantially.[1]

ORIGINS OF THE NUCLEAR POWER PROGRAM

Iran's interest in embarking on a large-scale nuclear power
program was prompted in large part by developments in the
world energy market in the 1973-74 period. The nearly fourfold increase in crude oil prices and continuing uncertainties
regarding supplies following the Arab oil embargo intensified
efforts within the major industrial countries to develop
cheap, plentiful, and indigenous sources of energy. Nuclear
power seemed to be the most attractive choice. Forecasts
based on cost comparisons with oil-fired plants at a time
when crude oil was selling within the $2 to $3 per barrel
range had already indicated a growing market potential for
nuclear power. With crude oil prices at more than $11 per
barrel, the competitive edge thought to be held by nuclear
power appeared substantially enhanced. Furthermore, the
political imperative of reducing dependence on imported oil
made the case for a nuclear option even stronger. Ambitious
plans were drawn up in a number of key industrial and developing countries, notably Japan, the United States, Brazil, South
Korea, West Germany, France, and Great Britain, which called
for sharply increased use of nuclear power.
      The same considerations and cost calculations were cited
as reasons for the development of a major domestic nuclear
power program in Iran. Oil prices, it was argued, would
continue to rise periodically, whereas the cost of nuclear
power had more or less stabilized. Rather than burn oil in
power plants, it followed, Iran should export oil to earn
foreign exchange for its development program and produce
electricity from nuclear plants at a lower cost. Moreover, by
developing domestic nuclear power, Iran could underscore its
call for a worldwide effort to find and develop substitutes
for fossil fuels, thereby preserving oil for more important
uses in the petrochemical industries. Nuclear power, it was
also argued, would help to diversify the country's energy base
and build a viable energy infrastructure in preparation for
the time when domestic oil production would start to decline.
There was the added element of prestige associated with the
construction and operation of nuclear plants.
      But at least two other important considerations also
weighed heavily in the decision to launch a large-scale nuclear program. First, Iran was under substantial pressure--or
perceived itself so--to recycle its increasing petrodollar
earnings through purchases of massive quantities of goods and
services from the major western industrial countries. Second,
the royal family and those close to it, who were regularly
paid huge commissions on foreign contracts to facilitate and
to approve major projects, stood to earn substantial kickbacks from the purchase of each of the multi-billion dollar

reactors. According to businessmen and government officials close to the Iranian nuclear program, commissions on the initial reactor purchases were expected to run close to an astounding 20 percent of the total contracts, or several hundred million dollars per reactor.[2]

The actual amount paid or the anticipated commissions have not been substantiated--and perhaps never will be. Nevertheless, large kickbacks were undoubtedly involved at the highest levels and played no small part in the secretive manner in which the Iranian nuclear program was drawn up and in the insistence of the Pahlavi regime on retaining the program despite growing recognition of its inappropriateness for Iran.

Military considerations probably did not contribute significantly to the decision to launch the nuclear program. The Iranian government probably believed that it could eventually move toward a nuclear weapons capability as a result of the massive investments in nuclear technology. However the acquisition of nuclear weapons was not an immediate or important consideration in starting up, and later retaining, the program. It was generally believed that, if necessary, there were quicker, cheaper and cleaner ways to acquire nuclear weapons, than through huge investments in reactors.

It was decided to install 23,000 MW_e of nuclear capacity within 20 years, that is, by 1994.[3] Significantly, once the decision was made to proceed with the nuclear program in principle, the findings of the Monenco study supported the government's choice of a large-scale nuclear option by concluding that nuclear power is the most economical source of power for base load and middle range operation down to about 4,800 hours a year or an annual capacity factor of about 55 percent.

But the Monenco study contained several misleading--if not erroneous--premises which determined its findings. For example, the study listed the capital costs for the construction of a 1,000 MW_e light water reactor in Iran at $550 per KW_e installed, plus an additional $140 per KW_e for interest payments during construction, for a total of $690 per KW_e installed. In fact, later estimates showed those costs to be substantially over $3,000 per KW_e installed.[4] Furthermore, while underestimating the cost of nuclear power, the Monenco study also significantly overestimated the cost of power generated from Iran's plentiful fossil fuel resources. For example, Monenco priced domestic natural gas at about $1.80 per thousand cubic feet, which was not only higher than the going delivered world price for natural gas, but was $1.65 more than the price Iran expected to net from its most favorable natural gas export scheme then on the drawing board. The Monenco study also overlooked other factors--infrastructural, political, economic, manpower, social and environmental--that should have been weighed in any objective assessment of the nuclear power option in Iran. But, despite its obvious short-comings, the Monenco study was probably the single most important study used by the government to justify proceeding with the nuclear program.

The Iranian Atomic Energy Organization was established in 1974 and negotiations were immediately launched with a number of supplier countries including the United States, Canada, France, West Germany, Great Britain, Australia, India and several African countries for technological training and assistance, and for the purchase of hardware and fuel. The first contract to purchase reactors was concluded with West Germany's Kraftwerk Union (KWU) for two 1,190 MW_e pressurized light water reactors to be installed on a turnkey (i.e., operationally ready) basis. KWU also contracted to supply the initial load of fuel plus reloadings for the first 10 years of operation.

Construction of these two reactors was well underway at Halileh near Bushehr on the Persian Gulf, with the facilities scheduled for operation in the early 1980s, when the country was thrown into political turmoil. Work on the reactors, which were 80 percent and 50 percent completed, respectively, came to a halt in late-1978 as a result of nationwide strikes by Iranian workers and the large-scale exodus of foreign technicians. Work on these plants has not been resumed; their future remains uncertain despite widespread sentiment that the entire nuclear program should be scrapped. According to the manufacturer, Iran has already made some $2.75 billion in payments on the $7 billion-plus project.

Two 935 MW_e pressurized light water reactors were also ordered from France's Framatome for installation at Darkhouin, near Ahwaz in the southwest, again on a turnkey basis. The Framatome contract, too, included a fuel agreement under which the French would supply enriched uranium for the plant for up to 10 years, if Iran requested it. There was an additional reprocessing agreement, according to which spent fuel from the plant would be shipped to France for reprocessing, and the recovered uranium returned for subsequent enrichment and use within Iran, or for resale to a third party. This agreement did not cover the return of plutonium.

On-site work on these reactors, begun in 1977, also came to a standstill following the revolution and will almost certainly not resume.

In addition to the reactors under construction, Iran had signed a letter of intent with KWU for four 1,200 MW_e air- or dry-cooled reactors to be installed in the central part of the country. A plan to sign a letter of intent with West Germany's Brown Boverie Company for two more reactors of similar size had also been drawn up. Negotiations for those six reactors were suspended indefinitely in mid-1978.

Finally, Iran had negotiated intermittently with companies in the United States for the purchase of nuclear reactors. Trade talks in 1975 covered the installation of six to eight U.S.-built reactors. But contracts were held up, at first pending Congressional approval of legislation governing U.S. nuclear export policies, and later pending signature of a bilateral nuclear safeguards agreement by the two countries. Needless to say, the issue of the bilateral agreement is now moot.

While talks covering reactor purchases proceeded during the 1974-78 period, Iran was also discussing investment in uranium enrichment facilities with several Western European countries and the United States. In one deal, Iran acquired a 10 percent share in the EURODIF gaseous diffusion enrichment plant then being built in Tricastin, France. Other shareholders include France, Spain, Belgium, and Italy. The plant became operational recently and is expected to reach full production capacity of some 10.8 million separative work units (SWU) by the end of 1981. Iran also agreed to subscribe to 25 percent of the shares of a similar enrichment facility to be built by COREDIF, another consortium including France, Spain, Belgium, and Italy. Subsequently, however, Iran and at least one other consortium member, Italy, reconsidered their commitment to the second facility, given the likelihood of excess enrichment capacity worldwide through the 1980s and their own reduced requirements resulting from downgrading of domestic nuclear programs. For some time the French government, hopeful that the COREDIF facility would be built in France, continued actively promoting the project, but without Iranian participation COREDIF is expected to be substantially reduced in size, postponed, or dropped altogether.

As for natural uranium, Iran acquired some 28,000 tonnes of ore for its reactors from several countries, negotiated joint ventures for exploration and development of deposits in others, and launched a 10-year, $300 million search for uranium at home.

The fate of these overseas and domestic investments remains uncertain.

CRITIQUE OF THE IRANIAN NUCLEAR POWER PROGRAM

Even as Iran moved rapidly ahead with its nuclear power program, prospects for nuclear power worldwide changed dramatically. The early euphoria over nuclear reactors gave way to serious rethinking about the desirability, and indeed the necessity, of dependence on a technology that was ever more controversial as to safety and security, especially after it became obvious that the nuclear power cost picture had changed significantly.

Within three years of Iran's decision to launch a major nuclear power program, it had become more and more obvious that nuclear power was no longer a relatively cheap means of generating electricity. Indeed, even in the industrial nations, soaring costs for capital investment and operation, including fuel, had whittled down any competitive edge over coal- or oil-fired power stations. Nevertheless, within Iran the myth of nuclear power as an almost infinite, secure, and cheap alternative to fossil fuels continued to persist in most circles, and certainly among the public at large. The growing nuclear power bureaucracy could not be expected to dispel that myth. Neither were the international conglomerates who manufacture and export nuclear technology inclined to do so. These companies, faced with declining sales at home, had turned to the very lucrative overseas markets. With each export contract for a 1,000 MW_e reactor expected to run into billions of dollars, the commercial stakes were high indeed, prompting the companies to market their hardware aggressively.[5] The supplier governments, too, promoted export of nuclear hardware and services to help their balance of payments and to keep their domestic nuclear industries afloat, offering substantial export credits when necessary to sweeten the deals.

By late 1977, following reports of major cutbacks in planned nuclear capacity elsewhere, pressure finally mounted in Iran for a reappraisal of the original nuclear targets. A small group of critics--energy specialists and economists from government and from academe--charged privately and later publicly that the nuclear heirarchy was not fully assessing-- or reporting--the growing costs and risks of a substantial Iranian commitment to nuclear power. Specifically, the critics challenged the persistent assertions of the Atomic Energy Organization and the government that nuclear power offered Iran a secure and cheap alternative to fossil fuels; they called, instead, for a careful evaluation of the country's other options.

Most of these experts had not been consulted in evaluating and planning the nuclear program. The nuclear power program was initiated and later closely directed by the Shah with a closed circle of domestic and foreign business associates and political advisers. Implementation of the program and efforts to legitimize and justify it at home and abroad were entrusted to the head of the Atomic Energy Organization and several of his deputies. Critics charged that nearly all these individuals were incompetent to run the program. Indeed, when that regime, gambling to stay afloat, began to clean house in the summer of 1978, the head of the Atomic

Energy Organization was fired following an investigation on charges of mismanagement and embezzlement.

That move reflected the uneasiness with which the government was beginning to view its nuclear program after 1978. In fact, as a result of increasingly vocal criticism, a small commission was set up in the prime minister's office to review the program critically and recommend changes. The general consensus of this commission was that the government should declare a moratorium on all new nuclear activities, including the negotiation of international nuclear cooperation agreements, thus allowing time to complete the study of nuclear power's potential role versus alternative sources of energy.

Political events overtook the work of this commission and other efforts at careful and objective reassessment of the country's energy options. But the principal arguments advanced at that time against the Iranian nuclear power program will probably remain valid for the foreseeable future. Those arguments are summarized below.

Uncertain Supply

Nuclear reactors will not provide Iran with a steady and secure long-term source of power. The present generation of light water reactors, which were slated to comprise some 15,000 to 20,000 MW_e of installed capacity by 1994, would have to be fueled with natural uranium, which has limited availability worldwide and which, for a variety of economic, political, and technical reasons may not be readily available to Iran over the life of its plants.

Given the potential link between the spread of civilian nuclear hardware, fuel, and know-how, and nuclear weapons proliferation, three principal uranium-rich countries--Australia, Canada and the United States--have already sought to impose strict conditions on uranium exports.

The uranium market is expected to remain highly politicized and, due to the likelihood of even greater intervention by the principal producers on security grounds, both unstable and unpredictable.

This instability will be further compounded by the fact that the bulk of the world's limited uranium resources will continue to be produced by only a handful of countries (currently the four largest producers account for nearly 90 percent of the non-communist world output) and the uranium market is expected to be dominated by these countries until the end of the next decade, even with the entry of several other important producers--Niger, Gabon, and Spain.

This concentration, if not an actual cartelization, in the uranium market has important implications for uranium prices. It is uncertain, for example, whether prices will remain constant in real terms during the coming years or whether they will rise substantially as in the period between 1973 and 1978, when they jumped five to sixfold due in part to market manipulation.

In addition to the uranium producers' cartel, Iran faces a second highly politicized, unstable and cartelized market for uranium enrichment services. The United States holds a virtual monopoly in enrichment services although the Soviet Union has been making some inroads into that market. Two other European enrichment projects are coming on stream--one, the URENCO joint venture between Great Britain, West Germany and the Netherlands, and the other, the French-led EURODIF consortium, including Iran indirectly. Even with Iran's indirect participation in EURODIF, Brazil will be the only developing country with direct access to its own enrichment facilities, if the planned West German facility is constructed.

Because the nuclear suppliers decided to severely restrict, if not altogether ban, any further sale of sensitive enrichment technologies that could be used to produce weapons-grade uranium, developing countries with light water reactors will necessarily continue to be extremely dependent for reactor fuel on suppliers of enrichment services. Even if the enrichment facilities were available for sale, economies of scale would preclude any commercial operation in the small developing countries. While suppliers have indicated some willingness to offer enriched uranium under agreed upon terms, as part of a non-proliferation bargain, such considerations as the temporary moratorium on new enrichment contracts by the United States in the mid-1970s, and Australia's domestic debates over uranium production, certainly raise questions about the long-term credibility of these guarantees.

Furthermore, plutonium from the back end of the fuel cycle is unlikely to be available as a hedge against the suppliers of uranium and enrichment services.

Spent fuel from light water reactors can be reprocessed to retrieve unused uranium and fuel-grade plutonium transformed from part of the original heavy uranium isotopes. Both can then be recycled back into reactors as fresh fuel. However, plutonium recovered through reprocessing is both highly toxic and weapons-grade, making the reprocessing highly controversial. One key country, the United States, has indefinitely postponed commercial reprocessing of spent fuel and has urged others to do the same; many, in fact, are expected to follow suit. But even if France and Great Britain for example, continue to operate their existing commercial reprocessing facilities, the terms under which reprocessing services might be offered to the developing countries remain uncertain. The sale of the facilities themselves will almost surely be barred for many years to come, due to concern over safeguards. Considering the high cost, spent fuel reprocessing, like enrichment, makes very little commercial sense for developing countries with small nuclear programs anyway.

Finally, Iran confronts yet another highly concentrated group of nuclear hardware sources--those which supply reactors and spare parts and the trained technicians to build, operate, maintain and eventually dismantle the nuclear facilities and dispose of their spent fuel.

The reactor market is dominated by about six conglomerates which, despite competition in overseas sales, are closely interconnected. The two predominant U.S. nuclear manufacturers, Westinghouse and General Electric, together share about two-thirds of the U.S. domestic market and have been heavily involved in the European and Japanese nuclear power programs as well. For example, the principal West German domestic nuclear reactor now operating is virtually identical to the General Electric boiling water reactor, while the principal export reactor is of Westinghouse pressurized water reactor design. In France, the Framatome conglomerate produces pressurized water reactors under license from Westinghouse, for both domestic use and export. In fact, until several years ago Westinghouse held substantial shares in Framatome itself. In the Japanese market, of the three principal nuclear reactor manufacturers, Mitsubishi holds a Westinghouse license, and Hitachi and Toshiba hold General Electric licenses.

While other countries including the Soviet Union, Canada and Sweden, have more or less independent nuclear industries, all have grouped together in the London Nuclear Suppliers Group mainly to set ground rules and restrictions regarding the export of nuclear technology.

Such interconnection and controls will significantly affect prices. Moreover, while they last, controls may result in joint embargoes (on the sale of hardware and services for constructing and operating nuclear facilities) against a country or group of countries, whether in response to legitimate safeguards concerns or in pursuit of commercial or foreign policy objectives.

A decision to embark on a major nuclear power program, particularly by a country lacking an indigenous nuclear base, entails dependence on a small group of highly politicized and commercially aggressive nuclear suppliers. Iran should, therefore, examine the risks, costs, and uncertainties with respect to future availability and prices of the nuclear hardware, fuel, spare parts, and skilled manpower needed to operate and maintain nuclear facilities, before assessing the trade-offs between these costs and any benefits that nuclear power might offer.

Infrastructural Bottlenecks

There are major infrastructural bottlenecks in the original blueprint to implement the nuclear program. For example, the 1,000 MW$_e$ reactors, which are increasingly constructed world-wide because of significant economies of scale, are ill-suited to Iran because of the limited size of the country's power grid.

An electric power grid requires sufficient idle or reserve generating capacity--whether the individual plants making up the system are oil, gas, coal, or nuclear--to prevent loss of load if one or more plants are shut down for repair, maintenance, refueling or other cause. The amount of that reserve generating capacity is a function of plant size. As the size of the plants installed in a grid increases, so does the requirement for reserve capacity; i.e., the loss of a 1,000 MW$_e$ plant requires more backup than the loss of a single, smaller plant.

Additionally, larger plants are considered to be less reliable than smaller ones; they break down more frequently, cause a greater disruption of the grid when they do so, and suffer longer shutdowns. These problems are particularly acute in the Iranian context, since the national grid has little, if any, reserve capacity. In the case of Iran's first two 1,190 MW$_e$ nuclear reactors, therefore, one reactor had to be built simply to provide the necessary back-up capacity for the other.

High seismic risk coupled with the absence of cooling water in much of Iran severely limits the number of possible nuclear reactor sites. The few sites available in southern Iran are situated several hundred miles from the country's principal urban and industrial areas and even from the national grid itself. As a result, there would be large transmission losses or the need for substantial investments, running into billions of dollars, for high voltage lines, or both.

Economic Drawbacks

Nuclear power makes very little economic sense in Iran at this time. Cost studies conducted in industrial countries indicating that nuclear power holds a competitive edge over most alternative sources of power, specifically coal, had originally been cited in support of the program. These studies, however, are not applicable to Iran and are misleading in an Iranian context.

Capital costs, which constitute the single most important factor in determining the final cost of power from nuclear reactors, have been substantially higher in Iran than in perhaps any other country in the world. Only part of the

higher costs in Iran can be attributed to expenditures on
infrastructure. In the industrial countries, capital costs
for a 1,000 MW$_e$ reactor scheduled to operate in the early
1980s have been variously estimated at between $700 and $1,000
in current dollars per KW$_e$ installed. In Iran, the comparable
figure for the first four reactors was estimated at the end of
1978 at over $3,000 per KW$_e$ installed.

For the two Halileh reactors, for example, the capital
cost breakdown in Deutsche mark was as follows:

Construction	5.4 billion
Contingency	0.8 billion
Infrastructure	1.6 billion
TOTAL BASE COST (actual)	7.8 billion
Escalation During Construction	3.1 billion
Interest During Construction	2.3 billion
TOTAL INDIRECT COSTS (estimated)	5.4 billion
TOTAL COSTS (estimated)	13.2 billion

The U.S. dollar equivalent of total estimated costs of the two
reactors was $7.5 billion (1978 dollars).[6] The cost per KW$_e$
installed was therefore about $3,150.[7]

For the two Darkhouin reactors, the capital cost breakdown in French francs was as follows:

Construction	9.6 billion
Contingency	1.0 billion
Infrastructure	2.9 billion
TOTAL BASE COST (actual)	13.5 billion
Escalation During Construction	8.1 billion
Interest During Construction	4.1 billion
TOTAL INDIRECT COSTS (estimated)	12.2 billion
TOTAL COSTS (estimated)	25.7 billion

The U.S. dollar equivalent of total estimated costs of these
two reactors was $6.4 billion (1978 dollars). The cost per
KW$_e$ installed was therefore about $3,435.

Even these high figures do not fully reflect the actual
capital requirements for the nuclear reactors. Additional
allowances should be made for owner's costs, such as consultants' fees; expenditures on site selection and training;
and systems costs, such as incremental high voltage transmission lines to connect the nuclear reactors to the national
grid and for building up reserve capacity. Systems costs for
the first four reactors could have run to several billion
dollars. Allowances are also needed for other externalities,
such as hidden subsidies and customs exemptions. Many of
these costs are not normally entailed in the construction of
alternative power generating facilities.

Another important consideration is that the foreign exchange component of the capital costs of the Iranian reactors
is probably over 90 percent, whereas the foreign exchange component in the industrial countries manufacturing most of their
equipment domestically and drawing on local labor markets is
only a fraction of total costs. Building reactors in Iran thus
mandates consideration of foreign exchange resource allocation
as well.

Finally, as pointed out earlier, nuclear cost studies
conducted in industrial countries for their decision-making
purposes generally compare costs of power generated from
nuclear reactors with those from coal-fired plants. This is
so because in the principal industrial countries, nuclear and
coal plants are considered to be the only means of generating
power that are technologically feasible, economically competitive, and for which the fuel supply is either indigenously
available in large quantities or at least reasonably assured
over the life of the facility. Comparison of nuclear power
with coal generally shows that while capital costs for construction of a nuclear reactor are higher than those for a
coal plant, in the final analysis, power generated from a coal
plant is somewhat costlier than that from a nuclear reactor
due to higher fuel costs. In Iran, on the other hand, the
competitive position of nuclear power must be matched not
against coal, but against indigenously available oil and, more
importantly, natural gas.

Yet no exhaustive study has been made of the cost of
generating power from natural gas in Iran. The limited evidence, however, would seem to place natural gas plants at a
significant economic advantage over other alternatives, including nuclear power. Capital costs for natural gas-fired
thermal power plants as well as for combustion gas turbines
have been estimated at several hundred dollars for conditions
that apply to Iran. The actual operating cost of these plants
has yet to be calculated, however, largely because it is not
known what price should be assigned to the fuel used. But it
can be safely stated that natural gas was and is the most
economical source of incremental electric power supply for
Iran under any reasonable set of assumptions.

Natural gas also has other advantages. There is greater
flexibility in siting of natural gas plants; smaller units can
be located throughout the country closer to points of consumption, thus reducing transmission costs and losses. Natural
gas is safer than nuclear power and presents fewer safety
problems. It is cleaner to burn. Natural gas plants can be
constructed much more rapidly. Increased use of domestic
natural gas prevents too great a dependence on outside sources
of fuel. Finally, the foreign exchange requirements for
natural gas are lower vis-a-vis nuclear power, not only

because capital investment costs are lower but because there is no requirement for importing fuel and fuel services from abroad.

PROSPECTS FOR NUCLEAR POWER

By the end of the summer of 1978, the government began to indicate a willingness to quietly reappraise, and even to cut back earlier plans. This shift reflected, in part, the growing concern about rapidly rising capital costs for nuclear reactors coupled with the fear that funds for the full program might no longer be available. The price tag, variously placed in 1978 between $80 billion and $120 billion, was a three to fourfold increase over the original 1974 estimate of about $30 billion.

The nuclear program had become increasingly unpopular and was showing signs of becoming a political liability domestically--not only because of criticism by some experts on technical grounds, but also because the public viewed the reactors as grandiose monuments to the post-1973 era of wasteful management of the nation's increased oil revenues. In addition, the Shah's offer in 1977 to store Austrian spent fuel inside the country had come under harsh attack from influential Moslem leaders, among others, as an effort to "turn Iran into a dumping ground for western nuclear wastes."

While the Pahlavi regime never officially announced any reduction in its original 23,000 MW_e target, it became increasingly clear that only four reactors actually under construction at the time would be completed on schedule, which would bring the total installed capacity in Iran to about 4,250 MW_e by the mid-1980s. Negotiations for additional reactors, including four air-cooled West German units for which letters of intent had been previously signed, and six to eight U.S. units, were quietly dropped.

The short-lived government of Shahpur Bakhtiar took a further step in January 1979 and announced the cancellation of the two French reactors for which preliminary site work had started in southwestern Iran. The effect of this decision was to limit the country's nuclear power program to two West German plants that were then about 80 percent and 50 percent completed, respectively.

Thus, even before the final outcome of the revolution was known, the Iranian nuclear power program suffered a significant setback as a result of interacting financial and political troubles. This setback turned into a rout after the revolution. The new head of the Iranian Atomic Energy Organization recommended the complete abandonment of all nuclear plants under construction for "political, economic, social, human and technical reasons."[8] That recommendation was probably affected to some degree by strong and vocal opposition to the overall nuclear program from members of the atomic energy body following the incident at Three Mile Island. It was perhaps the first time since the launching of the program that scientists and others working most closely with the program had demonstrated any strong opposition to the building of nuclear power plants in Iran.

The Islamic government has not yet made a formal announcement about the fate of the country's nuclear power program. There have been reports that some Iranian clergymen have advocated development of an "Islamic bomb." It is still difficult to ascertain how seriously these suggestions may be taken in Iran itself. At present, the government is probably more inclined to accept the political costs of such a decision than its predecessor was. Moreover, the notion of an "Islamic bomb" can be expected to have considerable appeal at home and could be used to divert attention away from other pressing national problems. The future direction of the nuclear programs in Pakistan and Iraq will also influence decisions in Iran about how to proceed, if at all.

The Iranian nuclear power program is still very much in its infancy, however, and even with considerable government backing, the development of a viable military program is still years away. Much could change during this time to affect the course of such a program. Even if the civilian nuclear power program is kept alive, influenced partly by military considerations that may or may not be realistic, it will be limited to the completion of at most one or two of the West German reactors that were already under way when the revolution broke out.

The outcome of the Iran-Iraq war may also help determine whether Iran ultimately completes these plants. Iraqi military strikes into Khuzestan could prove critical to Iran's electric power supply because of the vulnerability of the country's two largest hydropower plants located in that province (the 1,000 MW_e Karun Dam and the 520 MW_e Dez Dam). These plants represent more than one-fourth of the country's current installed power generating capacity; if they are significantly damaged, pressure could build to complete one or both of the abandoned reactors.

Yet a comprehensive assessment of the desirability of proceeding with the program as originally planned, or of radically altering or reducing it, remains to be made. Until such an assessment is completed and until lingering doubts are addressed and a national energy blueprint is drawn up, nuclear energy will continue to have an uncertain future in Iran.

Salient information on Iran's nuclear power program is summarized in table 10.1.

Table 10.1. Nuclear Fact Sheet

Member, International Atomic Energy Agency.

Non-Proliferation Treaty (NPT) status: signed, 1968.

NPT Safeguards Agreement in force.

Research reactors in operation: one 5 MW_e unit (since 1967).

Commercial power reactors in operation: none.

Reactors under construction in 1978: four.

Reactors likely to be completed by 1985: none.

Dominant planned reactor type: pressurized water reactor.

Uranium resources: unknown.

Approximate purchased uranium stocks: 28,000 tonnes.

Reprocessing facilities: none.

Uranium enrichment facilities: none in Iran but a 10 percent share in EURODIF plant in Tricastin, France, with Belgium, Spain, Italy, and France.

Total originally announced planned capacity: 23,000 MW_e by 1994 (announced in 1974).

Total expected capacity by 1994: 0-2,380 MW_e.

NOTES

1. See Bijan Mossavar-Rahmani, "Reassessing Iran's Nuclear Energy Program," paper presented to a conference on Iran-U.S. relations, Washington, D.C., October 1977. This paper was published in Abbas Amirie and Hamilton A. Twitchell eds., Iran in the 1980s, Institute for International Political and Economic Studies and SRI International, Tehran, Iran, 1978.
2. Interviews with present and former officials of the Iranian Atomic Energy Organization and prominent businessmen involved in the program, Tehran, April, 1979.

3. The 23,000 MW$_e$ figure represented a somewhat arbitrary
    target based on what the government believed national
    electric power requirements should be in the early 1990s.
    Specifically, in 1974 the government stated its intention
    to increase per capita power consumption in the country
    to the Western European level in about 20 years, and to
    provide about 40 percent of the total required installed
    capacity in the form of nuclear reactors. This brought
    the figure to 23,000 MW$_e$ by 1994.

4. Monenco put the total cost of the Iranian nuclear power
    program of 23,000 MW$_e$ at nearly $24 billion in 1974
    dollars. Later estimates placed the price tag at four to
    six times that amount.

5. The suppliers systematically underestimated nuclear power
    costs in their approaches to the Iranian government and
    only put forward substantially higher figures at the
    final stages of the commercial negotiations. Having
    committed themselves to the purchases, the Iranian
    negotiators then found it difficult for political reasons
    to pull out. For example, when France first approached
    Iran in 1974 about reactor sales, Iranian press reports,
    quoting French sources, placed capital costs at $200
    per KW$_e$ installed. When the contract was signed a year
    later, the base cost per KW$_e$ was nearly 10 times
    higher, at $2,000, and the escalated price (including
    escalation and interest during construction) came to
    almost $3,500 per KW$_e$ in current dollars.

6. The Deutsch mark and French franc figures have been
    converted to U.S. dollar equivalents based on end-October
    1978 exchange rates for two reasons: to obtain costs in
    a single unit of account for comparison purposes, and
    because Iran's crude oil exports are priced, and revenues
    therefore effectively received, in U.S. dollars. These
    figures should be used very carefully because the actual
    outlays for plant and equipment are staggered over the
    six- or seven-year construction period during which
    time exchange rates fluctuate.

7. In 1979, the new head of the Iranian Atomic Energy
    Organization put the total cost of the two West German
    plants at close to $7 billion, which is consistent with
    the above estimates. At about the same time, the manu-
    facturer of the plants, KWU, gave a lower estimate of
    $5.5 to $5.6 billion; those figures, however, apparently
    did not include costs of interest payments during con-
    struction.

8. The government should consider completing the containment
    structures of the two West German plants for use as stor-
    age silos for imported grain, since the site has access
    to an unloading dock on the Persian Gulf, roads to the

interior of the country, and much of the rest of the
infrastructure required for the implementation of such a
plan.

IV

Petrochemicals

11 Petrochemicals

INTRODUCTION

Iran is a relative newcomer to the petrochemical field. The petrochemical establishments of the industrial nations are already highly developed and extremely competitive, and enjoy the advantages of large domestic markets and sophisticated infrastructures within the economy.

Iran entered the petrochemical field from what was believed to be potentially a position of strength--having available a vast and secure supply as well as a wide array of petrochemical feedstocks. For example, Iran produces large quantities of associated natural gas that could be utilized for petrochemical manufacture. But while this associated natural gas often contains a substantial amount of NGL--which are among the most desirable feedstocks for petrochemicals--much of it has traditionally been flared and continues to be flared even today. Apart from this associated natural gas, Iran has many non-associated natural gas fields as yet un-touched. In addition to this great volume of natural gas, refinery gases and liquids are also available that can be used to make a variety of petrochemical products.

The incentives for employing these feedstocks to develop a competitive petrochemical industry in Iran once seemed compelling. Not only would domestic output of petrochemical products replace imports, but production in excess of domestic demand could bring in additional foreign exchange. The development of a sizable petrochemical industry would lead, it was argued, to the establishment of supporting secondary industries and to growth of the end-product sector. Owing to the large labor requirements of the industry, many new jobs would be created. Although the major producing units within

the petrochemical industry would be established wholly or in
large part by the government, the secondary industries in the
end-product sector would provide many opportunities for private business. Finally, owing to its geographical proximity,
Iran, it was reasoned, could gain access to markets in central
and southeastern Asia that would provide future export outlets
for petrochemical products.

Based on these seemingly sound considerations, Iran
developed ambitious plans for establishing a host of petrochemical facilities inside its borders.

PROJECTS IN OPERATION OR UNDER CONSTRUCTION

In 1961, construction of a modest nitrogenous fertilizer
plant was started at Marvdasht, near Shiraz. Products from
this plant were already being marketed when the state-owned
National Petrochemical Company (NPC) was set up in 1965 as an
affiliate of NIOC to plan and develop the petrochemical industry, and empowered to enter into joint venture agreements
with foreign concerns toward that end, if necessary.

By the end of the 1970s, NPC had six main operational
complexes, all situated near the oil fields in the south
including the Iran Fertilizer Co., Abadan Petrochemical Co.,
Razi Chemical Co. (formerly Shahpur Chemical Co.), Kharg
Chemical Co., Iran Carbon Co., and Iran-Nippon Petrochemical
Co. Another company, the Iran Ocean Co., was set up as a
joint venture to ship products from Iranian petrochemical
plants to international markets. In addition to several
expansion projects involving existing facilities, construction
of a new giant multibillion dollar complex in partnership with
a consortium of Japanese companies, the Iran-Japan Petrochemical Co., was nearing completion at Bandar Khomeini (formerly Bandar Shahpur), when the revolution erupted. This
project, the largest of its kind in the world, is expected by
both sides to be completed, albeit after a delay of several
years (see table 11.1).

NPC petrochemical projects in operation or in an advanced
phase of construction are the following:

Iran Fertilizer Co.: Operating near Shiraz since 1963, this
plant serves the domestic market only. The facilities, based
on natural gas, limestone and phosphoric acid as feedstocks,
presently have the following capacities, measured in metric
tonnes annually (MTA):

Urea	52,000 MTA
Ammonia Nitrate (26% N)	30,000
Nitric Acid	4,000
Soda Ash	53,000

Table 11.1. Petrochemical Projects in Operation
or in Advanced Construction

Project	Start-Up Date	NPC Share-holding in 1978	Capital Costs (million dollars)
Iran Fertilizer Co.	1963	100	57.0+
Abadan Petrochemical Co.	1969	74	57.4+
Razi Chemical Co.	1970	100	612.1*a
Kharg Chemical Co.	1969	50	41.7+
Iran Carbon Co.	1975	20	10.0+
Iran Ocean Co.	1977	50	50.0+
Iran-Nippon Petrochemical Co.	1976	50	80.4+
Expansion of Iran Fertilizer Co.	--	100	460.0*
Abadan Aromatics Project	--	100	690.0*
Iran-Japan Petrochemical Co.	--	50	1,833.3*
Phosphate Project (Phase I)	--	100	4.5*
LPG Processing Project	--	100	536.0*
Land Reclamation/Jetties	--	100	146.0*

+Actual.

*Projected.

aIncludes preliminary costs of $353.5 million for the planned expansion program.

Source: National Petrochemical Company of Iran (1978).

Sodium Bicarbonate	10,000
NPK Mixed Fertilizer	50,000
Sodium Triployphosphate	30,000

Abadan Petrochemical Co.: Located at Abadan, this petrochemical complex was a joint venture between NPC and B.F.
Goodrich of the United States, with the latter holding a
26 percent share. This plant manufactures raw materials for
the domestic plastics and detergent industries. Its products,
based on refinery gas and benzene, include:

Polyvinyl Chloride	60,000 MTA
Dodecyle Benzene	12,000
Liquid Caustic Soda	24,000

Razi Chemical Co.: This large fertilizer complex located at
Bandar Khomeini on the Persian Gulf was originally an equal-
shares joint venture between NPC and Allied Chemical Company
of the United States but became a wholly-owned subsidiary of
NPC several years ago. The facilities are based on natural
gas and phosphate rocks. Recently, a major expansion program
was completed and its annual production capacity now includes:

Ammonia	660,000 MTA
Sulfur	432,000
Urea	705,000
Sulfuric Acid	1,000,000
Phosphoric Acid	260,000
Diammonium Phosphate	263,000
Monoammonium Phosphate	186,000

Kharg Chemical Co.: This company was set up in 1967 as a 50-50
joint venture between NPC and Amoco, a subsidiary of Standard
Oil of Indiana. At present, the plant is designed to recover
some 230,000 MTA of sulfur and 370,000 MTA of LPG and light
naphtha from associated natural gas pumped in from offshore
oil fields in the Persian Gulf and a field on Kharg Island
itself. All its products have been exported.

Iran Carbon Co.: This project was set up as a joint venture
between NPC, the Industrial Mining and Development Bank of
Iran, the International Finance Corporation and Cabot Corporation of the United States. The plant, located in Ahvaz, has
a capacity to manufacture 16,000 MTA of various grades of
carbon black for the domestic rubber industry.

Iran Ocean Co.: A joint venture set up between NPC and
Gazocean of France, this company was formed in 1975 to ship
products from Iranian petrochemical plants to international
markets. The company took delivery of its first vessel, the

70,000 cubic meter Razi, in 1977. The vessel was intended for transport of liquid ammonia and LPG.

In addition to the complexes already on stream, several projects have been underway for expansion of existing facilities or construction of new ones. They include:

Iran-Nippon Petrochemical Co.: This complex is a 50-50 joint venture set up between NPC, Nissho-Iwai Co. and Mitsubishi Chemical Industries of Japan. The project is being implemented in two phases. The first phase, completed in 1977, involved the production of 23,800 MTA of phthalic anhydride and 40,000 MTA of dioctyl phthalate. In the second phase, 2-ethylhexanol will be produced for use as a raw material in the manufacture of dioctyl phthalate, which will, in turn, be available to the domestic plastic industry as well as for export.

Expansion of the Iran Fertilizer Co.: This expansion program was expected to be completed by 1981 and the major portion of its new products was slated to be consumed domestically. The additional capacity will include:

Ammonia	400,000 MTA
Urea	500,000
Nitric Acid (100% Basis)	200,000
Ammonium Nitrate (30% N)	250,000

Abadan Aromatics Project: Under construction within the Abadan Refinery premises, this project will utilize naphtha from the refinery for the manufacture of 760,000 MTA of aromatics. Fully owned by NPC from the start, this project was expected to go on stream in 1983. As a result of repeated Iraqi shelling, the fate of this project--like that of the refinery itself--is unclear. Its planned product mix was:

P-xylene	320,000 MTA
O-xylene	50,000
Cyclohexane	210,000
Benzene	180,000

Iran-Japan Petrochemical Co.: This project is a 50-50 joint venture between NPC and a consortium of Japanese companies consisting of Mitsui and Co., Toyo Soda, Mitsui Toatsu, Japan Synthetic Rubber and Mitsui Petrochemical, collectively known as Iran Chemical Development Co. The multibillion dollar complex, among the largest in the world, was well under way at Bandar Khomeini, adjacent to the Razi Chemical Co. facilities, when the revolution forced a suspension of construction work. Iran and Japan were renegotiating the terms of the project and limited construction had resumed when the Iran-Iraq war broke out, forcing Japanese engineers and technicians to leave the site once more.

The project, when originally conceived, was expected to cost less than $1 billion; by 1977, cost estimates had escalated to over $1.8 billion. Post-revolution estimates have put costs at $3.5 billion to account for the delays of many months but, realistically, the project may ultimately cost as much as twice that figure.

It is not known whether the Iranian government or its Japanese partners can raise the extra financing required for this complex, which was reportedly 85 percent complete when work halted. Both sides appear committed to the project, given the massive financial outlays already made; the Iranian government has exempted the project from the post-revolution nationalization of various NPC joint ventures. The Japanese government, for its part, also views completion of the complex not only as a matter of national prestige but a means of keeping a foothold in Iran at a time when Iran's political and commercial relations with most other industrial countries have deteriorated. That view, however, may prove to be shortsighted. Given the enormous escalation, the project will probably never make much commercial sense to either side--some analysts suspect it did not from the beginning. If completed, the complex may well be a fiasco of such magnitude that relations between the two countries may suffer for many years.

Associated natural gas from the Khuzestan oil fields and naphtha from the Abadan Refinery have been earmarked as feedstock for this complex. Three main core units have been planned. The first is a salt electrolysis plant for the manufacture of chlorine and caustic soda; it will use some 400,000 MTA of salt harvested from sea water. The second is a cracker for the production of olefins, ethylene and butadiene from natural gas. The third is an aromatics unit for the production of benzene and xylenes.

A substantial portion of Iran-Japan Petrochemical Co.'s products was expected to be exported initially but if domestic demand grew quickly and the development of downstream manufacturing operations were realized as planned, exports from the complex were expected to decline steadily. The final output of the complex is slated to consist of:

Caustic Soda (liquid and solid)	262,000 MTA
Ethylene Dichloride	170,000
Vinyl Chloride Monomer	150,000
Low Density Polyethylene	100,000
High Density Polyethylene	60,000
Polypropylene	50,000
Propylene	53,000
Styrene-Butadiene Rubber	40,000
Benzene	350,000
Mix-xylene	144,000
Liquefied Petroleum Gas	1,500,000

Before the revolution, NPC was also planning three other extensive projects, including a $600 million, 15-year program to explore for and develop phosphate resources in Iran; a $536 million project to carry 160,000 b/d of NGL obtained from associated natural gas to Bandar Khomeini to separate the ethane for production of olefins, and export the left-over LPG (63,000 b/d) and naphtha (43,000 b/d); and finally, a $146 million project to build a loading terminal at Bandar Khomeini and recover swamp lands for future plant expansion purposes.

NPC estimated in 1978 that these and other projects already under way or planned for completion by 1987 would require capital expenditures of some $14.2 billion at 1982 prices. NPC estimated that when all these projects reached full capacity in 1992, total petrochemical sales would reach $5.2 billion a year at 1982 prices, of which $3.7 billion consisted of domestic sales and $1.5 billion of exports. The export figure included $350 million in sales of naphtha and LPG.

Those projections are not likely to be met since construction work in the petrochemical sector, too, has been delayed by events leading up to and following the revolution, and the future of some of the projects remains highly uncertain.

IMPEDIMENTS TO DEVELOPMENT OF THE PETROCHEMICAL INDUSTRY

Despite the factors that appear to make the petrochemical industry a logical and attractive area of endeavor, there are problems and difficulties that Iran and most other developing countries face in their efforts to create a viable petrochemical industry.

The capital-intensive nature of petrochemical plants and the rising minimum scale of primary or basic producing units demand a level of production far greater than small domestic markets can absorb. However, the existence of highly developed and competitive petrochemical industries elsewhere severely limits the export potential for excess production from large plants. The alternative for a developing country is to build small plants to meet only its own domestic needs, which results in high unit production costs.

Lacking sufficient domestic demand for economically-sized (i.e., large) basic petrochemical facilities, NPC planned to build an export-oriented industry in two ways. First, it sought foreign partners to provide know-how and venture capital and to offer access to export markets. To attract such foreign partners, Iran offered five-year tax holidays as well as the infrastructure required for the growth of the industry. It also promised these companies cheap and

plentiful feedstocks. Thus, except for the Shiraz facility,
each one of the principal petrochemical complexes operating or
under construction in Iran initially included at least one
foreign partner.   Second, NPC hoped that cheap feedstocks
would lower its operating cost and make products from its
petrochemical plants competitive with those from plants already operating elsewhere in the world.

The price of natural gas sold by the government to NPC
was a mere $0.20 per thousand cubic feet for sour (i.e.,
sulfur rich) gas, and $0.25 per thousand cubic feet for sweet
gas.   LPG was sold at $2 per barrel.[1] Yet even with such
low prices, which did not cover the costs of gathering, processing and transportation--let alone an appropriate intrinsic
value for natural gas--high initial capital costs for the
petrochemical facilities and high operating costs wiped out or
severely limited any comparative advantage in export markets.

All NPC petrochemical facilities with the exception of
the Kharg Chemical Co. (profits totaling $11.3 million) and
the Iran Carbon Co. (profits totaling $1.2 million), operated
at significant losses in 1977.   But these two plants are not
representative of the potential profitability of the petrochemical industry generally.   The Kharg plant is merely a
rentier; i.e., it processes LPG delivered at low cost for
export at much higher world prices.   The Iran Carbon plant
similarly enjoys special treatment since it has a captive
domestic market for carbon black in the Iranian rubber industry.

NPC facilities as a group registered net losses in 1977
totaling $17.46 million on domestic sales of $214 million and
export sales of $81 million (see table 11.2).

Admitting that joint partnership with foreign companies
and low feedstock prices were not sufficient to ensure its
commercial viability as a large-scale, export-oriented company, NPC requested even greater support from the government
in early 1978.[2] Specifically, NPC asked that petrochemical
feedstocks be made available to the industry at zero prices;
the government provide additional direct subsidies to help
develop export markets for NPC products; and, given uncertain
prospects for such exports, the government meanwhile ensure
sufficient domestic demand for at least half of the products
from NPC plants by preventing imports of cheaper foreign
products. If these conditions were met, NPC officials argued,
and if all petrochemical plants in operation or in advanced
construction as of 1978 were still operating at full capacity
by 1982, total NPC net profits in 1982 would be $181.8 million
on domestic sales of $762 million and export sales of $1.28
billion.

Opponents of a petrochemical program in Iran--at least on
the massive scale planned by NPC--were skeptical that such
export levels could be realized.   More important, they argued,

Table 11.2. Sales and Net Profits/Losses of Petrochemical Projects in Operation or in Advanced Construction (million dollars)

Project	1977			1982		
	Domestic Sales	Export Sales	Net Profits/ Losses	Domestic Sales	Export Sales	Net Profits/ Losses[a]
Iran Fertilizer Co.	47	–	(7.6)	215[a]	–	71.0[a]
Abadan Petrochemical Co.	47	–	(7.8)	59	–	5.5
Razi Chemical Co.	91	34	(11.8)	129	140	22.5
Kharg Chemical Co.	–	43	11.3	–	52	15.1
Iran Carbon Co.	7	–	1.2	11	3	0.1
Iran Ocean Co.	–	3	(2.7)	–	14	0.5
Iran-Nippon Petrochemical Co.	22	1	(0.06)	54	2	1.1
Abadan Aromatics Project	–	–	–	47	194	20.9
Iran-Japan Petrochemical Co.	–	–	–	274	448	(16.9)
LPG Processing Project	–	–	–	–	427	62.0
Total	214	81	(17.46)	762	1,280	181.8

( ) Parentheses denote net losses.

aIncludes sales of output from planned expansion of the project.

Source: National Petrochemical Company of Iran (1977).

under existing and proposed direct and indirect government subsidies, NPC was not a profitable operation and it was exporting feedstocks at zero or negative prices while diverting scarce capital and human resources from other development programs.

Iran's petrochemical export potential was limited by the fact that the international petrochemical industry was already over-supplied, having built up a large capacity in the 1960s in anticipation of demand growth, only to be hit by higher oil prices and recession in the 1970s. This excess production capacity had prompted key industrial countries to set up import barriers to protect their own industries, on the one hand, while sharpening competition among established industrial country exporters, on the other. But despite this situation, nearly all key oil producers in the Persian Gulf and North Africa have engaged in petrochemical export projects, many with a distinct advantage over Iran. Algeria and Libya, for example, have the advantage of being close to Europe. Saudi Arabia can export large amounts of petrochemicals to developing countries at preferential prices as part of its aid program, thereby shutting other producers out of those markets.

Iran might try to compete with other OPEC producers in the Indian Ocean region or even Japan, but would soon have to confront such established exporters as Singapore, Taiwan and South Korea. Eastern Europe is building up its own domestic petrochemical capacity; it would not have been an attractive export market for Iran anyway because only a portion of the payments could be expected in hard currencies. The U.S. petrochemical industry is already highly developed; moreover, this country could not provide an assured market because of changeable import policies.

Heavy direct and indirect subsidies made a large export program unattractive in any case. NPC officials long argued that because much of the country's associated natural gas was flared and wasted, this natural gas was, for all practical purposes, a free commodity and should be supplied to the petrochemical sector at minimal cost.

In fact, of course, there is no such thing as free raw feedstock or fuel gas for petrochemical production, particularly in Iran. Iran's associated natural gas is sour and is located far from those sites which would be suitable for installing petrochemical facilities. Desulfurization and delivery of this natural gas to an appropriate plant location requires substantial capital investment for processing equipment and pipelines and adds to operating costs. Moreover, even the use of associated natural gas entails an opportunity cost in the form of forfeited alternative uses, such as piped gas or reinjection gas, once natural gas gathering projects start to be implemented.

LESSONS FOR THE FUTURE

One area for potential growth in Iran is the end-product
sector, where size is not as critical as it is for basic
petrochemical production. For example, plants producing such
products as polyvinyl chloride, polyethylene, synthetic
fibers, detergents, elastomers, and carbon black can be economically viable on a relatively small scale. The capital
requirements for such facilities are modest and the labor
input and value added can be relatively high.

Until the revolution, the Iranian private sector participated in setting up five important end-product petrochemical
facilities. These projects, which have since been taken over
by the government, are:

Pasargade Chemical Company: This company operates a relatively
small plant at Abadan with a capacity of 12,000 MTA of salty
rocks, 10,000 MTA of chlorine and 13,000 MTA of caustic soda.

Parsylon Corporation: This plant at Khorramabad has a capacity
of 16,000 MTA of nylon-6 fibers, now using imported caprolactam but later to be supplied by domestic facilities.

Sherkat Shemi Aliaf: Initially a joint venture between Bayer
AG of West Germany (50 percent) and Iranian private interests,
this company operates a plant in Tehran with a capacity of
8,000 MTA of nylon-6 fibers from imported caprolactam. The
capacity was slated to increase to 10,000 MTA, with a further
expansion of 20,000 MTA also planned.

Polyacryl Iran Corporation: Potentially the largest project of
its kind in Iran, Polyacryl Iran Corp. started as a joint
venture among private sector interests including the Behshahr
Industrial Group and Dupont of the United States (40 percent).
Sited outside Isfahan, the plant's planned capacity was 42,000
MTA of polyester fiber (staple and filament) and acrylic fiber
(staple only). Expansion plans were expected to lead to a
total synthetic fiber capacity of 100,000 MTA within five
years of start-up.

Persepolis Industrial Resins Company: Situated near the city
of Shiraz, this was first a joint venture between Iranian
private interests, the Industrial Credit Bank of Iran and
British Industrial Plastics, with a share distribution of
40-20-40 percent, respectively. The plant capacity is:

        Formaldehyde (37%), Urea/Formaldehyde
          and Melamine/Formaldehyde   35,000 MTA

Moulding Compounds	10,000
Urea/Formaldehyde Resins (Powder)	6,000
Phenol/Formaldehyde Resins (Powder)	5,000
Phenol Formaldehyde Moulding Compounds	5,000

The viability of the above projects remains to be assessed. But it cannot be emphasized enough that not all
petrochemical projects are inherently good investments;
therefore careful market and financial judgment must be exercised. Only those projects that can be supported adequately
by the domestic market in Iran in the reasonably near future,
or those which have a reasonably assured export market should
be pursued. Implicit in any policy for development of a
petrochemical industry should be the need to achieve acceptable levels of profitability and return on capital, weighed
against alternative uses of both capital and feedstocks. If a
new project cannot provide an adequate return, then the incentive to proceed with it is greatly reduced.

It is unlikely that Iran will enter into any new major
petrochemical projects or complete any projects not already
well underway, if not because of a more realistic assessment
of the pros and cons of proceeding, then because of the hur-
dles that stand in the way. Iran's petrochemical program,
together with the nuclear power program and the military
acquisitions program, were seen as the leading examples of
waste and mismanagement of national resources during the
Shah's regime, and therefore are still unpopular. It would
be politically difficult for any government in Tehran to
commit itself anew to one of these programs. Moreover, the
high capital and high operating costs (a large portion in hard
currencies) may well place any new petrochemical project outside of NPC's financial reach.

It may be some time before Iran is prepared to employ
large numbers of expatriates to build petrochemical facilities
and operate them. NPC has projected, for example, that at the
height of construction work on the Bandar Khomeini project,
more than 10,000 workers will be engaged on site, many of them
expatriates. NPC had also estimated manpower requirements for
operation of its petrochemical facilities at 10,500 in 1982,
split about evenly between blue and white collar employees;
the total required was projected at 15,500 by 1987. With the
heavy emigration of Iranian professionals since the revolution
and the delays in starting up or expanding technical training
programs, the required manpower will not be available in Iran
to proceed with even abridged versions of earlier plans.

NOTES

1. The world price for LPG was about $30 per barrel in 1980.
2. National Petrochemical Company, "Proposed Projects for the Sixth Plan and a Long-Term View of Proposed Projects for the Seventh Plan," NPC, Tehran, March 1978.

Guidelines for Policy

The uncertain Iranian political situation makes any assessment of energy requirements and options both tenuous and tentative. Once the uncertainties are removed and long-term national economic objectives are set forth, one can begin to improve the accuracy of demand projections and identify more definitively the corresponding requirements for energy supplies.

Meanwhile, on the basis of this and previous studies, the following general policy guidelines emerge:

- Expand domestic natural gas consumption rapidly and provide incentives to encourage a move away from refined oil products to natural gas once it becomes available.
- Facilitate and promote the use of liquefied petroleum gas in areas not served by natural gas, particularly in small towns and rural areas, as a substitute for middle-distillate products.
- Cancel the nuclear power program. Reactors are not practical in Iran today, nor are they expected to become so in the foreseeable future. Develop fossil steam power generators based on fuel oil and natural gas for base-load power generation, and combined cycle and combustion gas turbine units for intermediate- and peak-load generation.
- Develop the country's hydropower resources. The dependable capacity of many of Iran's potential hydropower sites will be relatively low, generally below 30 percent; thus, these sites will, with few exceptions, lend themselves best to intermediate- and peak-load service. Coordinate hydropower development with water development for irrigation.
- Prepare an extensive inventory of oil and natural gas resources, and carefully evaluate the potential for

enhanced recovery based on natural gas reinjection and
other methods.

- Refrain from exporting natural gas at least until domestic requirements are covered and world prices rise sufficiently to justify the export of surplus volumes.
- Encourage and promote energy conservation.
- Mount an ongoing and aggressive program of electric power plant construction to cope with the expected growth in electric power demand. Rapid expansion of the power transmission network will be needed as well, in view of the economies to be achieved by integrating the majority of these facilities into a single system.
- Coordinate national energy planning. Because the construction of new facilities requires long lead times, decisions will have to be well grounded and expeditious.
- Closely monitor the development of advanced energy technologies and continue to support limited research programs, particularly in the application of solar energy to Iran's rural needs.
- Set up an expanded manpower training program.
- Limit the petrochemical program to internal requirements and existing facilities until a more intensive assessment can be made of the pros and cons of petrochemical production.

Appendix

CONVERSION FACTORS USED

Heat Content

      1 kilocalorie = 3.9682 British Thermal Units (btus)

      1 million barrels per day of crude oil = 2.068 quadril-
          lion (10^{15}) btus per year

      1 cubic foot of natural gas = 1,000 btus

Oil

      1 metric tonne of crude oil = 7.33 barrels of crude oil

      1 kiloliter (cubic meter) of crude oil = 6.29 barrels of
          crude oil

      1 metric tonne of liquified petroleum gas (LPG) = 11.6
          barrels of LPG

Natural Gas

      1 cubic meter of natural gas = 35.315 cubic feet of
          natural gas

Note: Somewhat different conversion factors have been used by
the studies consulted, explaining slight variations that
appear in the data in this book. Other variations result
from inconsistent use of the Iranian and Gregorian calendars,
even in official sources.

141

Index

About the Author

Bijan Mossavar-Rahmani is an Iranian energy analyst and consultant currently based in Cambridge, Massachusetts. The
author was a Visiting Research Fellow at the Rockefeller
Foundation in New York between October 1978 and October 1980,
prior to which he worked in Iran in a number of capacities
including that of member of his country's delegation to OPEC.
Mr. Mossavar-Rahmani holds degrees from Princeton University
and the University of Pennsylvania and has lectured and
published widely on Iranian and international energy issues.